The Corporate Imagination

By the same author

The Economic Imagination: Towards a Behavioural Analysis of Choice

Money Matters: A Keynesian Approach to Monetary Economics, with Sheila C. Dow

The Corporate Imagination:

How Big Companies Make Mistakes

Peter E. Earl
LECTURER IN ECONOMICS
UNIVERSITY OF TASMANIA

Wheatsheaf Books

M.E. SHARPE, INC.
Armonk, New York

First published in Great Britain in 1984 by
WHEATSHEAF BOOKS LTD
A MEMBER OF THE HARVESTER PRESS PUBLISHING GROUP
Publisher: John Spiers
Director of Publications: Edward Elgar
16 Ship Street, Brighton, Sussex

First published in the United States of America in 1984 by
M.E. SHARPE INC.
80 Business Park Drive
Armonk, New York, NY 10504

© Peter E. Earl, 1984

British Library Cataloguing in Publication Data
Earl, Peter E.
　The corporate imagination.
　　1. Corporations——Growth
　　I. Title
　　338.7′4　　HD2746

ISBN 0-7108-0276-5
ISBN 0-7108-0281-1 Pbk

Library of Congress Cataloging in Publication Data
Earl, Peter E.
　The corporate imagination.

　　Bibliography: p.
　　Includes index.
　　1. Organizational change. 2. Organizational behaviour.
　3. Corporate planning.　I. Title.
　HD58.8.E18 1984　　　658.4　　84-5352
　ISBN 0-87332-283-5

Typeset in 10 point Times by Photobooks (Bristol) Ltd.
Printed and bound in Great Britain by
Butler & Tanner Ltd, Frome, Somerset

All rights reserved

Contents

LIST OF FIGURES AND TABLES		viii
PREFACE		ix
INTRODUCTION		xi

1	THE SIMPLE MECHANICS OF CORPORATE GROWTH AND DECLINE	1
1.1	Introduction	1
1.2	Managerial Goals and Fears	2
1.3	Product Portfolios and Lifecycles	5
1.4	Profitability as a Constraint on Growth	7
1.5	Growth as a Constraint on Profitability	10
1.6	Cycles of Corporate Instability	12
1.7	Slack in the Mechanism	16
1.8	Conclusion	19

2	CHOOSING THE BOUNDARIES OF A FIRM	21
2.1	Introduction	21
2.2	Coase's Original Analysis of the Nature of a Firm	22
2.3	The Roles of Complexity, Opportunism and Idiosyncracies	26
2.4	Linkages, Synergy and Hedging	30
2.5	Informational versus Technological Determinants of Strategy	34
2.6	Conclusion	37

3	THE MANAGERIAL IMAGINATION	40
3.1	Introduction	40
3.2	A Blinkered View of the World	41
3.3	The Impossibility of Optimisation	44
3.4	Recipes for Success – and Failure	46
3.5	Priorities	49

Contents

3.6	The Conceptualisation of Uncertain Outcomes	51
3.7	Crucial Decisions	55
3.8	Conclusion	56

4	CORPORATE AMBITIONS AND LEARNING	58
4.1	Introduction	58
4.2	Dogma and Learning	59
4.3	Experience as a Function of Aspiration Levels	62
4.4	The 'Two-Armed Bandit' Problem	66
4.5	Teamwork and Experience	67
4.6	Euphoria	69
4.7	Depression	72
4.8	Conclusion	74

5	THE STRUCTURE OF CORPORATE REVOLUTIONS	76
5.1	Introduction	76
5.2	Business as Usual?	78
5.3	The Myopia Trap	84
5.4	An Example of Profitable Defensive Investment	86
5.5	An Example of Unprofitable Defensive Investment	88
5.6	The Sequential Wearout Trap	90
5.7	Segment Retreat Strategies	92
5.8	An Extreme Example: The Convair 880/990 Airliners	95
5.9	The Selection of a New Strategy	98
5.10	Conclusion	102

6	DIVERSIFICATION AND RATIONALISATION	105
6.1	Introduction	105
6.2	Focus	106
6.3	Mistaken Focus	112
6.4	Uncontrolled Product Proliferation	115
6.5	Rationalisation Problems	119
6.6	Conclusion	122

7	LEARNING CURVES AND EXPERIENCE CURVES	124
7.1	Introduction	124
7.2	A Clarification of the Concepts	125
7.3	Employment Contracts, Incentives and Experience	128
7.4	The Effects of Disruption	132
7.5	Strategy Implications	134
7.6	Conclusion: A Cautionary Tale Concerning the Pursuit of Volume	138

Contents

8	**PRODUCT/PROCESS LIFECYCLE INTERACTIONS**	141
8.1	Introduction	141
8.2	Preferences, Prices and Product Obsolescence	142
8.3	Changing Skill Requirements Through Product Lifecycles	148
8.4	Changing Organisational Requirements Through the Cycles	151
8.5	Conclusion	154
9	**STRATEGY AND ORGANISATIONAL STRUCTURE**	156
9.1	Introduction	156
9.2	Chandler's Thesis	157
9.3	U-Form Problems and M-Form Advantages	159
9.4	The Indecomposability Problem	162
9.5	Problems of Control in Decentralised Firms	167
9.6	Conclusion	171
10	**DISAPPOINTING CORPORATE MARRIAGES**	173
10.1	Introduction	173
10.2	Strategic Mergers	174
10.3	'Bargain' Purchases	178
10.4	Whirlwind Romances	181
10.5	Integration Problems	183
10.6	Corporate Personality Clashes	185
10.7	Conclusion	187
11	**IMPLICATIONS FOR GOVERNMENT POLICY**	189
11.1	Introduction	189
11.2	Cumulative Causation and Slack	190
11.3	Balance of Payments Policy and Corporate Rejuvenation	194
11.4	Price Controls and Inflation	197
11.5	The Role of Regional Policy	201
11.6	Merger Policy	204
11.7	Behavioural Problems of a 'National Enterprise Board'	208
11.8	Concluding Thoughts: The Significance of Corporate Crises in Prosperous Economies	211
BIBLIOGRAPHY		216
INDEX		229

List of Figures and Tables

Figure 1.1 The Supply of Finance for Corporate Growth 9
Figure 1.2 The Effect of Corporate Growth on Profitability 11
Figure 1.3 A Damped Corporate Cycle 14
Figure 1.4 A Catastrophic Corporate Cycle 14
Figure 9.1 Organisational Structures 160
Figure 9.2 British Leyland Motor Corporation: Basic Structure, November 1974 166

Table 5.1 Returns to alternative strategies, given in arbitrary monetary units, where earnings decline is rapid in the absence of defensive investment 87
Table 5.2 Returns to alternative strategies, given in arbitrary monetary units, where earnings decline is slow in the absence of defensive investment 87

Preface

This book has been written for practising managers, and for academic scholars and students of industrial and management economics; but anyone interested in current policy debates about the future of modern-day capitalism should find it has something to offer. Like many of the companies it describes, it is a multifaceted yet partially integrated structure, though one which has to be organised into an hierarchical arrangement to make it manageable. To keep the integrated nature of the arguments uppermost in readers' minds, I have frequently given cross-referencing pointers (for example: cf. section -.-) as to where linked ideas and examples may be found. I have also chosen to refer to a relatively select group of company histories quite frequently, rather than to a broader sample from my collection of cases, in order to aid the development of this integrated picture and to demonstrate that corporate personalities do, indeed, exist as relatively durable structures against a turbulent environmental background.

The process of writing this book served to ram home to me the power of the arguments concerning barriers to organisational restructuring and revolutionary changes; for after much deliberation I forced myself to rearrange the contents on a number of occasions (it is a lot easier to do this with a book than with a company, but it is still a disturbing process to undertake!). In this connection, I feel I ought to point out that Chapter 2 was originally scheduled to occur much later in the book – either between Chapters 5 and 6, or between Chapters 8 and 9. In the end it was placed at the front of the book in order to focus readers' minds on the role of the manager as a coordinator in a world of turbulence and opportunism. But some readers might prefer to read it in one of its former positions, or even

Preface

to read it several times – for I believe it is of fundamental importance that they keep its themes in mind.

As with everything I have previously published, this book owes a lot to the impact of Professor G.L.S. Shackle's writings on my world view while I was still an undergraduate. Professor Brian Loasby read most of the original draft in the midst of a busy schedule and I am very grateful for his many detailed comments. I have also had useful discussions with Richard Shaw, Dipak Ghosh, Michael Corr, Mark Russell and Neil Kay. Neil was kind enough to supply me with prepublication drafts of his (1982) and (1984) books, which were to prove invaluable. My ideas on non-price competition were considerably firmed up by a lively response to a paper I presented to the Staff and Postgraduate Economics Seminar at the University of Kent at Canterbury in October 1982. Around this time I also presented some of the themes of the book to the final year Honours class of Management Economics students at Stirling; the entire group took an active interest (particularly when I became bewildered during a lecture on Marris' work and stumbled upon the ideas presented in section 1.6!) but Michael Ruck and Timothy Lennard deserve special thanks for their perceptive questions and comments. However, while I offer my thanks to everyone mentioned in this paragraph, I alone take full responsibility for the analysis that has ultimately emerged.

Finally, I would like to express my thanks to Eleanor Bruce, Ann Cowie and Catherine McIntosh for efficiently producing the typescript from a patchwork of paper, staples and tape; and to Edward Elgar and his colleagues at Wheatsheaf for their encouragement and advice, as well as the speed with which they managed to deliver the finished product.

Introduction

Economists first started writing about company behaviour in earnest around a century ago. The leading theorist of the day, Alfred Marshall (1890), produced a theory of corporate evolution which had as its central notion the idea that, in the long run, managerial fallibility was destined to result in the demise of every firm. Marshall saw firms within industries as having histories that paralleled those of trees within forests. Many would not survive even the initial struggle to establish themselves in their environments. Some might grow and prosper for a time but, sooner or later, senility would set in and they, too, would founder, their places being taken by other, relatively youthful producers. Some firms, like some trees, might live to ripe old ages but none would be able to grow indefinitely and thereby achieve a dangerous position of monopolistic dominance. Marshall's theory was originally built around the notion of the owner-run family business. However, the increasing importance of the joint stock company led him to argue that a removal of the need to rely on the ability of a family to produce generation after generation of skilled managers did not make corporate immortality inevitable. Joint stock companies would, he argued, be prone to stagnate for bureaucratic reasons, because a dispersed set of shareholders would experience great difficulty in ensuring that managers always gave of their best and moved with the times.

Nowadays it is rare for leading economists (as distinct from researchers in 'business studies') to write about corporate mistakes and how they come to be made. Several theories about why this is so might be offered. One which can rapidly be dismissed is that, with the advent of business schools and management consultancy firms, corporate failure has become a thing of the past. Directly opposed to

Introduction

this hypothesis is one which argues that modern corporations have to cope with an environment which is being made increasingly complex and uncertain by technological change, financial and political instability, the internationalisation of markets, and the growth of bigger (and, arguably, more mobile) firms. It is thus obvious that firms will make mistakes; there is no need for academic economists to attempt to explain why they occur. A third hypothesis seems to me to be the most likely explanation: the analytical toolkit used by the conventional ('neoclassical') economist of today is poorly suited to the investigation of corporate errors, because it focuses on the characteristics of equilibrium states rather than on the dynamics and dilemmas of unfolding historical processes.

This book, needless to say, does not use neoclassical analysis as a basis for understanding how firms go astray. Instead, its tools of diagnosis and prescription are derived from an alternative approach to economics known as behavioural theory, whose leading proponent, Herbert Simon, was awarded the Nobel Prize in Economics in 1978. Behavioural theory focuses on the ways in which uncertainty and complexity shape individual behaviour and affect the paths taken by economic systems. Conventional analysis, by contrast, starts by assuming choosers to be fully informed and able to handle unlimited amounts of information; its theories are only amended to incorporate more realistic informational assumptions if this is possible within its equilibrium-centred frame of reference. Whereas the conventional theorist uses simple, highly abstract theories and argues for statistical tests of their adequacy, the behavioural theorist employs a subjectivist, multidisciplinary case study-based approach to explanation (see Wiseman (ed.) (1983)). Consequently, behavioural theorists are often attacked for producing complex theories which lack general applicability. The title of this book should be sufficient to indicate that I believe it *is* possible to see broad patterns of behaviour at work in processes of corporate evolution. If such patterns did not exist this book would be very different; it would be more akin to a series of long lists of things firms could get wrong (such books, of course, do exist, but they are not produced by economists) than a web of interrelated theories constructed from a common, behavioural perspective. (This is all I shall say in justification of the methodology I employ, for I have justified my approach in detail on many previous occasions, in Dow and Earl (1981; 1982, ch. 13); Earl (1980; 1983a; 1983b; and 1983c, chs 1 and 3).)

The mistakes made in firms are not always fatal to the corporate

Introduction

entities involved, or even to the security of existing management teams. None the less, they are things to be avoided, for mistakes usually entail misallocations of resources. (I say 'usually' here, because some 'mistakes' may have what are felt to be socially desirable distributional consequences.) This book is thus provided with a practical rationale: if it can contribute to an understanding of the processes whereby large firms come to make mistakes, it may make it possible for decision-makers in firms and government to make fewer errors in future. A number of earlier books by behavioural economists have attempted to contribute to this end by writing about the formation of corporate strategies and organisational structures which, so it is claimed, will be conducive to business success (the classic text is Ansoff's (1968) *Corporate Strategy*). I believe that decision-makers may be able to learn still more about how to achieve success if they start by investigating how their peers have been lured into error; they are much more likely then to be stirred to inquire 'Is *my* firm behaving like that; do *I* really act in that way?' In explaining how firms make mistakes the book will, of course, attempt to point out how they might be avoided, but its emphasis is very different from that usually chosen by writers on corporate evolution and strategy.

The title should help to indicate that this book is a sequel to my (1983c) work *The Economic Imagination*, in which I considered at length how individuals cope with a real world which is far removed from the world of unbounded rationality and certainty that mainstream neoclassical theorists commonly assume to help simplify their own, everyday work as economists. My earlier book includes many implications for the design and marketing of products that will help a firm to prosper. But the ability of a business to meet the aspirations of its participants depends on much more than an ability to design products and interpret (or mould) consumer preferences. The appropriate *set* of investment projects and organisational structure must be selected as well. Individual production activities are often very hard to treat in isolation, either at any moment or through time. The physical linkages between them may be obvious (though they tend to be neglected by mainstream, reductionist economists), but significant also are the linked ideas they create in the minds of managers, for these tie them to particular courses of action, by processes of which they will often be unaware. Hence, having studied the ways in which choices in general are affected by personality factors and information handling problems, I feel it is time to move

Introduction

on to examine the origins of *corporate* personalities, and the implications for the long term fortunes of businesses of the ways in which they, as complex structures themselves, 'view' the world and 'learn' from experience. Although this book is a development of my earlier work, it has been written to be self-contained.

The thinking behind this book may become clearer if I give a short account of its origins, for although it may seem an obvious sequel to *The Economic Imagination* most of the research for it was carried out before that for the earlier book. In 1977-9 I was a research student at Cambridge and I had the opportunity to give some undergraduate supervisions to final year students on Current Economic Problems and on the Modern Business Enterprise. A popular topic for discussion in lectures and essay questions concerned the threat to western economies posed by Japanese firms and, increasingly, by those from Taiwan and Korea. Many faculty members were in favour of using import controls and providing massive state assistance to aid reconstruction; some even advocated direct state entrepreneurship. This view stood in sharp contrast to the rising free market ideologies of Ronald Reagan and Margaret Thatcher, which argued that strong overseas competition was essential to force domestic firms to be dynamic. Both of these views left me dissatisfied, for they seemed to take little account of the literature on processes of corporation evolution with which I had become fascinated as an undergraduate.

Both the Left and the Right seemed to view firms rather as if they were like donkeys with perfectly conditioned reflex responses to, respectively, carrot and stick incentives. For the most part, their discussions of corporate responses to incentives left out any discussion of the importance of corporate perceptions, attitudes, past experiences, aspirations, and organisational structures, in shaping eventual outcomes. The Left seemed to presume that decision-makers would notice 'carrot' incentives and know what to make of them; the Right acted as if a failure to respond to a mild push in the past was not indicative of a degree of corporate unconsciousness so great that a major blow would produce death rather than an awakening. My researches aimed at providing my undergraduates with a rather more perceptive analysis led me to discover that I was not the only one with such doubts (see Loasby (1967a, 1967c) and Cyert and George (1969), whose warnings have been ignored by most economists); that Marshall's comments about inertia in large firms had a modern-day relevance; and, most of all, that it can be helpful to see corporations as being prone to suffer from trying to 'run before they can walk', and

Introduction

tending to go through periods of emotional (as well as financial) depression, identity crises and marital (merger) problems, which parallel those in the lives of individuals.

The structure of the book is as follows. Chapter 1 is designed to serve as a bridge between the conventional economists's way of looking at the growth of large firms, and the alternative behavioural view which emphasises the discontinuities and cyclical aspects of corporate evolution. To build this bridge, I will take one of the most influential books on corporate growth – Robin Marris' (1964) *Economic Theory of 'Managerial' Capitalism* – and show how its steady-state model of the expansion of a large firm automatically generates cyclical behaviour if one makes it internally consistent by assuming that managers, and not merely shareholders and customers, are less than perfectly informed.

Chapter 2 is concerned with questions that managers will rarely pause to consider, namely, 'Why do firms exist at all, given that there are other ways of arranging production, and what light does an understanding of the nature of the firm shed on decisions about where a firm should draw its boundaries at any moment?' Boundary decisions are, or should be, the very essence of business strategy formation: for example, if a firm has spare resources, it can hire these out to other enterprises instead of involving itself in a new activity; if it requires inputs, it can make them itself or obtain them from subcontractors. But it is only very recently that solutions to these questions have been worked out by behavioural economists, so it is not surprising that many firms have groped their way to unfortunate boundary choices. The new solutions are subtle, intellectually exciting and deserve to be more widely known. Furthermore, they help focus the overall analysis on questions of knowledge, since they centre on the costs of taking decisions in a changing and uncertain world; on conflicts of interest; and on the possibility of one decision-making unit being unpleasantly surprised by the actions of another.

Chapters 3, 4 and 5 consider how corporate decision-makers actually attempt to cope with uncertainty and complexity, and why they often experience great difficulty in facing up to a need to bring about major strategic changes. In this group of chapters, as in the rest of the book, the analysis draws heavily not merely on the literature of behavioural economics but also from business history, psychology, organisational sociology, and the philosophy of science. These sources may sound disparate, but in fact they share common perspectives. They lend themselves naturally to integration, in what

Introduction

might be called (echoing, respectively, Kuhn (1970) and Lakatos (1970)) a 'paradigmatic' or 'research programme-based' view of human action. This group of chapters begins by focusing on the ways in which individual decision-makers process information as they make up their minds, and shows how thought processes may lead to poor decisions being taken. As the analysis proceeds, however, attention turns increasingly to the means by which a firm tends to acquire a distinctive personality of its own – a 'corporate imagination' – which significantly shapes the kinds of decisions taken by individuals who make up the corporate whole. This part of the book ends by showing how the often tortuous processes that lead to the abandonment of outmoded corporate strategies closely parallel the patterns outlined in Kuhn's work on the structure of *scientific revolutions*.

It is one thing to face up to the need for a new strategy but another to dream up and evaluate possible options. The next group of chapters (6, 7 and 8), therefore, are concerned with how firms do, and should, put new strategies together once they have come to perceive that their technological and market environments have changed. Chapter 6 shows how attempts to diversify often founder because of the managerial blinkering produced by previous strategies, and how they can get out of control and lead to a 'corporate identity crisis'. Chapter 7 is concerned with the possible misuses of learning curves and experience curves as strategic planning aids. Themes from this chapter are carried over into Chapter 8, which investigates the strategic importance of product and process lifecycles, and the interactions between them. These lifecycles are often poorly understood and get overlooked by some firms, causing them sometimes to pronounce their products as 'dead' rather than merely 'in need of repositioning'; to be taken by surprise when a rival product 'takes off'; or to carry the production of some lines from the initial development to market growth stages without realising the organisational implications of the changing scale of production.

With Chapter 8 having raised the issue of how production processes and organisational structures should be related, it is natural for Chapter 9 to be devoted to the question of how a multiproduct firm's internal structure should be related to its strategy. Organisational concerns also figure prominently in Chapter 10, where there is an investigation of why it is that attempts to change corporate boundaries by means of mergers and takeovers often have harmful long run effects on business performance.

Introduction

Finally, and predictably, given the book's origins, Chapter 11 explores the implications of the previous chapters for government policy makers who are attempting to stop processes of de-industrialisation. Parts of this chapter will delight proponents of the merits of market forces and the reduction of state intervention in industry; parts will appeal to advocates of industrial subsidies and the regulation of merger activities – the pursuit of the logic of the analysis does not lead me to come down firmly on one side or the other. This chapter might therefore be expected to hold a certain appeal for Social Democrats, but even they will probably find some parts of it controversial.

1 The Simple Mechanics of Corporate Growth and Decline

1.1 INTRODUCTION

Economists prefer, for the most part, to write about firms which always get things right, rather than firms which are fallible. This is not because the typical economist believes that firms do not make mistakes. Rather, it is a result of the methodology such an economist employs in order to reduce the possibility that she, herself, will make mistakes or end up with nothing to say. Mainstream economics is highly formal in nature and has as its focus the notion that it is not unreasonable or inherently misleading to theorise about economic systems as if they are in, or near to, or heading towards, some position of equilibrium or steady-state growth. The word 'mistake' poses a threat to this core idea, for it seems to carry with it a picture of systems prone to chaos rather than coherence, to entropy rather than order. Mistakes are necessarily bound up with complexity and uncertainty. Such features are at odds with the mainstream economist's desire to produce mathematical models which generate determinate outcomes, and which have as their essential elements stable, well-specified functional relationships.

Once an economist decides to investigate corporate evolution from a perspective that emphasises the sources of failure rather than the characteristics of success, the immediate difficulty consists in knowing where to start. There are so many things a firm might get wrong. Such an economist is faced with a predicament rather akin to that which would overwhelm an aspiring entrepreneur if she asked, 'What line of business, out of *all* those possible, is the one for me?' A 'big idea', related to something familiar, is necessary

The Corporate Imagination

to focus the attention; to provide a framework upon which discussions of matters of detail can be hung. In the present context, the familiar idea which will serve as a starting point is Marris' (1964) classic work, *The Economic Theory of 'Managerial' Capitalism.* Marris' theory is concerned with what a firm must do if it is to achieve continuous growth and profitability. Viewed from an alternative perspective, however, it can be seen as a theory which points to the areas where significant opportunities for corporate error lie.

This chapter thus begins as a seemingly conventional exposition of the elements of Marris' theory. Section 1.2 is concerned with the goals of managers in modern corporations, while section 1.3 introduces the product lifecycle concept (discussed in much more detail in Chapter 8). Section 1.4 examines the way in which growth is constrained by profitability, whereas section 1.5 introduces an organisational perspective and shows how realised profit rates depend on the rate at which the firm has been growing in the recent past. In section 1.6, however, as these elements are put together, the exposition ceases to be conventional. The removal of Marris' implicit assumption, that managers understand perfectly the organisational constraints on profitable growth, results in steady expansion ceasing to be the inevitable path for the firm to take. Paths of cyclical instability, and even cumulative collapse, become possible if the firm fails to get on the steady-state expansion path at the first opportunity, or does not learn how it is to be reached. With section 1.6 having raised the possibility of cumulative collapse following an initial mistake about how much growth a firm might handle, section 1.7 considers what escape routes might be possible so that the firm might live to fight another day. Section 1.8 is a brief conclusion, on the implications of the chapter for the nature of the analysis to be presented in the rest of the book.

1.2 Managerial Goals and Fears

Marris' theory of 'managerial' capitalism is one of a number of post-war theories that have attempted to consider the economic implications of the divorce of ownership and control in modern corporations. If managers do not own the companies they administer, it is possible that they will not wish to administer them in the best interests of their shareholders. If shareholders of large firms are dispersed, and each have only small percentage stakes in any company, they will find it difficult to ensure that managers operate in their interests. Individually, they will be unable to vote a new board into power. Collectively, they might be able to do so, but getting together in a concerted action will be costly to arrange. Furthermore, there is the added problem that they can never know for sure whether or not managers are deliberately acting against their interests. They do not have the specialist knowledge required to make a competent judgment of managerial performance. This is so even if an ambitious 'insider' manager asserts that the existing top management are acting against shareholder interests. Company directors, the only people shareholders have a direct right to dismiss with their votes, would appear to have scope for discretionary behaviour to suit their own ends. Two questions are raised by this possibility: what goals do such directors have, and what constraints do they face in trying to meet them?

Traditional theories of the firm argue that firms are run to maximise profits, or, to put it slightly differently, to maximise the present value of their dividend streams. Marris (1964, ch. 2) contends, by contrast, that directors are concerned with profitability only indirectly, insofar as it affects their security as board members, and their ability to achieve corporate *growth* (measured in terms of the growth rate of gross assets). Growth, in turn, is only a proxy objective: if the directors demonstrate their competence by successfully expanding their firms' interests to encompass new products, markets and technologies, *they* will be able to command higher salaries, prestige and power. As Marris (1964, p. 59) observes,

> It is difficult to accord the accolade of professional ability to a chief executive who competently maintains a constant output, with constant profits, constant product mix, and constant methods of production in a constant market!

The expansion of a firm frequently will also involve an enlargement of its organisational hierarchy; the pyramid of control becomes broader and taller. Directors are thus able to exercise power over more employees; their status is enhanced.

Since managers are presumed to enjoy their greater power, the conventional 'net advantages' analysis of wage determination would lead one to expect that, other things equal, higher posts would be paid less than lower posts. But it seems to be the case that there is a virtually universal belief that a manager must be paid more than his or her subordinates (see Simon, 1957a). Any corporate growth which increases the height of the management pyramid will thus provide a justification for directors to increase their own rates of remuneration (Marris (1964), pp. 90–9). The bigger the firm, then, the higher will be the remuneration of its executives. A study by Cosh (1975), using cross-sectional data for over one thousand UK companies, failed to refute this assumption of Marris' work: company size (measured by the natural logarithm of net assets) was the major determinant of the remuneration of chief executives. Furthermore, Cosh also found that profitability was a statistically significant determinant of remuneration in only seven of the seventeen industry groups he investigated. So long as they do not lose their jobs as a result of attempting to achieve corporate growth at the expense of profits, it seems generally in the interests of directors to aim for growth rather than profitability.

But, Marris argues, directors will not ignore altogether the effects of their growth-seeking policies on profit rates and share values. Low profit rates and share values which are allowed to persist will affect their chances of financing corporate growth by borrowing and by new equity issues. To the extent that they own shares in the companies of which they are directors (for example, as a result of stock-option schemes), they will need to consider the adverse impact of growth on their own share values and dividends, weighing this against the benefits they can expect to obtain from being in control of a larger company. But their biggest worry in respect of the consequences of allowing their profit rate and stock market valuation to fall concerns the possibility of a takeover raid. If they are to keep their jobs as directors they must not allow the value that existing shareholders place on their equity holdings (that is, the market price plus any extra it would cost to attract intramarginal holdings on to the market) to get depressed below the value to a single outsider (for example, another firm) of the assets behind the equity. It is a central assumption of Marris' theory that information problems ensure that takeover raiders are relatively scarce; were this not the case, no firm would be able to pursue *any* policy yielding less than the market discount rate. That it is not an unreasonable assumption seems to be confirmed by Whittington's (1971) study of UK quoted companies in the period 1948–60. Companies with poor profitability records survived for long periods without being taken over. Over the twelve years, 96 companies achieved average annual profit rates of less than

The Simple Mechanics of Corporate Growth and Decline

5 per cent, whereas the average for the 1955 continuing members of the sample population was 16.6 per cent. The threat of takeover reduces the conjectured boundary of managerial discretion somewhat, but does not eliminate it entirely.

If anything, capital market imperfections actually encourage managers to strive for growth at the expense of profitability, as a means of securing their own positions. The bigger a company is, the fewer other companies there will be that could reasonably expect to make a successful bid for it. This is borne out in the work of Singh (1971, 1975), who found that, except for members of the smallest decile of quoted companies, the best way a management team could enhance its chances of survival in statistical terms was by becoming bigger, not by becoming more profitable.

1.3 Product Portfolios and Lifecycles

As they try to expand their firms, directors have essentially three kinds of routes they can take. They can: (a) attempt to expand their penetration of their existing markets; (b) enter existing markets which previously they have ignored; (c) create and market new products. In the long run, the pursuit of option (a) on its own will be inadequate as a means of enabling them to meet their goals. Unless a market has its own underlying growth, a firm which tries to expand by market penetration alone will grind to a standstill once it achieves dominance, even if it is not forcibly brought to a halt by an anti-monopoly legislation long before it has a 100 per cent market share. Furthermore, a market which is growing and prosperous today, may be one that will be stagnant or declining tomorrow. Products (and, even more so, brands) tend to have finite lifespans of viability: they get superseded by new technologies, stigmatised by changes of fashion, and left behind by increasing affluence. Thus even to preserve its size, let alone expand it, a firm must continually be changing the products in its catalogue or reorientating its sales efforts in different market segments. Diversification is essential for survival in a dynamic environment. A major part of managerial efforts at the top level necessarily must consist in appraising precisely how, and how fast, the environment is changing, and the extent to which their competitive strategies can bring it under control.

This task involves much more than the estimation of cost and demand curves in rival markets, working out implied prices and profits, and then making the appropriate investment choice – which is how traditional economic analysis depicts managerial behaviour in static markets. In a dynamic world, costs are affected by 'learning-by-doing', while demand curves are neither stable nor reversible, since the preferences of customers (be they individual consumers or industrial users) are the products of experience and are continually changing. To work out which activities will be most conducive to corporate growth, managers need to be able to assess prospects for learning and the creation of wants, and understand the role played by processes of interpersonal stimulation in decision-making. Choice is much more than a series of adjustments to price changes amongst established commodities (see, further, Earl (1983b; 1983c)).

It is the fact that customer choices involve learning processes and various forms of crowd behaviour that leads Marris (1964, ch. 4) to place particular emphasis on the complications caused by the concept of 'the product life cycle' for the process of corporate growth. Once a product is launched, demand will not build up immediately, even if its price falls within the budget ranges of most consumers. Initially (as recently with VCRs and '3D' cameras), it will be purchased only by a limited number of 'pioneering' buyers, who are the first to become aware of the product and whose inquisitive tendencies overwhelm any anxieties about the prospect of wasting money on something unknown. In this stage of the cycle, the product often imposes a cash drain on the firm (despite its sales volume being relatively insensitive to price), owing to the need to engage in heavy advertising expenditure and dealer incentive schemes. A big question mark hangs over its future. If it is to be viable, it must acquire a mass market. Marris sees its viability as depending upon whether or not a chain reaction is caused as a result of pioneering consumers purchasing it and spreading word about it. As with an atomic explosion, a critical number of interactions between potential buyers is necessary before a market will explode. If there are only a few 'pioneers', would-be 'sheep' will not acquire enough evidence that the product is worth trying; but if the 'sheep' begin to try it, the market will take off on its own as other 'sheep' follow. If the product soon appears to be stillborn, dealers will cease to stock it and hasten its early death, whereas if it passes the 'critical mass' stage and becomes a 'star performer', it will effectively begin to sell itself and generate a positive cash flow (even though its price has to be lowered as the market

The Simple Mechanics of Corporate Growth and Decline

becomes more price-conscious owing to the appearance of competing brands).

In the take-off phase, a product is still requiring investment in its own, expanding production facilities, so its ability to generate cash for expansion in other areas is relatively limited. As its market matures, however, the product's own sales are no longer expanding and its net impact on the corporate cash flow is at its greatest. Instead of contributing to the attainment of managerial growth goals directly, the product now begins to permit the company to grow by diversification into other markets. Sooner or later (and identifying how soon is the big problem) the market will decline due to saturation and/or the appearance of yet other products in earlier life cycle phases. Demand dwindles to replacement levels and the product ceases to function as a 'cash cow': it can no longer be milked of its net earnings to finance expansion elsewhere. The time has come for the firm to consider investing in a new version of the product or leaving the market altogether. In the former case, this sector of its activities once more becomes a drain on its cash resources; in the latter case, disinvestment provides a one-off injection of cash to buy replacement assets.

Growth-seeking directors ideally would like to have catalogues of products consisting only of 'star performers' and 'cash cows'. The infancy and decline stages of product lifecycles (which, following the work in this area by the Boston Consulting Group, are commonly known, respectively, as 'question marks' and 'dogs') involve low or negative turnover growth and drain cash from other areas. But typically their product portfolios will include some of these. Judging when to get out of a market is not always easy, while it is quite often the case that it is not possible to buy oneself into the 'star' stage of a product lifecycle without first going through the 'question mark' stage as an innovative producer or paying dearly to acquire a firm which has done so. And, for many 'question marks', the answer, in a world of uncertainty, will ultimately turn out to be a resounding 'No!'

1.4 Profitability as a Constraint on Growth

The catalogue of products that a team of directors inherits from a firm's past growth plays a key role in determining how fast the firm will be able to grow in the future. The firm's present capacity to produce particular commodities, coupled with its competence in organisation and marketing, determines its profit rate. This, in turn, determines how must investment the firm can finance internally, and how much money it will be able to raise from the capital market to pay for further accumulations of assets.

To say that a firm's investment activities are constrained by its past performance seems obvious enough, but this central idea of Marris' analysis of corporate growth is actually fundamentally at odds with the traditional neoclassical analysis of the firm. The traditional analysis is built around the idea of a perfect capital market. If a firm wishes to raise money to finance a scheme whose prospective marginal return is above the market rate of interest, it will find it has access to an infinite supply of funds. If it can only offer schemes which, at best, offer prospective rates of returns that are less than the market rate, it will be totally unable to raise external finance. Furthermore, its directors will be ejected as a result of a takeover raid and will be prevented even from using internally generated funds on such projects. In a world of uncertainty, such a view of the supply of finance to firms is hopelessly unrealistic. Prospective returns to investments are not guaranteed to equal actual returns. Nor are would-be suppliers of finance necessarily going to be able to notice all the investment proposals of would-be users of finance. The past track record of a firm will tend to be used as a guide to the likelihood of its prospective returns being realised. And, in the clamour for funds, large firms will be able to stand out against the rest, particularly since they are likely to be more diversified and the repercussions of the failure of any one line in their product portfolios are not likely to be catastrophic.

The way in which a firm's past investments constrain its growth rate can be presented in summary form with the aid of a diagram, Figure 1.1, though it is inevitably a poor shadow of the rich analysis of the supply of finance in Marris' book. Suppose the firm has net assets of 100 and that these are associated with a product portfolio which it is able to manage in such a way as to generate a net rate of profit (that is, allowing for interest charges, depreciation and corporation tax) of 10 per cent. If it pays out nothing in dividends and obtains no external finance, it can expand its assets by 10 per cent. If its net rate of profit is only 5 per cent it can, by such a policy, only expand its assets by 5 per cent; and so on. If it pays out, say, half of its profits as dividends, its internal supply of finance function swings to the left, pivoting on the origin of the diagram. In this case, it can only

The Simple Mechanics of Corporate Growth and Decline

finance a 5 per cent growth of assets from a 10 per cent net rate of profit, unless it raises funds from outside. Cutting dividend rates releases internal funds but harms the company share price, as shareholders see expenditure being directed at less attractive, marginal schemes. Thus the directors will be wary of cutting them too far, for fear of a take-over raid.

Marris suggests that, in the long run, a firm will not be able to raise external finance, even in an imperfect capital market, unless it is able to generate a profit rate above zero. On average, over the life of the

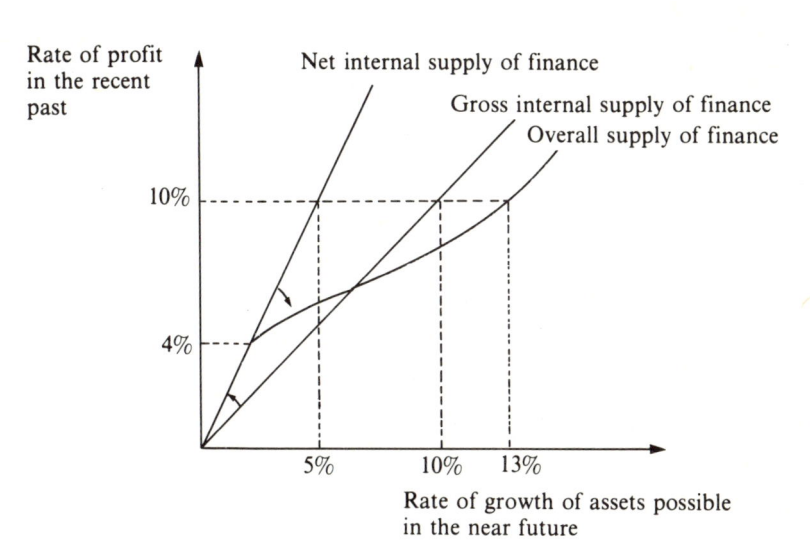

Figure 1.1 The Supply of Finance for Corporate Growth

firm, this may indeed be true, but loss-making firms will be able to extract external finance for reconstruction for a limited period. (This is particularly so when they are already in debt and suppliers of finance prefer to risk 'pouring good money after bad' to avoid immediate liquidation: as Keynes once put it, 'If you owe a bank one pound, the bank owns you; if you owe the bank a million pounds, you own the bank.') On Figure 1.1, the overall supply of finance function is drawn reflecting Marris' assumption: the firm needs a profit rate of 4 per cent before it can raise external finance. The slope of the function is drawn such that, if the firm has a profit rate of 10 per cent, it will choose to raise external funds on a scale sufficient to finance an 8 per cent growth in its assets, on top of the 5 per cent that it finances internally after paying a 5 per cent dividend.

The overall supply of finance function, on Figure 1.1, represents the maximum permissible growth rates of the firm's assets that are consistent with particular rates of profit, *given* a particular constant corporate valuation ratio (ratio of the market value of the firm to the book value of its net assets). If the directors were to choose a smaller proportionate use of external finance, and attempt a lower rate of growth for a given profit performance, the stock market would view this favourably; and vice versa. The greater the amount of loan finance a firm uses, the more its gross earnings are pre-empted as interest payments, and hence the more risky is its position. The more a firm finances its expansion by issuing new shares, the more it dilutes the voting power of existing shareholders; and vice versa. How far the directors choose to use external finance (and to economise on dividend payments) will depend on how far they think they can allow the valuation ratio to fall without leaving themselves open to an unacceptable risk of takeover. Given this tolerable valuation ratio and their recent profit performance, the position of their finance supply function and their maximum rate of asset growth in the present planning period, is fixed. The firm in Figure 1.1 chooses a 13 per cent rate of growth. *If* it is able to keep its profit rate at 10 per cent then, in the following period, starting from assets of 113, it could repeat the 13 per cent investment rate and expand its assets to 127.69; and so on. The obvious question is: will it be able to maintain its profit rate as it grows?

1.5 Growth as a Constraint on Profitability

As a firm buys assets and sets new investment schemes in motion, forces will be at work affecting the profitability of its constituent activities. Some of the products in its portfolio will move along a stage in their lifecycles. If many 'question marks' turn into 'star performers', but 'cash cows' do not turn into 'dogs', its profit rate will tend to expand. On the other hand, if 'question marks' and 'cash cows' turn into 'dogs', its profit rate will begin to fall. To the extent that the firm has been doing little investment in diversification in the past, its portfolio will tend to contain few 'question marks', but its 'star performers' will be turning into 'cash cows' as their markets

The Simple Mechanics of Corporate Growth and Decline

mature, and some 'cash cows' will be turning into 'dogs'. Consequently it will tend to have a relatively low profit rate. However, a firm which has been growing very rapidly by investment in diversification is also unlikely to be one with a high profit rate. This is because its product portfolios will contain many 'question marks' necessitating high research and development and marketing outlays. Furthermore, to the extent that a firm can only come up with a limited number of good diversification ideas at any one time, we would expect faster growth to entail more 'question marks' that fail to become 'star performers'. Between these two extremes lies the

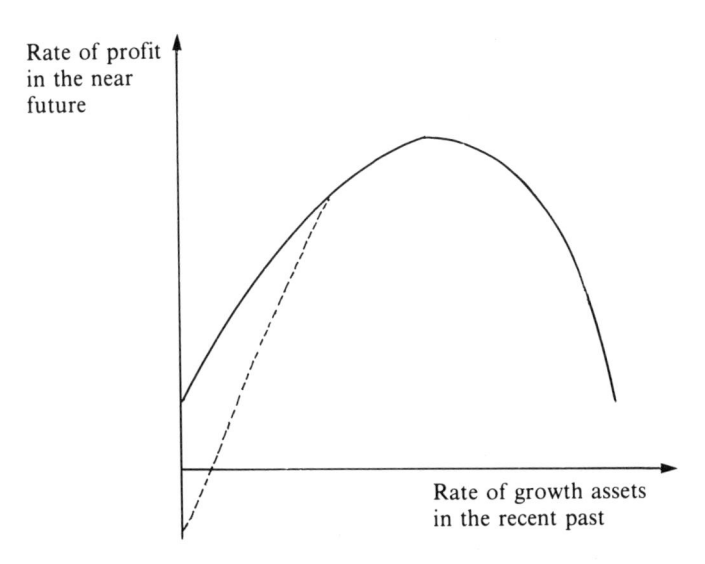

Figure 1.2 The Effect of Corporate Growth on Profitability

possibility of higher profit rates: a firm which has been growing at a rate that is neither so fast as to entail 'questionable' investments in new territories and technologies, nor so slowly as to be facing widespread market saturation in its catalogue of products, will, other things equal, tend to be relatively more profitable. Figure 1.2 is a graphical depiction of the pattern just described.

In Figure 1.2, the solid curve is the one to be found in Marris' work. The broken portion on the left hand side is perhaps how he *ought* to have drawn the curve to deal with the possibility that a firm may need to be growing to some extent merely to break even. If other firms are growing in the markets in which it sells, they will be enjoying increasing scale and learning-by-doing advantages (see Ch. 7) and will be able to undercut it, unless it too can expand its operations. The firm must expand, if only by market penetration, merely to keep its 'cash cows' from turning into 'dogs'.

On top of these 'product portfolio' considerations relating past growth with present profit rates, Marris places organisational considerations, largely derived from the work of Penrose (1959) (and which I discuss in more detail in Chapter 4). These centre on the idea that managerial efficiency depends to a great extent upon teamwork, and teams cannot be built up as effective units overnight. Up to a point, the influx of new talent at various levels in the corporate hierarchy will be conducive to profitability. Growth *may* bring fresh perspectives, and thus higher productivity in some activities, as personnel are promoted or newly hired. However, very rapid growth will lead to all manner of complications. Marris (1964, pp. 116–17) makes this point very vividly by pointing out that if a firm tried to grow at an infinite rate (assuming it could raise the funds to do so), employees with, on average, an infinitesimal length of service would not even know each other's names.

To a certain extent, diseconomies of growth can be overcome if a firm expands by means of merger rather than by assembling personnel, physical assets and market goodwill from scratch. But even here there are limits: directors can only contemplate or execute a limited number of possible mergers at any one time. To the extent they rush into mergers without properly appraising the costs and benefits, they are likely later to find they have made disappointing 'marriages' (see Ch. 10). Furthermore, if they are busy seeking out or arranging mergers, directors cannot be keeping such a watchful eye as they might have done on the existing activities of the firm or on schemes involving internal growth.

1.6 CYCLES OF CORPORATE INSTABILITY

The common practice of economists is to build up, separately, supply and demand functions, join them on a single diagram, and find (usually) an equilibrium solution. In section 1.4 a supply of finance function was constructed, showing how rapidly growth-seeking

The Simple Mechanics of Corporate Growth and Decline

managers might be able to expand the assets of their firm without subjecting themselves to an intolerable risk of takeover. But, so far, I have presented nothing on the demand side that corresponds to this supply of finance function. Readers familiar with Marris' work will wish to maintain that the relationship depicted above on Figure 1.2 is what Marris would call a 'demand for finance' function. I would prefer to label it as a 'managerial constraint on growth', for despite its appearance, it is not the same as Marris' demand for finance function. And the difference is a rather significant one. Let us consider it, how it arises, and what are its consequences.

Marris' book is inconsistent in its treatment of questions of knowledge. It allows shareholders to be ill-informed about corporate operations and consumers to be lacking pre-specified preferences for commodities. Managers are allowed to have limited project appraisal and team-constructing abilities at any moment (though not in the long run). However, there is one thing about which they are not unsure in his theory: managers understand perfectly well how the rate of growth achieved by a firm affects its subsequent profitability. They are trying to pursue policies that are sustainable in the long run, so they will not attempt to obtain more finance, for capacity growth, than they know they can safely handle; nor will they obtain any less.

In section 1.5, I drew the 'managerial constraint' on growth as an *ex post* feature, depicting what would happen to profitability if, in the event, particular growth policies were chosen. I made no claim that it was something of which managers were perfectly aware, or could discover. Indeed, I would go so far as to say that an unmoving function of this kind really does not exist to be pinned down by experimentation. Marris, it must be stressed, is able to call the curve, that I shall label as a 'managerial constraint', a 'demand for finance function' only because he assumes it is fixed and is something that managers perfectly understand. Marris' managers, that is to say, know how much growth they can handle without jeopardising particular profit rates and future growth possibilities; and, because they never make mistakes, their firms grow at steady rates, with constant profit rates. By assuming this, Marris is able to treat the firm as a set of *simultaneous* equations and, effectively, to remove history from his analysis: his firms *are* growing at particular rates with particular profit rates; they are not firms which *have been* growing at particular rates and which now stand poised *ready to try to grow* at particular rates and meet profit rate *expectations* (cf. Shackle (1982), p. 437). The business history and economic theory contributions

The Corporate Imagination

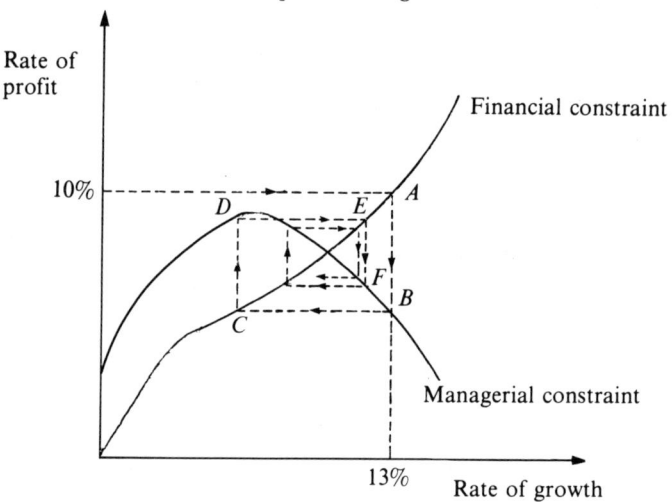

Figure 1.3   A Damped Corporate Cycle

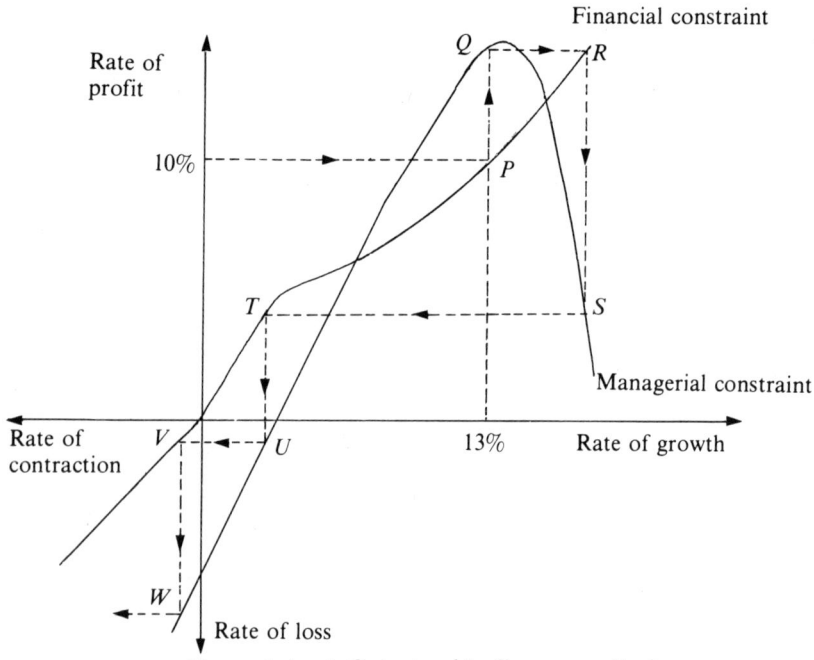

Figure 1.4   A Catastrophic Corporate Cycle

The Simple Mechanics of Corporate Growth and Decline

discussed in the rest of this book all serve to suggest, by contrast, that if one *must* treat a firm 'as if' it is a mechanism, reducible to a set of equations, a more useful perspective is to be obtained by assuming that managers are not perfectly aware of the 'managerial constraint' on successful growth. Of course, to presume they are not perfectly appraised of the nature of this constraint is not to presume they are entirely ignorant of it. However, their conjectures about it (along with those of the capital market) will largely make themselves felt in the supply of finance function.

So let us now, at last, lay Figure 1.2 on Figure 1.1 and watch as our managers, limited in their abilities to manage growth, struggle to meet their goals. Many possible evolutionary paths are possible, depending on the precise shapes of the curves representing the financial and managerial constraints. Two contrasting paths of corporate evolution are presented in Figures 1.3 and 1.4. The curves representing the finance supply functions are identical in these diagrams, but the firms face different managerial constraints on profitable growth. In both cases, having achieved 10 per cent profit rates in the recent past, the directors decide to embark on investment schemes involving a 13 per cent growth in net assets (point A on Figure 1.3; point P on Figure 1.4).

The firm in Figure 1.3 bites off more than it is immediately able to chew. Realised profits are pulled down to B by organisational problems. The next batch of investments are less ambitious (C) and the firm is pleasantly surprised by its subsequent performance (D). As a result, it expands its attempts at diversification once again (E), but again oversteps the mark and suffers from a (somewhat smaller) dose of corporate indigestion (F). So long as the functions do not move (which, in reality, is unlikely), the firm will eventually attain stable growth and profits at the rates indicated where the two curves cross: that is, Marris' result is achieved.

Figure 1.4, by contrast, presents a sorry tale of a firm for which one big mistake eventually proves to be fatal. An attempt to grow at the (unlucky!) rate of 13 per cent seems to be very successful (Q). The trouble is that euphoria sets in (cf. Minsky (1975) and Dow and Earl (1982), ch. 11) and the firm attempts to grow at a rate of around 20 per cent in a short space of time (R). The managerial constraint bites savagely: profits fall (S) and investment has to be cut back severely (T). Unfortunately, the firm operates in markets where scale and learning effects are important. The slower growth rate does not enable it to keep up with its rivals. It is squeezed further and losses result (U). (By this point, it should be added, the teamwork constraint on growth will be tending to operate in a reverse way: growth-seeking staff of the highest ability will be leaving in search of greener pastures.) Once it makes losses, the firm's decline accelerates: the external capital market fails to provide further funds because the firm's future prospects seem hopeless as its rivals expand their market shares and further cut their costs. It cannot even keep its net assets intact (V) if it pays no dividends to shareholders. Its losses become ever larger (W), particularly since the drain of ambitious management personnel continues and its products become socially stigmatised. It cannot survive.

1.7 SLACK IN THE MECHANISM

Or can it? To a behavioural economist, elements in the economic system and, indeed, the system as a whole, are not appropriately to be seen as fully specified, taut units. The histories taken by these elements are not predetermined in a mechanical way by their initial endowments of resources and possibly misguided beliefs. Various forms of slack provide some, if not always enough, room for manoeuvre. The initial mistake made by the firm in Figure 1.4 need not be fatal if its directors are able to shift either their finance function or the managerial constraint, via some form of slack uptake.

Various forms of slack exist in firms. The kind most widely discussed in behavioural economics is what Cyert and March (1963, pp. 36–8) have called 'organisational slack'. They see the firm as a coalition of individuals with partly complementary and partly competitive interests, which remains viable so long as it generates returns (in financial or non-pecuniary terms) that are sufficient to enable the minimum requirements of those involved – what they term 'transfer earnings' – to be met. Many participants in a firm will, at any time, be prepared to settle for less than they are getting, or to put more in than they are doing at present. Their excess returns or unused contributions, summed together, comprise the firm's organisational slack.

It is important to realise that this form of slack does not arise from any conscious decision of the firm as a whole. It arises out of the efforts of individuals seeking to meet their own ends, exploiting specialist knowledge as they do so. Shareholders, for example, may

The Simple Mechanics of Corporate Growth and Decline

not tell directors that they would tolerate a cut in dividends without selling out to someone else. Directors thus cannot be sure how far it is safe to risk squeezing dividends to finance expansion. In bad times, when a failure to invest will result in the collapse of the firm, and with it their directorships, they may reduce dividends and thus take the risk that this will cause the shareholders to get together and remove them. But in good times, they will not risk their positions in this way. (In this connection, it is interesting to note the findings of the Ryder (1975) investigation of the collapse of British Leyland. From 1968 to 1974 its pre-tax profits were woefully inadequate: its highest earning rate as a percentage of sales was 4.2 (1969): the average was a mere 2.3 per cent. Yet despite this, BL management distributed £70 million, from a net profits total of £74 million, as dividends in the period 1968–74. The failure to use this possible form of organisational slack seems to have been the result of a belief that to cease paying dividends would preclude any prospect of new equity issues: that is to say, the BL management did not see dividends as a source of slack. As it happened, they only raised £49 million by a rights issue in 1972.)

Other possible forms of organisational slack include: concealed quality reductions in outputs, which buyers *might* not detect; lower staffing levels to which unions *might* agree, if pushed; distress borrowing facilities which a firm's bankers *might* provide, but which they have not openly promised; financial reserves which managers are known to hold and which other parties do not attempt to appropriate, because they *might* be necessary to safeguard these parties' interests in a crisis. A somewhat subtle example of organisational slack, enjoyed by managers at the expense of customers, is evident in the work of Brown (1957), on innovation in the US machine tool industry. He notes (1957, p. 411) that, in testimony before the House Naval Affairs Committee, Ralph Flanders remarked:

During the good years he (the machine tool builder) must set aside reserves in order to retain his engineers and mechanics to redesign his line and improve it, so that he may quicken that demand by offering a machine so much better that it renders his earlier products obsolete.

Brown then reports that, in his own interviews,

Executives of machine tool firms repeatedly expressed the opinion that if sufficient research were undertaken major improvements on specific machine tools would be forthcoming. Many of the executives knew, or believed they knew, what the next improvements would be, how they should be designed into the machine, and when this would be done.

Coalition members do not attempt to test theories about the 'slack returns' being enjoyed by other parties in normal times, because the decisions involved are not guaranteed to be reversible. Furthermore, what the other coalition members will be prepared to accept is not independent of their external points of reference: whether or not an attempt to cut staffing levels results in a strike and lost production will depend partly on the overall state of the economy.

Organisational slack is a result of ignorance, but ignorance of a special kind, which it is convenient to label, following Williamson (1975), as *information impactedness*: the information relevant to a decision is not freely available, because people who have it do not find it in their interests to make it available. But there is another form of ignorance – due to an absence of search for, or poor appreciation of, alternative schemes of action – which also provides the origins of a form of slack. This differs from what Cyert and March call organisational slack in that its uptake does not involve losses being felt by any members of the coalition. I will call this form of slack 'X-inefficiency', after Leibenstein (1966, 1969, 1976), but I recognise that, by confining the use of Leibenstein's term in this way, I will surprise some readers: the term 'X-inefficiency' is typically used, illogically, to encompass aspects of productivity determination which include organisational slack, as if *any*thing resulting in productivity being below what is possible is a bad thing. Organisational slack, however, should only be seen as 'bad' if one does not approve of its distribution between members of a particular coalition; for, as Loasby (1976, p. 119) observes, it exists as a result of individual choices.

Evidence that organisational slack and X-inefficiency exist, and are taken up by firms attempting to escape from the cumulating consequences of mistaken policies, is widespread. But probably the only author hitherto first to set up a mechanistic analysis of corporate growth and decline, and then use a discussion of slack uptake to explain how firms escape from the processes of decline, is Jack Downie (1958) in his book *The Competitive Process*. Downie was concerned with the welfare implications of competition between firms of widely differing sizes. Large firms might be able to obtain

The Simple Mechanics of Corporate Growth and Decline

positions of monopoly through the mechanistic exploitation of scale economies: if a firm got ahead in the competitive race, it would tend to wipe out its competitors, by the transfer of their markets to its own clutches, as it lowered its prices. Against this 'transfer process', however, he set the possibility that threatened firms could find new ways of doing things, shifting *their* cost functions as they did so, or better products to make. This he called the 'innovation process'. If enough slack existed in the system, and was taken up in time, one would observe a continual jostling for leadership within markets, rather than an inexorable trend towards monopoly. In many ways, Downie's vision of the competitive process was a modern-day version of Marshall's view. It has been one of the major influences on the shape of the arguments in this book.

1.8   CONCLUSION

In this chapter I began by considering Marris' famous attempt to construct a deterministic model of the modern corporation, a model whose deterministic nature precluded corporate fallibility. I then went on to show what could happen to a firm whose directors did not anticipate correctly the effects that policies designed to achieve high immediate rates of growth would have on future profitability. By introducing uncertainty into the model, I produced corporate fallibility and lost determinism. The firm did not necessarily adjust smoothly to the working through of product lifecycles or changes in personnel. It *might* make mistakes, and these *might* be fatal. In fact, the evidence available in company histories suggests that, in general, firms do not grow at steady rates. Of course, this is partly the result of macroeconomic instability, or of an inability of managers to think of new uses for investment funds. But only partly. Most companies also exhibit cyclical behaviour that results from mistaken decisions. To understand how these errors come to be made, we need to consider in detail the nature of the managerial constraint on growth. It is not enough to see the firm as a mechanism; we need also to look at 'the ghost in the machine' (cf. Koestler, 1975) and examine how it thinks, how its personality constrains its adaptability in turbulent times. But, before we do so, there is something we should recognise in order to prevent ourselves from making a major mistake: so far we have taken the existence of firms for granted, as if it is inevitable that production should be arranged *in* firms *by* managers. Since this is not, in fact, the case, and since many corporate mistakes centre on decisions to arrange productive activities within a particular firm instead of within and between several firms, we may profit by pausing to consider, in rather abstract terms, the role of, and rationale for, the firm.

2 Choosing the Boundaries of a Firm

2.1 INTRODUCTION

The viability of any set of production schemes will generally not be invariant with the institutional arrangements under which they are put into operation. And, if it looks viable to implement a particular set of investment projects within a firm, it is by no means the case that this is a wise thing to do. Far greater returns *may* be available if the firm makes more use of external resources in the production and distribution of the set of projects, and uses its spare internal resources in some other activity. In this chapter I am going to try to show how choices about the boundaries of firms should be made and, indeed, why firms exist at all.

This issue originally received attention as long ago as 1937, in a paper by Ronald Coase. But the full implications of Coase's work have only been explored much more recently, by Williamson (1975) and Kay (1982, 1984). It is too early for most managers to be aware of this new academic analysis, yet the analysis itself has been presented, for the most part, as descriptive – as if strategists were aware of the relative merits of alternative ways of drawing corporate boundaries, and reasons for them, before the academic economists had worked them out. The prescriptive element in this new work relates mainly to anti-trust legislation and competition policy. The authors do not take great account of the possibility that firms, like Topsy, may have 'just growed', without properly weighing up the factors that form the building blocks of their new theory. Successful firms *may* do so, and drive out those who do not, but I believe that many long run survivors themselves go through troubled times because they fail properly to consider how a firm *should* draw its boundaries. It is thus to be hoped

The Corporate Imagination

that the work of Williamson and Kay may enable strategists to ensure their firms survive in future more on the basis of judgment than luck (cf. Alchian, 1950). The present chapter is a highly compressed account of this new work and readers are therefore advised to consult the primary sources if the ideas appeal to their imaginations.

The rest of the chapter is structured as follows. Section 2.2 is concerned with Coase's original analysis of the nature of a firm. Section 2.3 then shows how Williamson developed Coase's main theme in order to deal with the possibility that traders might be deceitful, and how he explained the emergence of hierarchical control systems within firms. Section 2.4 explores Kay's incorporation into this framework of the significance of linkages between production activities and the effects of technical change. The role of linkages in focusing the attention of corporate strategists has also been discussed in recent work by Moss (1981) which clearly cannot be ignored. Now, some aspects of Moss' analysis of corporate strategy are highly commendable (see section 6.2), but I am rather concerned about the validity of his attempts to challenge the logic behind the work of Coase and Williamson with a series of arguments which, themselves, seem logically flawed. The alternative conclusions at which Moss arrives are particularly interesting since, compared with his rivals, he makes a great use of business history works in justifying his analysis. As a description of how some firms *do* think, Moss' work may well be correct, but, as an analysis of how they should think about their boundary choices, it is frustrating: he so nearly comes to understand the arguments of Coase and Williamson and then misses their basic point. By examining, in section 2.5, how Moss gets his emphasis wrong, I hope to reduce further the prospect of managerial errors. Finally, section 2.6 is a short conclusion.

2.2 Coase's Original Analysis of the Nature of a Firm

Ask any manager, 'Why does your firm exist?' or, 'Why are firms necessary?' and watch her pause in surprise. It may take her quite some time to think of a reply, for she is likely to take the existence of her firm, and firms generally, for granted. When she does put an answer together it will be very different from the analysis presented in this chapter. She will tend to talk about the products that her firm produces, the particular set of skills embodied in it, the story of the original entrepreneur, the interests of shareholders, and so on. She

Choosing the Boundaries of a Firm

usually will not talk about transactions costs, opportunism or the difficulties of drawing up contracts.

A firm is an institution, a legally constituted entity involved in the production of goods and/or services for sale *in* the market, using inputs purchased *from* the market. If production is arranged and coordinated *in* a firm, it is not being arranged and coordinated *in* the market, for the market is *outside* the firm. But 'in' and 'outside' have no necessary spatial connotation in this context. In a spatial sense, for example, part of a factory may be 'in firm A' but in a legal sense it may be 'in firm B', with firm A merely holding a title to the right of access to a flow of services from it over a particular period. If a firm buys up another firm that supplies its raw materials or components, part of the production process has been internalised and removed from the market, even if the inputs are still ordered following exchanges between the same personnel, and delivered on the same trucks. If a supplier fails to deliver goods specified in a contract arrived at in the market place, the customer can resort to the courts to obtain redress. If an internal supplier fails to carry out a command, the people involved cannot be taken to court unless, in letting down another part of the organisation, they have broken contracts which were agreed to in the market. To understand the nature of a firm in *economic* terms, therefore, one requires an understanding of the costs of arranging and coordinating production with different kinds of contracts, and of the costs of enforcing contracts. This is the chief message of Ronald Coase's (1937) classic paper, 'The Nature of the Firm'.

For Coase, the essence of a firm is that a set of contractual arrangements exists between a group of resource owners, in which their precise input and output obligations are not completely spelt out. If production is arranged according to a set of fully specified contracts, covering all the contingencies that could arise during their period of existence, this production is not to be thought of as taking place within a firm. The essence of a firm is that the coordination of economic activities is achieved, not by the price mechanism, but by discussion, commands and bargaining within a bureaucratic organisation. Internal forces, within a set of partially specified contractual ties, supersede the market mechanism.

A means of coordination is necessary because the production and market environments are not static. Consider what happens when a breakdown occurs in an integrated system. (I have memories of a school trip to the Ebbw Vale steelworks, during which the leading edge of a tongue of sheet steel twisted as it hurtled down the rolling track, jammed in the coiling device at the end and caused the rest of the sheet to concertina to a standstill. While it was being cut free, all the previous stages of the process had to be slowed down or stopped, and hot steel was cooling down between the furnaces and the rolling mill.) In a 'firm', people will usually have *some* prior idea of what they must do to aid the repair, or while the repair is being carried out. But *precisely* what happens depends on decisions taken there and then – decisions about who should do what and, privately, in the minds of those affected, about how to respond to the new commands.

With an appropriate set of contracts, such a breakdown could be handled without any need for new decisions. The fact that a breakdown had occurred would be announced and people would simply look at their contracts, to which they had agreed previously at a particular set of market prices, to see what they were supposed to do if this contingency arose. They would then act accordingly. There would be no need for managers if production were arranged in this way. But the owners of the capital resources would need to be very skilled to put together the appropriate contracts and get them agreed with the workers involved. If the contracts failed to take account of contingencies which actually did arise, they would have to be scrapped and new ones concluded – possibly in the heat of a crisis. The longer the period embraced by a set of contracts, the less surprising it would be to find them failing to match environmental conditions because particular contingencies had not been anticipated. Attempts to preclude such difficulties by widening the span of possibilities covered by the contracts would not be guaranteed to succeed, but they would be costly to design and negotiate. Large parts of the 'small print' in such contracts would be redundant; not just because only one contingency could arise at any moment, but also because certain events would, if they actually occurred, clearly narrow the channels of possibilities or block some of them altogether.

The costs of drawing up and agreeing upon complex, long term contracts could be substituted for the costs of using short term, but still fully specified contracts. These would cover fewer possibilities and contain fewer redundant clauses but, in a world of surprises, they too might frequently be inappropriate. Attempts to reduce the number of occasions when this happened, by making the duration of contracts almost infinitely short, would lead to negotiation costs rising towards infinity. (Imagine the difficulties of trying to keep production going during turbulent periods, while simultaneously trying to arrange new employment contracts every few hours or

Choosing the Boundaries of a Firm

minutes!) And even the shortest possible contracts would not be sure to leave the capital owner in the best position to deal with a *kaleidoscopic*, discontinuous environmental shift (cf. Shackle (1974) and the correspondence between Keynes and Townshend in Keynes (1979), pp. 288–94 – where the discussions concern the theoretical rationale for liquidity and the importance of money, but where the arguments are essentially the same).

Some commonplace examples may help vividly to illuminate what can happen when expectations are disappointed in minor respects and parties to contracts insist on implementing them to the letter. Prima donnas, concert pianists and rock stars are prone to refuse to perform because their dressing rooms and stage arrangements are not as specified in their contracts. Such performers can afford the luxury of hiring skilled contract lawyers to safeguard their positions. Trade unionists, by contrast, may vent their discontent by 'working to rule' in such an extreme way that it is almost as if an outright strike has been called. In the railway industry, for example, minor, safety-related ommissions that would normally be overlooked may be used as justifications for holding up a train. If the show is to go on, or trains are to run, despite disappointed expectations, attitudes must be flexible. Contractual incompleteness promotes a flexible frame of mind and thus makes for organisational slack.

The rationale for the firm should now be obvious in situations of environmental instability and significant transactions costs. Relatively vague and open-ended contracts are cheaper to draw up and negotiate, and may enable unforeseen situations to be dealt with as they arise. Employment contracts, for example, give both sides some flexibility to try to mould the job to suit prevailing conditions. An illusion of permanence is given by an agreement that such contracts may be terminated by either side at, say, a month's notice; there is no need to negotiate terms or even mention the existence of the contracts at the start of most months. Equity financed investment offers similar benefits. The firm using it is not obliged to offer specified dividends, whereas, if it uses debenture finance, specific interest obligations must be met. Furthermore, if it uses equity issues to finance the purchase of machines instead of leasing them, these machines cannot be snatched away when a leasing arrangement runs out. The individual equity owner, on the other hand, is not tied to a specific asset (or, worse, part of a specific, indivisible asset). Her prospects of being able to sell out her interest in the activity in question are thus enhanced, unless there is a general desire to sell her kind of equities.

In bad times she may receive no dividend, but in good times there is no specified ceiling to the dividend the directors may care to offer.

The examples of employment contracts and equities serve, however, to remind us that a firm is not an institution which economises on the costs of contractual specificity without causing other costs to be incurred. Workers may find themselves unexpectedly made redundant, while, if a firm goes bankrupt, equity owners may look jealously upon debenture holders standing ahead of them in the queue of creditors. Furthermore, as is evident in the breakdown example, the very vagueness of the contracts holding the firm together means that chaos may ensue if the parties involved differ in their interpretations of how they should each respond to changing conditions. A coordination mechanism is required and this will absorb resources. Contractual vagueness also means that affected parties may be unsure as to when they have been breached. In short, markets may be less than ideal as means of arranging production but, on some occasions, coordinating mechanisms that supersede the market may be even worse.

2.3 THE ROLES OF COMPLEXITY, OPPORTUNISM AND IDIOSYNCRACIES

Coase's original work on the boundaries of a firm was left with its implications waiting to be explored for almost twenty years. Then Cyert and March (1956; 1963) built on Coase's idea of contractual incompleteness, by viewing firms as imperfectly specified coalitions of people with competing interests; who were sometimes disadvantaged by the incompleteness of their information; who might be prepared to give more or receive less than they were presently getting. On this view, even customers were 'members' of the coalition comprising a firm, until they changed their spending behaviour and went to join other coalitions. The work of Cyert and March emphasised the conflict of interests amongst coalition members, and made organisational slack (cf. section 1.7) a central feature in explaining how firms could cope with change without fragmenting into separate resources to be traded in the market. This emphasis on the goals and information resources of individuals became a central feature of the work of their one-time pupil Oliver Williamson (1975) (though, surprisingly, he makes very little direct reference to them). Williamson also attempted to explore the costs of different forms of coordination mechanisms which might exist within the boundaries of a firm.

Central to Williamson's work is the idea that knowledge is dispersed and idiosyncratic. For this reason, it may be very difficult to write it down properly so that it can be transmitted, at a price, to those who might like to have it (cf. section 6.2). Inarticulacy is not the only problem here. Williamson also emphasises that people often behave in an opportunistic manner, deliberately concealing and misrepresenting that part of their knowledge which they *could* attempt to transmit. The presence of opportunists would greatly complicate any attempt to arrange production through a system of highly specified contracts, for situations might arise where it was difficult to decide *precisely* which state of the world had come about. Some rival states might seem almost identical on the surface yet have entirely different ultimate ramifications for the various parties involved. If the complexity of the distinctions between such states were such that it could not properly be written down in an unambiguous manner, intricate contracts could still founder in a sea of litigation. But, with loosely specified contracts to hold production arrangements together, opportunists may be able to get away with 'delivering the goods' that they could, and would, deliver were more precise requirements laid down. On the other hand, however, uncertainty about the minimum that has to be delivered before the recipient will cancel the contract, *may* lead to the attenuation of tendencies to shirk: the recipient may be an opportunist, too, and trick the supplier into providing better than her tolerable minimum standard of output (cf. section 7.3). (Note: any 'buyer' is also a 'seller', even if it is only money that he or she is 'selling'.)

Now, buyers and sellers of goods and services can attempt to behave with opportunism both when using markets (for example, when one firm buys from another, or a consumer buys from a retailer), and within the boundaries of any particular firm (for example, the firm's sales staff may attempt to disguise their own poor productivity levels by blaming poor sales figures on the design and quality of the products they are supposed to be selling). The strategist's problem, then, is to decide which activities to internalise in order to meet her aspirations – and there is no guarantee that her personal aspirations will correspond to her firm's publicly stated goals. The firm can make, lease or buy its inputs; it can sell its outputs to ultimate consumers or intermediaries, or it can lease them; it can produce merely an intermediate physical commodity or it can produce a fully finished product; it can license its ideas to other manufacturers.

Opportunism will only be a serious problem if the number of potential participants in a transaction is small. In a large group context, the credibility of a would-be opportunist may be challenged by rivals who can claim to possess similar specialised knowledge yet offer a superior deal. Consider, for example, the predicament of a firm that is not confident of its own ability to exploit a new product which it has developed (cf. section 8.5). One option is to license it to another firm. But it may be suspicious that the licensee could reap large spin-off benefits from the experience it enjoys while producing the product. These benefits lie in the future and will depend on how the licensee firm exercises its own idiosyncratic skills. For this reason, the spin-off advantages cannot be specified in the licensing contract and used as a basis for the firm demanding a higher royalty. However, if the number of potential licensees is high, there will be competition for the prospect of obtaining the spin-off benefits and this will enable the firm more confidently to hold out for a high royalty rate.

The number of relevant potential parties to a contract will depend on the frequency of the firm's requirements for the services in question and on the urgency of its requirements. With an urgent, one-off purchase, the firm will not be able to 'shop around' to assess the credibility of a particular initial quotation that is alleged to be 'reasonable'. Furthermore, the potential supplier may judge that the firm may not be able to use its internal resources to manufacture the required product, and that it would not be worthwhile for the firm to invest in specific machinery to make it. When there is a prospect of repeated sales, a potential supplier will tend to be deterred from attempting initially to exploit the buyer's ignorance; in this situation the buyer may find search worthwhile. Buyers, too, will be deterred from being seen to attempt to exploit their suppliers if they hope to continue to purchase inputs in the market place. For a one-off deal, it might make sense to encourage a supplier to tool up for bulk production prior to a firm contractual commitment, and then to order at a lower rate than promised, thereby to extract a knock-down price deal. But suppliers would be unlikely to get caught twice in this way, unless, that is, a dogmatic desire to go ahead with a project blinkered them to the repeated possibility of opportunism (cf. the Howard Hughes/Boeing/Convair episodes in section 5.8).

When repeated purchases are made by a firm, suppliers who

successfully obtained a first-round contract will be able sometimes to command, for later orders, returns higher than the minimum they would accept. Their 'slack' earnings would arise from the specialised knowledge of their customer's bounds of tolerance, and internal strengths and weaknesses, gained during their first-round experiences. Once again, such suppliers might be deterred from attempting to exploit their superior knowledge when tendering for renewed contracts: they might fear that other, would-be long term suppliers could offer attractive introductory deals in order to put themselves in similar positions in respect of third-round contracts. However, consider the position of the buyer, who may have found the original deal entirely satisfactory (cf. section 3.3). There will be costs involved in putting a new contract out to tenders. The risks of experimenting with a cheaper but as yet untried supplier could be considerable – deliveries, for example, might be late and hold up the production process in a costly way; while attempts to preclude such a problem with a complex contract could be expensive to arrange and could still end in costly litigation. In the light of such considerations, the buyer might not ask for tenders and, even if they were sought, might prefer the lesser risk of giving an unnecessarily attractive second-round order to the original supplier (cf. section 4.4).

Williamson suggests that when opportunistic behaviour is likely, firms *may* find it worthwhile to internalise the activities in question, either by merger or by internal growth. He reasons that if the future position of a supplier depends on the performance of a larger corporate whole of which it is a part, then the supplying unit may be more afraid to attempt to behave with opportunism. But, then again, it may not. Once a firm has its own sources of supply or its own selling outlets, it will have to bear the costs of keeping them idle, or of selling the assets involved at a knock-down price, if it ceases to use them. Once internalised, suppliers or intermediaries may find their abilities to exploit their idiosyncratic knowledge greatly enhanced. Whether this is actually the case will depend significantly on the kind of organisational structure employed. The firm's chosen structure will also affect its costs of superseding the market as a coordination mechanism.

A broad distinction may here be made between peer group and hierarchical structures. In the former, all the parties involved – and the elements may be individuals or a group of firms which have come together to promote a joint project – have the same status, even though their roles are to some extent specialised. The peer group system has obvious advantages over the market where physical or informational assets are indivisible, or where teamwork makes individual productivity contributions impossible to pinpoint. An individual unit, for example, may lack the resources to finance and operate a large investment singlehandedly (or be unwilling to concentrate resources on a single project). Other, would-be contributors could in principle, hire out their spare resources of finance, production capacity and personnel for specific rates of remuneration. But the possibility of opportunism or contractual failure could make a consortium arrangement much more attractive to all concerned. Each member of the group would give up some possibility of reaping the benefits of opportunism, in return for a specified share of a possibly larger whole.

In a peer group arrangement, coordination is still rather costly in terms of resources, for everyone has to be consulted about a decision that will rebound on everyone else. Furthermore, an individual who is not satisfied with the way some of the other members are performing cannot expel them except by coming to some agreement with a majority of the rest of the members, or by buying them out. A threat to withdraw altogether may carry the cost of losing rights to future pay-offs to resources previously sunk, because such rights were not specified in the original agreement. Such considerations will often make it preferable for some parties to insist on an hierarchical form of organisation, as a condition of internalising a productive activity. High level authorities can attempt to attenuate opportunism at lower levels by playing them off against each other, and by threatening to remove them or deprive them of resources for future development. Such a departure from the democratic processes of a peer group also reduces the resource costs of reaching decisions, for there are fewer channels of communication. However, as will be shown in sections 7.3 and 8.4, an excessive formalisation of roles may inhibit responsiveness to change and produce an atmosphere which is not conducive to high levels of productivity in the system.

2.4 Linkages, Synergy and Hedging

The significance of opportunism or a failure of detailed contracts to account for a contingency which actually arises is clearly enhanced if activities are linked together. However, the internalisation, within a single firm, of activities which involve strong linkages is not something which can be achieved without cost: in turbulent times, market or technological conditions may change suddenly and throw the future of an entire integrated firm into jeopardy. It is this conflict, between the risks of being caught out in a market-based means of coordination and the risks of an integrated system of internal coordination being 'mugged' by environmental change, which has been the subject of recent work by Neil Kay (1982; 1984). But before I explain how Kay has extended the Coase/Williamson analysis, it may be helpful if I give a quick preview of how strategy formation will be described in section 6.2.

In section 6.2, I will use Moss' (1981, chs 2 and 3) analysis to suggest that managerial attention will tend to focus, as a result of the perception of bottlenecks and unused resources, on new activities that are in some way related to the existing operations of their firm. Strategy formation will be depicted as a problem-solving activity which tends naturally to link activities together. Managers will be portrayed as asking themselves, 'What can we do with these spare, but relatively specific, resources?' or, 'How can we remove the bottlenecks that are causing some of our resources to be lying idle?' Vertical integration might be a way of overcoming the deficiencies of input suppliers (who might include marketing intermediaries) or users of the product. Diversification into areas which could use up idle resources would enable the firm to enjoy a head start over firms starting from scratch in these areas.

Kay adds to the analytical significance of linkages by making use of a concept associated with Ansoff's (1968) normative work on strategy (which is nowhere mentioned by Moss), namely, *synergy*. If the net revenues a firm can earn from a set of activities are greater if they are undertaken together than if they are underatken separately, synergy may be said to exist (see Ansoff (1968), pp. 74–6). Synergy *can* be associated with the exploitation of underused resources already contained within a firm, but it can also be sought when new resources are being incorporated into a firm's structure. Suppose, for example, that strategists perceive that their firm's sales division has improved its efficiency through learning-by-doing and is no longer working at full capacity. In taking on new activities, they will naturally wish to choose projects which make use of their sales division's particular marketing skills. Insofar as management experience in the sales division is transferable between projects, management synergy can be enjoyed. Sales synergy may come via the use of common distribution channels, sales administration, advertising, sales promotion or reputation. The use of the sales division's spare human resources may, for example, involve the sales staff in marketing new products, with the aid of spare 'capital' embodied in the firm's existing trademark. If new products have to be designed or new manufacturing capacity installed, investment synergy and operating synergy, respectively, may be gained if the new products share, say, technologies or raw materials – even if the firm has no resources already sunk in these areas.

In principle, synergy can be traded between firms. In the example just described, for instance, the strategists might have opted to sell sales consultancy services to use up spare human resources without adding manufacturing resources to their firm. Another market-based solution might have been to renegotiate the contracts of their sales staff, so that, instead of receiving their annual pay rise, they were given the right to spend part of each week acting as consultants to other firms on their own account. In practice, however, such arrangements might be open to abuses which could not easily be taken account of in contractual form. In the former case, the buyer of the selling services might be suspicious that poor sales resulted from the fact that little attention was being given to its products. In the latter case, the firm might fear that its 'part-time' sales staff would take it easy and blame poor sales on the arrival of the decline phase in its product's life cycle, while simultaneously passing expertise to its competitors.

Contracts to trade synergy are particularly likely to be hazardous, and hence prone to breakdown, when the gains from trade are unevenly distributed (see Kay (1982), pp. 45–6). A sales consultancy arrangement might earn relatively little for the firm with spare capacity in its sales division, but the sudden abandonment of it might be disastrous for the firm that had purchased the service. Furthermore, if the sales staff could pick up production secrets whilst 'acting as consultants', and if they chose to pass these secrets to their employers, the firm that had used the consultancy service might also find itself faced with a new rival to its own product. In this case, the firm supplying the consultancy service has little to lose, and much to gain, if it pulls out of the arrangement or behaves with opportunism. It would be almost impossible to design an enforceable contract to prevent this firm from making use of any production or research secrets it acquired in the course of its 'consulting' activities, unless these secrets were sufficiently *un*idiosyncratic that they could be covered by patents. Furthermore, selling an idiosyncratic product is an inherently uncertain business: a contract involving payment by results might be unsatisfactory to the firm supplying the selling service if the manufacturer could not deliver as a result of a strike, or if the product was rendered obsolete during the period of the contract; payment by the hour would open up the possibility of shirking by the consultants, whose idiosyncratic input skills would be difficult to specify in a contract or, if specified, could be appropriated by the manufacturer.

Evidently, a firm with spare resources in its sales division could have a hard time finding trusting (or, for that matter, trustworthy) customers for its 'sales consultancy' services. Firms in need of such a sales input might be prepared to forego the low price that synergy would make possible and, instead of purchasing this firm's services, might prefer to develop their own sales functions or use a third party intermediary with a reliable reputation, thereby to safeguard themselves against the prospect of being let down or 'mugged'. Such behaviour would leave the firm with the spare resources in the position of being able only to exploit synergy potential internally. It could do this either by internal growth or by merger. The internal growth route might preclude it from enjoying operating and/or investment synergy which, in an atmosphere of greater trust and environmental stability, could have been traded on a reciprocal basis in the market. Greater overall synergy might be released by a merger agreement – at least insofar as opportunistic tendencies on both sides were attenuated out of concern for the overall well-being of the larger merged unit. But even when a corporate marriage is arranged to exploit synergy in an atmosphere of greater trust and reduced transaction costs, it will rarely be possible for *all* potential synergy ties (Ansoff lists sixteen sub-varieties in all) to be open to exploitation within the broader corporate boundary.

Difficulties of exploiting synergy in the market place will often make it rational, then, for firms to become multiproduct operations and engage in merger activity. But the possibility of trading synergy, which Kay's (1982) book is the first to mention, should not be overlooked. It is all well and good to try to internalise synergistic activities if conditions are stable. But if conditions change in respect of one product in a linked set, or in respect of a common synergy link (for example, if there is a technological shift), the entire set of activities may be jeopardised. If synergy has been traded, the catastrophe may not be so great, because its effects will be shared between a number of firms. If synergy cannot be traded in an acceptable manner, it is not necessarily desirable for a firm to try to internalise a number of activities that may release synergy: the other message of Kay's work is that, in a turbulent world, a firm should not 'put all its eggs in one basket'. Rational diversification may also involve *hedging*, so that, as activities are internalised, they do not all exploit the same linkages.

The synergy/hedging explanation of diversification choices is, as Kay points out, less applicable when diversification involves vertical integration. Synergy is only likely to be available in this context if the products involved are technologically idiosyncratic (for example, where a knowledge of how to sell them requires a knowledge of how they are made). The business of extracting and selling raw materials will not usually have much in common with component manufacture and marketing, nor with assembly, nor assembly with the distribution of the final product to consumers. Certainly, the activity of selling, for example, will occur at each level, but the skills, means and media involved in selling raw materials, components and finished goods are different. With selling functions, vertical integration is unlikely to release synergy benefits as such; rather, it is likely to permit the *replacement* of some sales functions by internal managerial co-ordination, with possible attendant reductions in opportunistic behaviour. Similar coordination benefits may also be possible from internalisation in respect of operating and research functions, rather than a sharing of resources being made possible. Vertical integration should only take place, that is to say, if there are contractual problems involved in securing, via the market, supplies of inputs or customers for outputs, *and* if the risks of insecurity opened up by transaction difficulties are not outweighed by the risks of creating a monolithic structure which could be rendered obsolete by technological change or shifts in customer preferences.

2.5 Informational versus Technological Determinants of Strategy

The information-based analysis of strategy proposed by Coase and Williamson has been challenged by Moss (1981, pp. 156–60), who proposes an alternative analysis built around the well-established idea of comparative advantage and the notion that technological differences between activities determine comparative advantages. I suspect he would feel that Kay's subsequent work is similarly flawed.

Choosing the Boundaries of a Firm

In this section, I will explain how Moss makes his challenge, and what is wrong with it.

In his analysis of vertical integration strategies, Moss (1981, p. 120) begins by arguing that

> In order for there to be transactions in any commodity, it must in general be possible to store the commodity over time and move it from place to place. . . . Goods and services which lack storability, or portability, or cognizability can be produced within integrated production processes and therefore within a firm, but they cannot enter into exchange.

Given such a starting point, it is hardly surprising to find Moss (pp. 159–60) attacking Williamson's (1975, pp. 83–4) analysis of vertical integration in the steel industry in terms of transaction costs. The fact that steel comes hot from furnaces and has to be rolled when hot obviously favours a *spatial* integration of furnace and rolling operations. So too, does the bulk of steel relative to its value, for this would make the storage and transhipment of cold steel slabs prohibitively expensive. But, as I pointed out at the start of section 2.2, spatial integration does not necessarily involve integrated ownership.

Moss himself considers the possibility of furnaces and rolling mills being run independently. He argues that the high fixed costs involved in both operations mean that shortage costs – due to a lack of demand for hot steel produced by furnaces, or the lack of a supply of hot steel inputs for a rolling mill – will be considerable. For this reason, he concludes that

> technological factors make the cost of any contractual failure very considerable indeed for both parties. . . . [F]or this case at least the information costs which Williamson deems crucial to his conclusions appear to result from the physical characteristics of the commodity in question and the technical characteristics of the processes in which the commodity is produced and used (Moss (1981), p. 160).

To be sure, transactions costs *are* exacerbated by technological considerations. But Moss makes no attempt to consider another way of reducing the risks of shortage costs, to either furnace or rolling mill operators, which would avoid a need for vertical integration. His analysis proceeds as if independent steel furnaces and rolling mills would each be owned by individual risk bearing units. Nowhere does he point out that shortage risks could be spread if the units were owned by groups of shareholders with diversified portfolios, but that portfolio diversification is hindered by the transaction costs involved in using stock exchanges. Furthermore it is far from obvious that vertical integration will necessarily be beneficial to both operators. This will only be the case if tendencies towards opportunism are attenuated, with the result that shortages are less of a problem and that attempts to deal with them are less protracted. In the absence of such reductions in coordination costs, vertical integration might merely result in a concentration of existing risks and a heightened dependence on a single product and technology.

Moss' analysis is no less incomplete when he attempts to encompass less extreme situations, where storage and transhipment are possible. His argument essentially is that intermediation is promoted by indivisibilities, so the internalisation of activities is less likely to be worthwhile if products are portable and standardised. The less bulky, perishable and idiosyncratic a commodity is, the larger will be the minimum efficient scale for handling it. However, 'if the demands of any of the users of a commodity are of sufficient size, then the users will be able to overcome indivisibilities in exchange and to supplant the intermediary' (Moss (1981), p. 137). If a firm fails to internalise a level of production despite its involvement with it having passed the minimum efficient scale of handling internally that level, then this is to be explained by comparative advantage (pp. 158-9). That is to say, given the resources available to her firm, the strategist is deemed to have decided that she can achieve a greater return by integrating forward instead of backward, or diversifying horizontally instead of vertically.

On the surface, Moss' arguments look fine; they make it seem obvious that, in a market characterised by small scale production and an absence of product differentiation, intermediation will be economic and vertical integration will not occur. But here we should surely ask, 'Why do the small producers not merge and then internalise the function performed by the intermediary?' Transactions cost analysis would argue that this may be precluded because, individually, the firms involved cannot see that the reductions in transactions costs obtained by using internal coordination mechanisms might be greater than the costs of: (a) bringing the many parties together; (b) agreeing the terms of the merger in a 'fair' way; and (c) becoming tied to a particular kind of process which might be rendered obsolete. Once again, Moss takes for granted existing arrangements at different levels in the production process, instead of considering the implications of alternative forms of horizontal ownership arrangements for his arguments about the rationale of vertical integration.

Let us now turn to consider Moss' use of the comparative advantage idea to explain why a firm may fail to internalise activities despite having exceeded, in the use it makes of them, their minimum efficient scale. Here, his arguments turn on the assumption that the volume of resources available to the firm is *given*. This is perhaps to be expected, since Moss, like Marris, lists Penrose (1959) as a major influence, and the major theme of her work is that managerial problems limit the volume of resources and activities associated with a firm *at any instant*, though not in the long run. But it is the growth-seeking managers themselves who have to guess where the limit lies in the short run, a point which seems to have escaped from Moss' analysis. Moreover, Penrose's arguments about the limits to the rate at which managers will wish to increase their command over resources are actually based on the kinds of informational and contractual concerns that are so central to the Coase/Williamson/Kay analysis. The idiosyncratic nature of knowledge embodied in a firm, and possessed by owners of resources outside the firm, is such that it is neither possible nor desirable to attempt to expand a firm at an infinite rate by drawing up fully specified blueprints for an extensive system of internal organisation. It is usually better to grow gradually in a less formal manner and make the most of learning that arises 'on the job'. Furthermore, opportunism and inarticulacy amongst people with experience of existing technologies mean that it is inherently impossible fully to specify, at any moment, the technological systems that Moss places at the centre of his analysis. And precisely which *new* technologies emerge will depend upon the incentives open to participants in existing production processes. The form of these incentives depends on the contractual arrangements under which production is carried out.

2.6   CONCLUSION

The intention of this chapter has been to show that there are, in principle, many different types and combinations of institutional structures within which production and distribution can be co-ordinated. The message of the modern theoretical contributions to our understanding of this aspect of the economics of the firm is that precisely which institutional arrangements will be appropriate to a particular context depends very much on the transactions costs that are involved. Weighing up these costs is no easy matter, even for the firm that is wise enough to attempt to evaluate them, for they arise out of uncertainty and ignorance: they will vary in ways that depend on the number of possible contingencies which seem worth anticipating; on the risks of opportunism and unreliability amongst the parties involved; and on the risks of arrangements being rendered obsolete by changes in technology or customer preferences. These factors will, in turn, be affected by the number of potential parties to the rival types of institutional arrangements.

Some readers may feel that I have failed to demonstrate conclusively that informational determinants of rational strategic choices are not best to be thought of in the way suggested by Moss; that is, as being rooted in the technological characteristics of products and production processes. If pressed on this point by Moss, I would suggest a compromise, namely, that in a world of complexity, it is impossible to say that *either* the cost of information *or* technology is the prime determinant, for they are inextricably woven together. However, I hope that my critique of Moss' extreme 'technological' perspective has made clear the dangers of thinking about strategy in a way which does not take account of transaction cost analysis. If one starts with a focus on transactional problems associated with alternative institutional structures, the technological issues will usually come automatically to mind. If one focuses primarily on technological images, one is likely to end up thinking merely of conventional institutional alternatives. Moss' own tendency to take the resources and ownership structures of firms as given is evidence of this. If one is not used to thinking in terms of more subtle forms of corporate relationships, such as implicit contracts, joint enterprises, consortium arrangements and leasing or licensing deals (see Richardson (1972) and Mariti and Smiley (1983) for examples of these), strategic choices will seem deceptively clear cut.

There is an instructive parallel to be drawn between the boundary choices of firms and those of ordinary households. Some couples may feel perfectly able to exploit their common interests and complementarities without finding it necessary to agree, via a marriage contract, on the joint ownership of all their assets. Some bring up children out of wedlock without much difficulty. Some enjoy satisfactory relationships without even sharing the same house. Some find that marriage is a costly institution to dissolve when they grow apart, or that it is no guarantee that a partner will not behave with opportunism. Marriage is in no way rendered 'technologically inevitable' by accommodation indivisibilities and physical linkages between couples (sex is a synergy-rich activity!). But many couples will report that marriage seemed 'a natural thing to do at the time', though later they have come to regret it. As Chapter 10 will show, the same is often true with corporate marriages. However, to understand why mergers often turn out to be disappointing, and to see why internal growth is often also a painful process, requires us to explore in detail how managerial coordination mechanisms work and how they break down. So, mindful of the nature of the firm, let us now turn to consider how managers think and act.

3 The Managerial Imagination

3.1 Introduction

Complexity, turbulence and uncertainty are the three characteristics of the modern business environment that make successful decision-making difficult. When many things may plausibly be argued to be things which *could* happen, because it is far from clear which chains of events might prevent them from coming about, it is perhaps not inappropriate to view differing propensities to achieve success and failure as originating in differences in endowments of luck and intuition. Achievements in business could often so easily have been entirely different: in a slightly changed, 'doppelgänger' world, 'mistakes' might have produced glittering successes. These episodes of business history one can observe with suspense, but from them patterns cannot be inferred. However, there are others which an onlooker with some understanding of decision processes can fit into a pattern; the mistake can be seen looming on the horizon as a trap, and the managerial actors then proceed to step right into it. Some mistakes, that is to say, are made not merely because successful decisions are difficult to take, but also because the mechanisms for taking decisions are faulty. The purpose of this chapter is to consider how the mechanisms of choice work and how they can lead decision-makers astray.

Attention will be focused on how the individual chooser sees her environment and processes information. Chapters 4 and 5 will shift this somewhat reductionist view of choice back into a structuralist, corporate perspective, recognising, after John Donne, that 'no man is an island unto himself'. The present emphasis on the individual decision-maker makes the overall analysis easier to manage, but it has a greater significance, which is explained in the conclusion, section 3.8. The rest of the chapter is divided up as follows. Section 3.2 is concerned with the limited number of dimensions in terms of which decision-makers see their environments. Section 3.3 argues that complexity and uncertainty make optimising behaviour impossible and generate an important role for external reference standards in deciding whether a decision is a good one. Section 3.4 is concerned with another result of the impossibility of optimisation: the use of 'recipes' for success, which can very easily result in failure as environmental changes occur. Section 3.5 considers the shortcomings of priority-based decision processes that are used when the recipe approach to choice is inappropriate. In the light of this, sections 3.6 and 3.7 examine how choosers do, and should, conceptualise the possible sequels to big decisions taken under uncertainty.

3.2 A BLINKERED VIEW OF THE WORLD

Decision making is necessarily an activity which looks forward into an unknowable and as yet undetermined future. As Shackle (1961, 1979) has been at pains to emphasise, choice involves using the *imagination* to form theories of cause and effect and then decide which of the set of hypotheses thus formed to subject to testing. To understand how managers make mistakes it is thus essential to consider first how they come to form images about particular schemes of action and their possible sequels. In this context, the work of an American psychologist, George Kelly (1955, 1963), which has much in common with that of Shackle, is particularly enlightening.

Kelly's starting point is to suggest that we may find it useful to see people in everyday life 'as if' they are *scientists*, who seek to predict and control their environments by processes involving theory construction and experimentation. That is to say, we may gain insights if we, ourselves, do not theorise about people as if they are 'utility seekers', but instead try to see them as inquisitive agents who want: to understand how things relate and work (some more so than others – like academic scientists, their interests will tend to be to some extent specialised); to see where they, personally, fit into the 'scheme of things'; and to discover the extent to which they can shape their environments so that these fit in with their images of particular 'ideal' structures. The more inflated a person's theory of her position in the cosmos, the less afraid she is of turning up evidence which threatens to invalidate this image, or of finding herself in a situation about which she cannot theorise adequately, the more aggressive she will be in her attempts to unfathom things which she finds particularly fascinating. Henry Ford, for example, asked the big question, 'Can I bring motoring within the grasp of the typical American if I adopt this set of policies?' The evidence suggested he could. Sir Freddie Laker tested the theory that he was skilful enough to bring transatlantic air travel within everybody's grasp. The evidence suggested, with a vengeance, that his theory was faulty: he was like a scientist who had blown up his laboratory (though his experiment produced some lasting benefits for consumers).

Any scientist necessarily has to build partial models of reality in order to be able to see anything at all. When we speak of *business* activity we are using a partial model even before we get down to details; we do not attempt to reduce everything that happens to the level of physics; we leave out any consideration of many linkages despite the fact that the universe is an integral structure and in the long run it is likely to be dangerous not to see it in an 'ecological' way. The things that we see as separate features are only separate in our minds, because we think we can discern repeated patterns that stand out as distinct features from the mass of background noise. The market for the Model-T Ford was a pattern, a theoretical *construct*, in the mind of Henry Ford, but it was, ultimately, a pattern which fell to pieces, despite Ford's last ditch attempts to hold it together in 1926 by advertising the car for the first time, under pressure of a sales crisis (see Selznick (1957), pp. 109–10).

In constructing patterns in our minds, we do so in a 'compare and contrast' manner, in respect of particular attributes that come to mind as relevant. An investment scheme, for example, can only be seen as 'dangerous' because it shares certain characteristics with other activities which are seen also as something other than 'safe'. Kelly calls these characteristic attributes 'constructs', to indicate that we put them together for ourselves: we do not have to see the world in identical ways and, where we *do* actually arrive at similar conclusions, we need not be doing so because we have experienced the same set of events in the past. But just as one pattern, or 'element', of reality can only be described in this relativistic way, so the constructs in terms of which a person views it are only meaningful as lower level elements themselves because such likenesses and dissimilarities exist: if activities do not differ in terms of whatever it is that safety and danger subsume (which will not necessarily be something that has a universal currency), the construct 'safe/dangerous' is meaningless.

Kelly argues that an individual's personality is usefully to be seen as an organisation of construction subsystems – interconnected sets of constructs in terms of which aspects of reality will be appraised. A manager will use different sets of constructs to appraise a business decision, the purchase of a new car, her spouse's behaviour, and so on, though some constructs may appear in several subsystems. The constructs acquire contextual relevance if seemingly related elements are normally construed in terms of them; these elements (for example, particular cases of business catastrophe from the past) provide the points of reference that make the constructs meaningful. Some sets of constructs and elements will be particularly closely correlated in the mind of the decision-maker, so much so that they can be thought of as nearly enough a separable whole – a *dimension* for thinking about particular puzzles. A newspaper editor, for example, might see events in terms of their 'political', 'human interest', 'industrial relations', 'South African', and a variety of other, dimensions.

But the frightening thing about these constructs and dimensions, and the elemental reference points we use to view the world, is that they are remarkably few in number for any construction subsystem. Techniques for identifying them (described in Kelly (1955) and Slater (1977)) suggest it is unusual for a person to think in terms of more than *two* dimensions and ten to fifteen constructs. Here I speak from experience. I allowed a psychologist friend to investigate how I see 'people', after being made to think of ten people I knew (including my actual and ideal selves in relation to elemental stereotypes). She was surprised to extract twenty constructs from me, and the computer analysis (using the UMRCC (1981) programme) revealed that my ten element/twenty construct matrix contained four significant dimensions. The fact that I had a more complex 'person' subsystem than most people did little to remove my alarm when I looked at the data from other subjects she had investigated. Many 'obvious' constructs in their subsystems were not in mine, and vice versa. Worse still, her thirty subjects (I was the trial run for a carefully conducted, larger scale investigation) had between them a total of 101 constructs for viewing people (see Axford, 1983) but even this did not include all the relevant attributes that might be used. The models people construct of aspects of reality are indeed very partial. Even the most brilliant manager has a highly constricted viewpoint, despite the fact that she will have learnt to see more constructs and useful dimensions to the analysis of business problems. The present book may help lesser managers to shake off some of their blinkers and make fewer mistakes.

3.3 THE IMPOSSIBILITY OF OPTIMISATION

The fact that managerial viewpoints are blinkered suggests that managers should not be thought of as engaging in optimising behaviour (except as an approximation that may sometimes be useful), even if they are trying their hardest to take good decisions. They suffer from what Herbert Simon (1957b) has called 'bounded rationality'. This term connotes more than just the problem of blinkering outlined in the previous section, and which is an aspect of the finite capacity of humans to process information. Managerial decisions are apt to be bad not merely because relevant dimensions and constructs somehow were not on the perceptual agendas of those involved, with the result that problems come to be mis-identified and solutions mis-appraised, but also because the number of options considered is restricted. The boundedly rational decision-maker, furthermore, is not guaranteed even to recognise that it is time to change her behaviour (see Loasby, 1967c). To be a global maximiser, like the 'as if' agents in the theories of neoclassical economics, she would have to be scanning all relevant possibilities continuously. Clearly this is impossible in logical terms, for the decision-maker cannot take decisions in a costless way: if she is weighing up options she cannot be scanning for problems to solve or potential solutions; while she can never know what the pay-offs to search will be, when she tries to work out how best to make use of her limited decision-making capacity. Behavioural theorists, unlike neoclassical theorists, are not willing usually to presume it safe to model decision-makers 'as if' they are optimising agents. Rather, they ask how people made up their minds, given that they only enjoy a limited form of rationality.

A decision-maker cannot say: 'This is the best decision that can be taken in these circumstances'; but she can say: 'I think this decision is possibly good enough to enable me to meet my aspirations.' She cannot optimise, because maximal points of attainment are impossible to identify, but she can, as Simon puts it, 'satisfice', by seeking to attain particular target outcomes. In the world of business it is not necessary to maximise profits or growth to survive, but it may be necessary to meet particular minimum levels of attainment. And, as in a race, the minimum performance levels that are satisfactory depend upon the quality of the opposition. Relative success, rather than absolute success, is what matters (cf. Alchian (1950), p. 215).

Aspiration levels, seen from the standpoint of Kelly's work, are predictions from the decision-maker's theories of what she ought to be able to attain in respect of particular goals, or of the minimum standards that will be necessary to meet other targets. And, like images generally, they will be formed with reference to other elements in the system. Managers seeking to ensure their firms' chances of survival will tend to copy each other's targets for quality control, research and development, productivity levels and so on; or aspire to have slightly higher targets, in order gradually to squeeze their rivals out of business. As theoretical constructs, aspiration levels may be revised once 'sufficient' evidence has been accumulated to suggest that they are too high or too low. But this evidence can take a long while to build up in the minds of decision-makers, just as in academic science or when statistical testing procedures are being used. Consequently, although aspirations tend to follow the attainments of reference elements, they do so with a lag, often shifting discontinuously as an evidencial threshold is crossed. It is then that slack will be taken up, unless, that is, the decision-makers find it easier to deal with a failure to meet aspirations by changing their reference points, their dreams of what might be possible.

An example of the latter is the then Chrysler boss John Riccardo's decision, in 1978, that the only way of escape from the nightmare of cumulative collapse was by selling Chrysler's European interests. He judged there was so much wrong with the company that its managers could only hope to engage successfully in search for ways of improving its performance if they reduced the scale of their task simultaneously with obtaining a cash infusion. The sale that made this possible ended 'Lynn Townsend's dream that Chrysler would one day become an independent, multinational, full-line producer of automobiles' (Moritz and Seaman (1981), p. 192). John Riccardo's abandonment of the pretence that Chrysler was in the General Motors/Ford league was a response to impending catastrophe, but many such corporate crises actually have their origins in the psychological mechanisms that shift aspirations and reference points in response to previous attainments, whether they be good or bad. It is, however, convenient to leave detailed discussions of these processes till later (see, particularly, Ch. 4 and sections 5.2 and 5.3).

3.4 RECIPES FOR SUCCESS - AND FAILURE

Having chosen her aspirational targets, the manager still has to decide how to meet them. She does not need the best possible decision, merely one that, over the relevant time horizon, will generate results that are 'good enough'. The search for possible options and the processing of information might be undertaken by a variety of means, each of which involve lower level decisions of various kinds (for example, has search gone far enough; how should a particular option be evaluated?). In seeking to understand how managers work out what to do, behavioural economists make a broad distinction between carefully reasoned (though inevitably blinkered) *deliberative* choice processes - which are discussed in sections 3.5 to 3.7 - and *programmed* or, to use Steinbruner's (1974, ch. 3) term, 'cybernetic' choice mechanisms - which are the subject of this section and which economise dramatically upon a manager's information handling capabilities.

Someone choosing in a programmed manner avoids the conceptualisation of alternative options and their prospective outcomes, in sharp contrast to the conventional economist's view of choice. Instead she behaves as if she has a list of possible occasions for action and a 'menu' containing individual 'recipes' for dealing with each occasion. Each recipe is her personal *policy* of how she will proceed when the occasion arises; it is a programme for action which will be carried out when she perceives the appropriate occasion for a choice has arrived. In effect, then, the choice has been made long in advance of its need being felt, rather as would have to be the case if production were organised through fully-specified, long-term contingent claims contracts (cf. section 2.2).

Programmed choices may be made at a variety of levels. To cope with everyday office life, for example, a manager may have a policy of 'dealing with correspondence (in all except for certain specified cases) immediately, as this is the only way of preventing a mountain of confusion from building up'. Another manager, in the same situation, might 'reply only when a reminder is received (except in certain specified cases), for letters that work their way towards the bottom of the in-tray without provoking a follow-up aren't worth answering'. In the 'certain specified cases', other policies will be brought into operation. For a higher level example, one can note a one-time recipe for success in the Bowater paper company: 'Our policy is, and remains, that we control not less than 60 per cent of our requirements of all raw materials' (Reader (1981), p. 244) – a recipe which was, till its shortcomings become apparent, even extended to encompass shipping facilities.

The hierarchical structuring of policies often results in means and ends being merged. That is to say, many stated corporate 'goals' can be seen also as policies, themselves comprised of collections of 'sub-recipes', which may help promote success in reaching higher level aspirations. For example, in its attempts to survive in the car market, Mercedes-Benz has for a long time had a 'product quality goal' as a recipe for success, one of whose ingredients is the policy of incorporating as standard equipment all significant automotive innovations as soon as they appear, whether the public demands them or not, and regardless of the increase in costs that they involve (see Perrow (1970), pp. 167–70). Having pioneered features such as fuel injection and anti-lock braking systems, the company remains in business, though the precise contribution of the various policy elements is difficult to quantify: other, untried recipes *might* have produced even better results had they been tried.

And therein lies the problem. When the proof of the pudding is in the eating, but no one knows for sure how the ingredients interact, it is by no means easy to decide what changes to make in the recipe if the taste suddenly goes sour as an environmental change occurs. Holmes (1978, p. 161) notes, for example, that the fall of the dollar against sterling in 1973 led some UK exporters to switch to sterling invoicing. At the time this seemed rational, but in retrospect it seems to have been unwise, given the path taken by the pound; Holmes' detailed case study investigations show how firms brought up on fixed exchange rates were often poorly adept at taking pricing decisions in a world of erratically floating currency parities. All too often, managers tend to get trapped into adhering to 'tried and trusted' recipes, even when they are open-minded enough to wish to learn how to do better. How this happens is more properly dealt with in the next chapter (in section 4.4), for there the focus is on learning in firms. But it seems appropriate to end this section by highlighting how the kind of blinkering discussed in section 3.2 will prevent managers from realising that, because they have made no change in their behaviour, they have begun to use a recipe for disaster.

The Corporate Imagination

The difficulty is most likely to arise when managers have a one-dimensional view of their business environment and all their policy recipes are attached to it. Henry Ford's view of the car market up to 1927 focused on costs and how to cut them; it did not contain a significant 'marketing dimension', which might have alerted him to the impending death of the Model-T Ford as a viable product. Given the magnitude of the crisis that resulted, one might have expected Ford's experience to become an image-forming element in the cognitive frameworks of all managers. It did not. Eddie Rickenbacker, the famous World War 1 pilot, who ran Eastern Airlines as a one man show from 1935 to 1959, seemingly failed to see the relevance of this major automotive happening of 1926–7 in the context of civil aviation in the late 1950s and early 1960s. Once again, a one-dimensional construct subsystem, focused on costs and how to cut them, was very successful for many years, but eventually proved a disaster.

Rickenbacker was an expert at eliminating X-inefficiency but an incompetent at producing what the public wanted in the long run. The ingredients in his recipe included tight scheduling and overbooking, to maximise the use of aircraft; delays in introducing faster and more comfortable aircraft; and cabin services that were spartan in the extreme with seats five instead of four abreast. Until the late 1950s, Rickenbacker's recipe worked very well, despite causing so much customer discontent that an informal pressure group, WHEALS – We Hate Eastern Airlines – emerged, and appealed to the Civil Aeronautics Board. But his success had been contingent upon the fact that Eastern enjoyed a near-monopoly on its most profitable routes. It was this monopoly which attracted interlopers offering superior standards of service, who were, eventually, aided by the new Civil Aeronautics Board policy of giving busy routes to small operators. Rickenbacker relinquished executive power in 1959, just before the crisis became apparent, but he did not end his active chairmanship of the board and his policies continued. By 1963, Eastern's loss was 15 million dollars and one-third of its trunk-line traffic. At that point, Rickenbacker finally departed for good and the innovation process could begin. A new executive was given a free hand and copied the customer-conscious policies of the interlopers. With this new recipe for success, they eased Eastern back to a 24 million dollar profit in 1967 (see further, Perrow (1970), pp. 147–50). Interestingly enough, Eastern were later to revive some of the ingredients of Rickenbacker's recipe when they pioneered the shuttle, using superannuated aircraft and offering zero service – other than the guaranteed unbooked seat.

3.5 PRIORITIES

Most people, at one time or another, end up saying, about someone else, that they have 'got their priorities wrong'. They do so without realising the vast body of literature on the theory of choice assumes that preferences are not structured on a priority basis. Central to this literature is the notion of substitution, the possibility that one attribute may be traded against another (see Lancaster (1966) and Fishbein (1963) as the seminal works in, respectively, economics and marketing). Marris' formal model of the firm, for example, depicts managers as being prepared to trade higher growth rates for lower profit rates, the terms of the trade-off depending upon the risk of takeover that is involved. For each rival scheme of action that comes to mind, the manager works out an expected utility by weighing one attribute against another. She then chooses the scheme with the highest expected utility. A strategy involving a very high growth rate might be selected in favour of a more balanced strategy, despite having a very low prospective profit rate (and hence a bigger danger of takeover), because the way the growth/profits/takeover threat attributes compensated against each other enabled the former to achieve a higher total score. If this theory is to be used to rationalise behaviour that would commonly be regarded as indicative of a *misordering* of priorities, the rationalisation must run in terms of a badly skewed *weighting* of attributes.

The behavioural economist prefers to take the 'commonsense' description seriously at face value. In a world of bounded rationality and satisficing, it seems to make much more sense. A 'compensatory' view of choice depicts the chooser 'as if' she can weigh up essentially noncommensurable attributes in her mind in common units, and store the scores for each scheme in her mind (like a multimemory pocket calculator) until she has to make the final choice. In the behavioural analysis of deliberative choice, the chooser is seen, by contrast, 'as if' she sets an aspiration level for each attribute she finds relevant, and ranks these attributes in order of priority. Choice amongst rival schemes on her agenda then becomes a filtering activity. She does not trade one goal against another but asks herself which of those schemes she has in mind as possible options will meet her first priority, regardless of how well they perform in other respects. Those that fail this test are removed from the list. Those that pass are subjected to a second stage test at the second priority aspiration. The process continues until only one scheme is left. If this happens before she has got 'sufficiently far' down her priority list, search will be instituted, to see if there exist a scheme which would possibly meet even more priorities, in order and with no gaps. I should add that this 'as if' description is only an attempt to encapsulate what happens 'at the end of the day' in a deliberative choice process. The costs of performing evaluations at high-level priority filters may be significant. For this reason, the decision-maker may choose to start the filtering process by looking at less important priorities in the first instance, and only later return to consider whether or not the scheme thus implied as the winner actually meets the higher-ranking aspirations. Obviously, if it is likely that very many schemes meet these top priorities, it may seem worthwhile to risk the possibility that a *preliminary* choice might, in the event, not meet them. But it is most important to realise that such a 'shortcut/backtrack' procedure is not the same thing conceptually as working out expected values along the lines proposed in the orthodox compensatory theory. In the priority analysis, the key thing is the *number* of aspirations likely to be met in the desired order, not the *sum* of prospective scores on the set of possible outcomes.

Conventional economists seem generally to be horrified by the priority-based view of choice (or lexicographic model, as it is commonly known), for it seems a remarkably intolerant way of taking decisions. But all around us are examples that are difficult plausibly to rationalise in terms of a compensatory model, but which are easily understandable in terms of a priority-based model with high aspirations at particular points – any decision-maker who is, for example, a six foot five vegetarian will soon find the set of driveable cars, adequate clothes and restaurants is frustratingly restricted.

In the context of corporate decisions, two kinds of priority structures would seem particularly prone to cause disasters. Firstly, there are those that accord a high priority to the preservation of the decision-maker's self-image – her theory of where she fits into the scheme of things. Some activities will be impossible to undertake without destroying this image, or without threatening someone else's self-image (see section 5.9 and Earl (1983c, chs 6 and 7) for details). This suggests that role of the 'face-saving compromise' is not to be underestimated in boardroom rows or industrial-relations disputes.

Secondly, it would appear that decision-makers often shoot for their goals in priority order in a temporally much more separated way than the basic description of the process appears to credit; and they only monitor attainments, in respect of goals other than those being

The Managerial Imagination

attended to, at discrete intervals. This is what Cyert and March (1963) call 'sequential attention to goals'. It gives an added perspective on the cycles of corporate instability discussed in sections 1.6 and 1.7. To look at targets separately makes a good deal of sense if one is not dealing with organic structures and if the targets are strictly separable. However, in a firm, what is attempted in respect of one goal (such as expansion, product development or inventory levels) will feed back upon other goals (such as profitability targets). The managers cannot always stand still and work out the many ramifications of particular schemes. Instead they are driven either to attend to things one at a time (often mixing cybernetic procedures, for reaching each goal, with their longer run attempt to act according to priorities in a more deliberative way) or to divide the task up between different parts of the organisation. But when linkages are ignored, partial actions or recommendations are almost inherently likely not to add up to a coherent whole. This is a theme to which I will often return in subsequent chapters of this book, for it seems a powerful way of explaining the tendency of firms to go round in circles, fighting different 'fires' and shifting from one perspective to another (see especially section 5.2).

3.6 THE CONCEPTUALISATION OF UNCERTAIN OUTCOMES

So far, in speaking of the manager's views of whether particular schemes will enable her to meet her aspirations, I have considered possible outcomes in very simple, dichotomous terms; as if, that is to say, they are construed as *either* adequate *or* inadequate in respect of *particular* targets. But what if the answer to the question, 'is this good enough?' is, 'possibly'? How, then, does the decision-maker choose? This is a question to which I devoted a good deal of attention in Earl (1983c, ch. 4). In the present context, therefore, I shall outline briefly the answer at which I arrived, before contrasting it with the orthodox analysis of choice under uncertainty, and then exploring its limitations in respect of successful decision-making.

In essence, I argued that the decision-maker proceeds, in respect of a particular attribute, as if she: (a) asks herself what outcomes she considers might possibly be associated with pursuing a particular course of action; (b) considers how *surprised* she would be if each outcome occurred (remembering that only one *can*, in the event, do so, and it may not even be one she has thought possible, or even thought of at all); and (c) asks herself how much surprise she can *tolerate* in respect of either each of these imagined outcomes, or each of a pair of 'gambler aspiration levels' (one either side of her normal 'dichotomising' adequate/inadequate aspiration level for that attribute: a 'loss avoidance' gambler aspiration level on a capacity utilisation conjecture might be the break-even level; her 'dichotomising' target might be, say, 80 per cent capacity utilisation; and her 'gain' gambler aspiration level might be 90 per cent capacity utilisation). Her set of conjectures about possible outcomes, mapped against the surprise they would cause, is her theory of what could happen; her set (or pair) of surprise tolerance levels, mapped against possible (or two particular) outcomes is her mould of tolerance. All she then has to do is to ask 'does this theory fit the mould?' If it does, in the sense of possibly 'inadequate' outcomes (for example, capacity utilisation below 80 per cent) seeming sufficiently unlikely (that is, they would cause *more* than particular tolerable degrees of surprise if they occurred) and possibly 'more than adequate' outcomes seeming sufficiently likely (that is they would cause *less* than particular tolerable degrees of surprise if they occurred), the scheme thus envisaged is acceptable, despite uncertainty, in respect of the attribute/goal in question.

This method of taking decisions in the face of perceived uncertainty, which I adapted from Shackle's (1949, 1961, 1979) earlier work, is conceptually very different from the probabilistic approach to decision-making that is taught to today's business-studies students. The difference between the two methods closely parallels the way in which the priority-based choice model runs counter to the compensatory theory of choice. The probabilistic method of choice uses subjective probability weights to make prospective good and bad outcomes commensurable. (These weights might be thought of as representing an imaginary statistical distribution of the outcomes that could result if the actions in question were repeated time and again.) Thus, for example, a 'high probability' of bankruptcy may be outweighed by a 'high probability' of outstanding success, despite 'low probabilities' being assigned to intervening probable outcomes. Indeed, this may be so to such an extent that the scheme involved dominates over another which has 'low probabilities' attached to extremely good and bad results and 'highly probable' intermediate results.

But one is dealing with the mutually exclusive outcomes of unique decisions – a bankruptcy is final; a glittering success may change the

The Managerial Imagination

structure of an industry. A bankruptcy is a bankruptcy whether a manager brought up according to conventional doctrine assigned it a 'probability' of 0.05 or 0.5. This doctrine may drive managers to implement schemes whose sequels they are poorly equipped to handle (even if additional techniques such as sensitivity analysis have been applied), for it encourages them to focus their attention away from the key question, which is whether or not they will be able to cope with the different kinds of situations that might arise. A person's ability to cope with extremely bad results is something altogether distinct from her ability to handle success, however great that might appear in prospect.

The consequence of training managers to take decisions on the basis of the probabilistic analysis may therefore be that they focus their attention largely on the prospects of highly weighted, 'probable' *good* outcomes, which might be associated with the choice of a particular course of action, and do not much consider how they would deal with conceivable catastrophic outcomes which together achieve a lower weighting. However, it is perhaps desirable that they should be trained to face up to uncertainty in this misleading way, rather than not at all. The probabilistic analysis at least has the merit of encouraging a decision-maker to consider alternative visions of the future; to ask herself whether or not she ought really to consider ranges of possible outcomes, instead of merely dichotomising images in respect of a target reference point. As Carter (1954, p. 52) warns,

the human mind does not . . . carry very easily a picture of a continuous variable. Attention will at once be concentrated on *typical outcomes* in imagined future situations; the first Rule of simplification being that all variables must be reduced to a few discrete values. . . . We may find that, in looking at a fairly close date, a man's calculations are based on a *single* typical outcome. He has made up his mind about what will, he thinks, happen; he has no side glances at alternative possibilities [emphasis in original].

All teachers of business policy will be familiar with this problem: students are sadly prone to treat sales projections as gospel truths in case-study work, instead of realising that demand curves should be seen as conjectural *bands* of possible sales levels at particular possible prices.

It was an awareness of this tendency to ignore uncertainty which led the Shell International Petroleum Company to develop the technique of planning on the basis of 'scenarios' (see Jefferson (1983) for an 'inside account', and Chandler and Cockle (1982)). Scenarios are internally consistent, detailed stories of what *may* occur in the future, based on building blocks such as: macroeconomic growth prospects; possible political shifts and public policy changes; changes in social behaviour; demand prospects; supply prospects, relating to costs, capacity and competitive developments; and possible technological shifts. It was through the use of this technique that Shell began to anticipate and allow for a decisive eventuality which came as a complete surprise to many other large companies, namely, the OPEC oil price rises of 1973–4.

Proponents of the use of scenario planning techniques at Shell have met with some opposition. This is because the methodology deliberately illuminates uncertainty, whereas most people expect a planning aid to assist in the reduction of ignorance about the future. As Jefferson (1983, p. 146) notes,

Most people want to know what *the* future will be, what *the* result of a decision will be, and dislike being confronted with the realities of uncertainty. Even where those realities are grudgingly recognised they may be put on one side because administrative convenience, or unwillingness to take responsibility, call for a single set of assumptions to be handed down from above. For many people the opportunity of working with more than one scenario . . . is not perceived as offering scope for choice and responsibility but as opening up the risk of error [emphasis in original].

Experience at Shell suggests that people can only cope with two or three scenarios before becoming confused and apathetic. Furthermore, if one of these is in the nature of a middle course, 'base case', people tend to ignore the others and accord it an excessive degree of certainty. A *pair* of extremely optimistic and pessimistic scenarios (Shell at one time had the 'Belle Epoque' and 'World of Internal Contradictions' scenarios) may therefore be a suitable device for forcing executives to focus on the bounds of possibilities, and hence on the situations which they might be able to exploit to their advantage or be forced to confront if they make particular strategic choices.

The remarks of Carter and Jefferson make me feel, in retrospect, that the analysis of choice I proposed in sections 4.6 and 4.7 of *The Economic Imagination* should have been presented partly as a prescription as to how some people *should* think, rather than merely as a description of how others, who *have* faced up to their ignorance about the future, *do* think.

3.7 Crucial Decisions

Whether or not we regard the decision-maker as someone who typically focuses on single outcomes or on ranges of possible outcomes, it is important to consider how her images of the future are formed. In crucial decisions, particularly, making up one's mind is no easy matter, even if a relatively undemanding technique for processing information is used. Often such a decision makes the chooser feel trapped on 'the horns of a dilemma'. In this section I will attempt concisely to convey what happens as a person agonises over an important choice, and how this relates to corporate error. Readers interested in a more detailed analysis should find Steinbruner's (1974, ch. 4) work especially helpful.

What the decision-maker sees is heavily channelised by her frame of reference. This is defined by her relevant construction subsystem: the correlated elements and constructs that comprise her perceptual dimensions. But the particular images she sees within this frame (fuzzy as these may be) are formed by her unconscious cognitive processes. These processes have to deal with a number of problems which her logical powers alone cannot handle. Firstly, there may be uncertainty about how the schemes she has in mind will perform in respect of particular goals. Logic may determine the bounds of possibility, but not her precise theories. Secondly, she may be uncertain about the appropriate ordering of particular goals in relation to her priority system. Thirdly, she may have nagging doubts that her own world view is blinkering her to important perspectives and from finding major inconsistencies. She is, that is to say, worried about whether or not her choice is justifiable, either to herself or, on the 'million lemmings can't be wrong' principle, to her social reference group, the people whose opinions matter to her. Her cognitive processes have to concoct this justification, by making some arguments seem more plausible than others; shutting her mind to others; decrying some things as irrelevant or impossible – in short by managing her logic so that she has a case for making a choice that will ensure she can meet, without gaps, her important, 'core' priorities, some of which she would find it hard to admit to herself or others. In this context, her most important goal will be to preserve her theory of her 'self' within tolerable bounds. Her cognitive processes will manage her perceptions to ensure she does not see herself acting excessively at odds with her self-image.

Now, the actions which her cognitive processes will find easiest to accommodate will not be independent of what she has done in the past, or what her reference group are currently saying. Her credibility as a decision-maker will depend partly upon how justifiable her past decisions were (Wolf, 1970); for, so long as the future is unknowable, any claims she makes about proposed schemes of action may be open to question by someone. Errors which are not judged by her reference group as easy even for an expert to make, will be in particular need of justification: they will affect a manager's promotion prospects and her company's ability to raise external finance (cf. section 1.4). Such errors will threaten her core constructs, so her mind will make schemes with 'possible' outcomes, that could save her reputation, seem deceptively plausible: that is, her cognitive processes will make her 'sink good money after bad' in an effort to challenge a claim that a mistake has already been made. Her construct system cannot stand the immediate damage a confession of ineptitude would entail, and thus she is driven to justify schemes she would normally dismiss as too hazardous. This problem seems to me to be so important (notwithstanding any 'fudging' by my own cognitive processes to highlight its significance!) that it warrants a chapter-length discussion; this will be provided in Chapter 5.

3.8 CONCLUSION

This chapter, like Chapters 1 and 2, serves as something of a scene-setting device. Readers should now have a broad picture, not only of the nature and role of the modern large, multiproduct firm, but also of how managers within it think and choose. In the rest of this book, I shall frequently write as if the performance of a firm depends on how that firm, conceived as a whole, thinks; on how its cognitive processes work. Such a holistic perspective is often very enlightening; for many purposes, a firm is most usefully to be seen as 'more than the sum of its parts', as a structure which will carry on in pretty much the same way if individual elements are amputated or replaced by others. This is what the main title of the book is intended to convey. But, this said, it is important also to recognise that the destinies of even some of the largest of today's corporations are shaped by the world views of individual decision-makers. A particularly fascinating example is Eric Bowater, who dominated the Bowater Corporation for around forty years. Reader's (1981) centenary history of this company is in many ways more a biography of Eric Bowater and an analysis of his managerial imagination. The story behind his managerial activities makes only too clear the role of the managerial self-image in shaping corporate performance, and it seems appropriate to end this chapter by recounting it.

During World War 1, Bowater's army dugout was hit by a shell. For three years after this event, he could only walk with crutches, but then he went to see a leading neurologist. The latter, as Reader (1981, pp. 19–20) recounts, decided his symptoms were physical manifestations of mental stress and boldly ordered him to cross the room, which he immediately did. Shocked, he saw his illness as unreal and shameful. He was overcome with a desire to prove himself, and thus decided to take an active part in the growing family business.

For the most part, his judgment was brilliant but, as Reader (1981, p. 314) observes, this in itself led to a problem:

The measure of his dominance of Bowater's affairs was apparent as soon as he died. He left no directions as to who was to succeed him and the Board had taken no steps to choose a successor themselves, although they had known for some months that, in all probability, a successor would soon be necessary. Not only Eric, it seems, but also his close colleagues were unprepared to face the possibility that he might be mortal.

For many companies, though happily not for the Bowater Corporation, the failure to smooth the transition from dominance by a single managerial imagination to collective control turns out to be a fatal mistake, since it leads to infighting between individuals who lack the overall vision of the departed individual. In the turbulent environment of modern capitalism, no firm, however large, can survive indefinitely without a sense of where it is trying to go.

4 Corporate Ambitions and Learning

4.1 INTRODUCTION

This chapter develops further some of the themes of Chapter 3, in an attempt to answer two questions: how do new experiences cause managers to ask different questions of the world from those which hitherto they have asked, and how do the processes whereby they learn lead them into error? The wording of the first question may seem a rather odd way of saying 'How do managers learn from experience?' However, the 'obvious' wording seems illogical from the standpoint of Kelly's theory of personality, which formed the backbone of Chapter 3. Kelly (1963, p. 171) argues that experience 'is a set of personally construed events'; it is 'the extent of what we know – up to now. It is not necessarily valid'. From a Kellian perspective, therefore, a person cannot be said to learn from experience; rather, 'it is the learning which constitutes experience' (p. 172). To be consistent within a forward-looking analysis of choice, one must see learning as the change in experience from one period to another. The focus of this chapter is on how managers' mental constructions of what has happened affect their constructions of what may be possible, and subsequently impact on their choices of hypotheses to test. As in the previous chapter, it will be seen that corporate errors can often be accounted for in terms of psychological processes, rather than merely being put down to the difficulties of taking good decisions.

The rest of the chapter is structured as follows. Section 4.2 examines the role of dogmatic beliefs in determining what a firm can and cannot experience. Sections 4.3 and 4.4 consider further barriers to experience: respectively, the setting of modest and vaguely specified aspiration levels, and a gambling trap known as the 'two-armed bandit' problem. Section 4.5 adopts a more obviously corporate perspective and considers the interactions between teamwork and experience. The arguments of the preceding sections are then brought together in an investigation of corporate instability in terms of 'emotional' responses to experience: section 4.6 considers the perils of corporate euphoria, while section 4.7 examines the consequences of corporate depression and loss of self-esteem. Section 4.8 is a brief conclusion.

4.2 Dogma and Learning

In business, as in every other inquisitive activity, the proof of the pudding is in the eating: before one can attempt to learn, one must have a prior belief in a particular theory. Popper (1976, p. 51, emphasis removed) makes the point very plainly: 'there can be no critical phase without a preceeding dogmatic phase, a phase in which something – an expectation, a regularity of behaviour – is formed, so that error elimination can begin to work on it'. The willingness to make a dogmatic commitment is an essential ingredient of business success; for even mock-ups and test marketing exercises do not entitle a manager to generalise about what *will* happen when a product is put to the test of the market. William Morris, for example, succeeded in reaping the full benefits of the British motor transport revolution only because his intuition disagreed fundamentally with the conventional wisdom. The economics press in the 1920s arrived at pessimistic conclusions about the market for cars, having looked at income-tax data from a perspective that underestimated the importance of the used-car market and tendency of businesses and the rich to replace cars every year. Morris' intuition was that the prospects for the market were those of expansion; that saturation was not in sight (Overy (1976), p. 69). And only when he acted upon his belief that a mass market existed did the statistics become available to test who was right.

In believing that he was right and everyone else was wrong, and in being prepared to risk what he had on the basis of this belief, Morris was the epitome of the entrepreneur as portrayed in Casson's (1982) recent work, where 'the essence of entrepreneurship is being different – being different because one has a different perception of the situation' (1982, p. 14). He was fortunate that, unlike many other entrepreneurs, his vision did not systematically lead him astray, and that his picture of the market was broadly correct at the time. In this section I will begin to consider how some dogmas may lead to errors of learning; the difficulties of judging market life cycles will be addressed later, in Chapter 8.

Dogma precedes criticism, but criticism itself is not independent of dogma. When a manager learns something about her business environment, she revises her earlier theories about it in the light of what she has seen. But her perception is selective. What she sees happening depends on what she is looking for, on the constructional templets she lays over the world. Experience is inevitably theory-laden: as Popper (1976, p. 51) puts it, 'there is no such thing as an unprejudiced observation'. Not only this, but the manager is also forced to contend with a problem known to philosophers of science as the Duhem–Quine thesis (after Duhem (1906) and Quine (1951)), which states that it is impossible to say whether or not a single theory has been falsified, since one cannot test a single theory without taking many others for granted.

When a theory a manager holds about the world of business is apparently contradicted by events, the Duhem–Quine thesis holds that there may well be nothing wrong with it as such; it may merely be that parts of the theoretical apparatus used to test it – such as the firm's accounting and reporting mechanisms – are themselves not behaving in the expected way. The same may be true when an expectation seems to be validated – false information could be painting too rosy a picture. But the manager cannot test the efficacy of her firm's information systems without assuming that still more theories are not leading her astray. The Duhem–Quine thesis means that a person can only say that a particular *set* of theories she holds is or is not inconsistent with a particular body of evidence framed in the light of some of the theories in this set. Obviously, it *could* be the case that the whole bundle of theories is defective when an inconsistency is observed, and that a return to a complete new set of first principles is in order. But a manager who attempts this every time her expectations are disappointed is likely rapidly to end up in a state of complete bewilderment.

Lakatos (1970) argues that academic scientists get round the Duhem–Quine problem by dividing their world views up into two distinct sections: a 'hard core' and a 'protective belt'. The former is a set of propositions which the scientist makes a dogmatic methodological decision not to lay open to empirical challenge. The latter is the body of 'auxiliary' hypotheses which she is prepared to modify in the face of anomalous empirical observations or logical difficulties. For Lakatos, then, a scientist's 'research programme' is a two-level hierarchy. The dogmatic decision about which level to assign certain presumptions thus determines what kinds of revisions a scientist will be able to make in her world view when she encounters problems. Some kinds of criticism will be deemed as inadmissible because they relate to the validity of hard-core assumptions and procedures.

The hierarchical use of dogma is also a central feature of Kelly's theory of personality. The organisation corollary of his theory (which is implicitly embodied in the discussions of priorities in sections 3.5 and 3.7) states (1963, p. 56) that 'each person characteristically evolves, for his convenience in anticipating events, a construction system embracing ordinal relationships between constructs'. In effect, Kelly is asking his readers to picture the mind of a person as an information gathering and processing organisation, structured on the basis of a hierarchical system of authority relationships between theories – just as a person, in the role of a manager, is an information processing element within a higher level organisation called a firm. Like managers in firms, theories in minds occupy fairly inflexible positions in the short run, but, in the long run, depending on how they seem to have performed in their organisational contexts, they may be promoted, demoted or even discarded altogether. From this standpoint, a parallel should become apparent also between a firm's information systems and the cognitive processes that shape images in the mind (see section 3.7): sometimes, but not always, third-level theories may be able to appeal directly to first-level authorities and discredit a second-level theory, despite the attempts of the second-level to manage images to the contrary.

It is the short-run inflexibility of information-processing hierarchies that gives a person or firm a discernible personality. The organisational perspective on minds and firms implies that the most difficult policies to change will be those that relate to the core (self-image) constructs of people in positions with a veto over what is allowed to happen. In section 3.4, I mentioned, as an example of a recipe for success, the Bowater policy of '60 per cent control over raw materials'. This is also an example of an almost unshakeable theory. It originated in 1937, as a result of the company being forced to seek a special dispensation to renegotiate long-term supply contracts for newsprint, after it had been severely out-manoeuvred by the Scandinavian pulp cartel. Eric Bowater felt personally humiliated by what happened and was determined not to be exposed to that kind of risk again (cf. section 2.3). The avoidance of a perceived past error thus became a major choice criterion: 'never again'. As Reader (1981, p. 244) observes, 'his belief in the necessity of self sufficiency was emotional as well as rational, as little likely to be shaken by argument as any other article of faith equally firmly held'. Twenty years later, as pulp prices began to drop, and the demand for newsprint was falling short of supply, the belief could no longer be so rational. But it was a belief which had a mass of evidence supporting it; a belief which could only be shaken to its foundations by a crisis on a grand scale (cf. section 4.6 and Chapter 5).

Now, it may be the case that an organisation's set of authority relationships between its elements is so inflexible and so out of line with its environment that a return to first principles *is* needed. Some of the lower level elements may be suitable to form new superordinate constructs in a revised system, yet such a revision may be impossible because of the existing hierarchical pattern. In such a situation, as Loasby (1983, pp. 116–17) points out, the organisation, be it a mind or a firm, may find learning impossible. The core constructs/elements cannot be revised to match the environment, even if subordinate ones are discarded or pushed around. The necessary restructuring may only be possible after the death of the organisation. Loasby notes that the failure of, for example, management and union negotiators in some firms to adopt alternative approaches, when their current methods have a dismal record of failure, may be

because a more effective method would require so radical a change in their conceptions of the 'opposition' as to threaten their whole interpretation of the economic and social system (1983, p. 116).

He goes on to conclude (p. 117), grimly, that

Some principles an organisation must have, if it is to remain an organisation; some principles a person must cling to, whatever the evidence, if he is to remain a person. Some changes are simply not possible, even if the alternative is death.

4.3 EXPERIENCE AS A FUNCTION OF ASPIRATION LEVELS

Central to Kelly's analysis of the 'person as a scientist' is the idea that how much a person can experience depends on how difficult are the questions that she asks, or is forced to ask, of the world. A person's theories will have limited ranges of applicability but these ranges cannot be discovered, except by accident, without aggressive testing, which involves risking failure. It is only when failure occurs that the person will be able to see she has misjudged the range of convenience of a construct and that some creative, problem-solving, theory-forming activity is in order. Translated into the language of behavioural economics, Kelly's point is that a firm's experience – and hence what it may be capable of achieving in the near future – is a function of its aspirations. To experience a lot and be driven to be creative, a firm's personnel must set their aspirations high enough for seemingly soluble problems to be generated by inadequate attainments. The word 'seemingly' is very important here; in section 4.7 I will be dealing with the kinds of breakdown that result from the generation of problems to which the people involved can see no solutions.

A firm which consistently meets its aspirations, and raises them each year by so little as to stay within the ranges of convenience of its existing recipes for success, will fail to enlarge the scope of its vision or reduce the extent of its misinformation. It will be rather like the case of the veteran school administrator described in Kelly (1963, p. 171) as having 'had only one year of experience – repeated thirteen times'.

If a firm experiences very little that is new, this may reflect the fact that the performance levels of its rivals, that it uses as reference points when forming its aspirational theories, also consistently fall far short of what is possible. Indeed, a strong case can be made for saying that much of what is presently wrong with British industry, in terms of relatively poor productivity, design, quality, delivery and innovation, arises as a result of many British firms using each other's performances as reference points during the 1950s and early 1960s when a seller's market existed, instead of looking at overseas performances as a guide to what was feasible. That a healthy home market did little to stimulate improved performances in these areas is only too clear in the two classic studies of British firms in this period, Turner's (1969) *Business in Britain* and PEP's (1965) *Thrusters and Sleepers: A Study of Attitudes in Industrial Management*. Particularly evident in the former is the fact that the seller's market led to a lack of experience in the art of salesmanship, typified by the BMC director quoted as saying that, up to 1964, 'the industry had twenty years when the public would take anything at any time or price. If you could turn out things with an engine and four wheels you couldn't go wrong' (Turner (1969), p. 64).

The Corporate Imagination

The failure of British firms to look overseas for examples of what might be achieved was compounded by what one might call the problem of 'corporate arrogance'. Many firms in the PEP study simply used their *own* past performances as reference points. That is to say, these firms adjusted their aspirations to their own attainments – in keeping with what many naïvely believe to be the general view of behavioural economists. These businesses, classified as 'sleepers' by the PEP study, were often very hostile to the idea of finding out about their relative performances by using the services of the Centre for Interfirm Comparisons. High aspiration, open-minded firms ('thrusters') were typically keen users of performance ratio data and of consultants – facts which were reflected in their usually superior performances relative to the rest of UK firms (PEP (1965), pp. 60–3; 206–7). Another aspect of corporate arrogance is what Michael Edwardes (1983a, p. 282) has described as 'the "not invented here factor" ... a myopic disease that causes engineers and others to assume that anything that owes its parentage *to others* is inferior – is "foreign" or suspect in some way' (emphasis in original). But whatever its form, arrogance is a barrier to experience which is as potent as it is difficult to remove, for it relates to a decision-maker's self-image.

A justification, commonly used for not taking account of external reference points, is that a particular investment scheme is unique and therefore not easily compared with another (see Loasby (1976), pp. 103–4). It is a justification which will crumble away when a product is a copy of something else. This has been evident in the performance of BL's Cowley car plant. Workers have proved themselves capable of matching Japanese quality levels as they assemble Honda Ballades as Triumph Acclaims; yet the same personnel could only turn out erratic standards of finish in the Morris Ital/Marina, which was commonly judged to be a stop-gap model with an 'inherently' dated design (see Edwardes (1983b)). That is to say, the fact that quality was not 'designed into' the Marina helped the BL workers feel secure in the claim that their standards of quality were not strictly comparable with those in Japan, but now such a pretence is untenable.

In fact, the design inadequacies of the Marina can themselves be traced to a failure clearly to spell out in detail precisely what kind of car was being designed, and at which market segment it was aimed. Certainly, plenty of theories were falsified during the design of this car (see Turner (1971), pp. 192–207), and much search was prompted

– mainly as a result of a failure to control costs and think far enough ahead. But the lack-lustre attributes of the final product seem to result from the fact that the designers started with the idea that they were, in a broad sense, trying to compete with the Ford Escort, and finished by attempting to tackle a rather fuzzy impression of the Ford Cortina. By contrast, Ford's repeated success in designing cars that are good all-rounders (which means that they are likely to do very well in priority-based choice processes) has not been achieved without its personnel being given a good idea of what is expected of them in respect of a long list of product attributes. The Ford philosophy is that 'Without commitments you wander round loose, spend unlimited funds without meeting objectives, make some things superb but others terrible' (Ron Mellor, quoted in *Sunday Express* (1982)).

The role of well-specified expectations in shaping how much a company experiences is illustrated by the study of investment proposals and decisions undertaken by Williams and Scott (1965). Their findings were consistent with the predictions of satisficing theory: it was the falsification of expectations that led managers to engage in search for ways of making forecasts come true. However, the actual state of the world – whether or not failure had occurred – was often difficult to decide upon, particularly if the investment schemes were complex with long gestation periods. Initially, it was often difficult to distinguish teething troubles from more permanent problems. Later, the effects of a given scheme tended increasingly to become obscured by those of more recent, related ventures.

The difficulties mentioned by Williams and Scott are related to the Duhem–Quine problem, but an even more basic problem in specifying success or failure is that often scales of comparison will not exist in any formal sense. For example, Ron Mellor's set of targets at the 'thrusting' Ford Motor Company included ensuring that the steering on the Sierra had a 15 per cent better 'feel' than its rivals: it is very hard to imagine how this would be assessed. It is difficult to avoid the conclusion that it will often be inherently impossible precisely to specify objectives so as to bring out the limitations of the theories framed for dealing with them, even if many other theories are taken for granted. But it is clearly a mistake not to attempt, at least, this task – unless, that is, such precision as is achieved follows or leads to unnecessary internal bickering: precision has costs as well as benefits (cf. section 2.2).

4.4 THE 'TWO-ARMED BANDIT' PROBLEM

When managers fail to meet their aspirations and are driven to discover potential alternative recipes for success, or to reconsider hitherto rejected options, they have a choice of potential experiences before them. They can persist with their existing recipes and lower their aspirations into line with what they now believe to be the more modest range of convenience of these recipes (possibly changing their external reference points as they do so). Alternatively, they can attempt to see whether another set of recipes – altogether new, or partially duplicating the earlier set – will have a wider range of applicability and enable them to meet their recently unattained targets. If the former strategy entails a mere revision of aspirations in the direction of attainment levels the existing set of recipes has once reached, they will be likely to discover little beyond a more precise definition of the bounds of applicability of this set of recipes. They will, furthermore, be lowering their sights, possibly ending up with less than they might have achieved. Will they wish to add to their experiences by trying the new set of recipes?

In seeking to answer this sort of question, Rothschild (1973) has used the analogy of a gambler faced with the choice of two betting machines – hence the title of this section. The gambler's experience with one machine is such that she feels certain of a particular probability distribution of pay-outs (in this context she can replicate experiments to discover the distribution, so the critique of probabilistic notions is less applicable) and she is willing to lose a particular sum in pursuit of the pay-outs it will 'probably' deliver. The other machine is a new one, on which she has no experience, and which actually has an objectively more favourable pay-out distribution. However, she can only discover this distribution by experimentation, which involves her in sacrificing the chance of a certain pay-out probability on the familiar machine. Rothschild argues that if the gambler has a positive discount rate (that is, if she values present winnings over future winnings) she may end up never playing the objectively more favourable machine. Her choice always hinges upon what she believes about this machine; *if* she does try it she receives not merely a pay-out (if she is lucky), but also some information which she can use to assess the validity of her expectations. The other machine yields no such information. If, in the first instance, her assessment of the odds makes her judge the optimal policy to be playing the old machine, her information is unchanged the next time she has to decide which machine to play. Thus, as Rothschild (1973, p. 1305) observes, 'If the machine whose payoff probability is known is ever played, it will be played forever. The optimal policy is in the form of a stopping rule.' For the odds to be changed in favour of the new machine, the gambler would either need to find the old machine ceasing to function as expected (for example, due to its wearing out or the environment changing), or she would need to observe the fortunes of someone else who judged the machine worth playing.

A manager who continually fails to improve her attainments, because her decision resembles the two-armed bandit case, has a lot in common with someone who has a phobia. She avoids the new experience because it *might* be worse then the one usually confronted (even if this one fails to enable her to meet certain aspirations) and consequently fails to find out that she can handle it, that it does enable her to meet her aspirations. For such a manager, the fact that other managers are using different recipes for success and reaching higher performance levels will often be a less persuasive reason for a change of policy than observations of the fortunes of a rival, with a belief in the merits of trying a different one-armed bandit, would be to a gambler. The element of uniqueness in business, emphasised in the previous section, makes schemes difficult to compare directly even if (and this often is not the case) performance data are available. In itself, the observation that other firms are doing different things will not *prove* which policy is best. It shows merely that these firms may have had different experiences, hold different beliefs about the future, or have access to different resources.

4.5 TEAMWORK AND EXPERIENCE

The daily operation of a firm's activities and planning of its future growth path both involve the cooperation of groups of individuals. This cooperation is only likely to be successful if the parties involved have a good deal of confidence in each other, or, to put it slightly differently, if they can predict how their colleagues will construe events and act upon them. A person suddenly dropped into a managerial slot from outside will be limited in his or her ability to get things done at first, since he may be unfamiliar with the firm's currently-employed set of recipes for success; may not know the operational jargon of the firm or the details of the activities in which it is involved; and may not be able to take for granted that his subordinates will implement his commands or his superiors will understand his proposals. Sir Michael Edwardes' feelings on arriving at British Leyland illustrate this point, which economists associate most with the work of Penrose (1959),

> At first I felt able to trust only three people in a company of about 198,000 and I would bet that the feeling was mutual – at that stage 197,997 didn't know what to make of me, and it took a few months for mutual trust to develop. The three people had come with me from Chloride . . . (Edwardes (1983a), p. 12).

Penrose uses this problem to explain why the growth of a firm is limited in the short run, but not in the long run. And, as we have seen (section 1.5), Marris makes use of her analysis in his theory of the firm, arguing that the costs of creating a team to plan and administer growth will tend to pull down the profit rate as the growth rate is increased. The importance of this argument will become particularly apparent in the next section, when I consider the problem of corporate euphoria; but before that I would like to make a few comments on the problems of mixing in teams people with different experiences.

Many companies suffer unnecessary periods of decline because they fail to recuit personnel from outside at high levels. In the short run, this policy seems to have many advantages over one which involves hiring personnel from other firms. The latter policy can often cause great confusion at first, as the new managers suffer a 'culture shock': even a company in the same line of business will not necessarily think entirely as another does, though its set of hard-core presumptions is likely to exhibit a greater degree of overlap than would the set of a company operating in a completely unrelated set of activities. Internal promotions may also generate a better atmosphere among the management team. But a company which promotes only 'company men', who have, at an early age, been introduced to its set of blinkers via an intensive management induction programme, is likely to be ill-equipped for spotting environmental changes or dealing with them. Such managers are likely to have developed excessively one-dimensional world views. The dismal performance of GEC in the first fifteen years after World War II is an example which illustrates this contention only too vividly.

The pre-war success of GEC depended heavily on the use of cartels.

Corporate Ambitions and Learning

This recipe was undermined by the 1948 Monopolies and Restrictive Practices Act. The first two post-war Chairmen (Harry Railing (1943) and Leslie Gamage (1957)) were both old men when they achieved this office, and both had been with the company through the cartel period (since 1905 and 1919, respectively). During this period it had not been necessary for them to criticise the achievements of their predecessors. Their attitudes were far too inflexible to adapt to the new environment. Below the level of the board the problem was just the same: as Jones and Marriott (1970, p. 199) observe, there was an 'unwritten rule not to appoint men from outside GEC, so that the atmosphere became thoroughly in-bred' . . . and managers 'were too thoroughly imbued with the ways of their bosses to have much initiative themselves'. It took the fresh perspectives of the young Arnold Weinstock, using experience gained on a smaller scale in the fast-moving new market for televisions, to shake the company out of this rut of decline.

At the other extreme, as will be shown in Chapter 10, attempts to mix several corporate world views which share almost no common core of beliefs are also likely to be disastrous, even in a changing environment, for the company will be unable to present a unified front. Adaptability seems to require an *overlapping mix* of perspectives, a mix which is never allowed to solidify. So long as maverick personnel, hired from outside, can overlap with established managers' beliefs sufficiently far as to avoid confusion, all parties will gain, for they will be able to swop related constructs for seeing their environments, which otherwise they might never have used. To put it another way: a continuing dialectic within a firm is an aid to long-run survival, but not a dialectic so strong as to entail continuous internal bickering and chaos.

4.6 EUPHORIA

When managers are surprised by the ease with which they have been able to meet their aspirations, their response is often to become euphoric; to adopt the attitude that 'the sky's the limit'; to conclude that the time is ripe to move into 'another league' with an altogether different set of reference standards. Once an original set of external reference standards seems outmoded, it is far from obvious how far to revise aspirations in an upward direction, so such responses are not surprising. Euphoric attitudes are likely to be contagious; for not only will companies be using each other as reference points for what is possible, they will also be using the activities of their rivals as indicators of what is necessary to stay in the competitive race, and their investments will fuel aggregate demand, tending to make sales projections self-fulfilling at the level of the economy as a whole.

From the standpoint of the theoretical analysis presented so far in this book, one can read euphoric episodes in business histories with alarm. Consider, thus, the following three cases. Jones and Marriott (1970, p. 228) present a table showing the capital commitments of AEI rising from £2.9 million in 1953 to £20.2 million in 1956, and note (p. 229) how the 1958 annual report listed the timing of their coming in to service of twenty-six new factories or major extensions and details of twenty-one other important additions to the firm's manufacturing capacity. Reader (1981, pp. 250-1) notes how the Bowater paper firm in 1952 embarked on an expansion programme, for completion eight or nine years later, to cost £124.5 million, of which 'prior charge issues' provided about 72 per cent of the necessary capital. Such heavy borrowing ratios were entirely within the Bowater tradition, but the company's estimates of being able to afford this quantum leap in the scale of its operations required a growth rate of at least $3\frac{1}{2}$ per cent a year in sales over the period. Turner (1969, p. 153) describes how ICI, having failed to achieve rapid expansion by taking over Courtaulds, embarked on a massive internal growth programme into the mid-1960s: 'in the four years from 1964 to 1967, almost £600 million was spent; by 1966 total investment was almost three times what it had been in 1963'. In each of these three cases, it is entirely correct to be alarmed at the surges in investment, for each ended in an abrupt slow-down in growth, in a manner reminiscent of the hypothetical examples in section 1.6.

The experiences of AEI, Bowater and ICI (and other companies that space limitations preclude from any detailed discussion) point in the direction of the following lessons. First, managers are prone to forget earlier mistakes associated with sudden surges in growth, a fact which supports the cyclical analysis of corporate evolution presented in Chapter 1. The Bowater cash crisis of 1961–2 (Reader (1981), ch. 14), for example, was the second one associated with dramatic expansion to which Eric Bowater had been a major party (the first being in 1926 – see Reader, pp. 46–8). And, even as I write, there are signs that the Bowater Corporation's policy of aggressive expansion financed by borrowing has once again run into difficulties. As the *Financial Times* (31 March 1983) reported on the day the final dividend was halved, 'The group has spent consistently beyond its means and, in spite of two rights issues in the mid-70s, its balance sheet has continued to deteriorate.'

Secondly, and in keeping with the work on financial instability by Minsky (1975, 1982), it seems that euphoric managers fail to leave themselves enough room for manoeuvre on the demand side, as they sanction long-term investment outgoings before the revenue has been generated to pay for the implied expenditure flows and debt repayment obligations. In particular, they fail to anticipate economic downturns occasioned by government 'stop/go' policies.

Thirdly, euphoric behaviour appears to be a characteristic of 'thrusting' firms, where managers are full of bright ideas about possible areas of expansion (cf. Reader, p. 273). The trouble is that top management then fail to choose between proposed schemes, with regard to the resources available. Their proponents do not feel a responsibility to consider the effects on the corporate whole of too much expenditure being sanctioned in too short a time and, rather than choosing between proposals, the people at the top try to carry out all of them. Jones and Marriott (1970, p. 229) have a comment from an executive of the BTH division of AEI in the late 1950s which makes the picture only too clear:

'In factory development and capital spending the directors of the company just went mad and everybody looked at things through rose-tinted spectacles. [The chairman, Lord] Chandos had effectively said to us: "I know nothing about engineering but I can raise any money you want."'

Fourthly, even in a large company, a lack of experience and skilled management personnel can indeed hold up profitable growth; but managers in the real world, in contrast to those in steady-state growth models of firms, fail to anticipate the scale of the problem. The consequence is often that investment projects come on stream later than expected, with much higher costs. Thus they hold up the generation of cash while increasing the need for it. The Bowater crisis of 1926 resulted because the first manager of their Northfleet paper mill demanded changes in the design of the half-built plant: he discovered that there were no facilities for direct unloading of pulp from ship to shore. Transhipment costs were simply not on the agendas of the company's managers, nor, seemingly, on those of the suppliers, Armstrong-Whitworth. The delay as the plant was redesigned and the contract renegotiated (at a much higher price) very nearly bankrupted both companies. The crisis at ICI forty years later was on a grander scale but had similar roots: the firm was attempting to prove several new technologies simultaneously; at the height of its investment spree it was spending £4 million a week and the industries supplying the equipment could not keep up with its orders. As Turner (1969, p. 155) notes, the price of this was that, at one point, over £100 million of equipment was over six months late.

Fifth and finally, firms in a euphoric mood fail to estimate the organisational demands of a larger scale operation. Managers used to being able to do everything themselves fail to realise that they are coming to focus on individual goals to the exclusion of other matters, and the latter, left undelegated, go by default (cf. the end of section 3.5). Jones and Marriott (1970, p. 241), for example, note that, within AEI, in 1960-1

The overheads of Hotpoint got out of hand and manufacturing became inefficient since Craig Wood [the managing director] concentrated so much on promotion, discounts and packaging; he became volume happy and sales did indeed continue to shoot up, but profits shot down.

There is an extensive literature associated with the kind of organisational problems bred by euphoric expansion; it is, however, appropriate to delay any discussion of it until Chapters 9 and 10.

4.7 Depression

The negative counterpart of corporate euphoria is corporate depression. A firm's behaviour becomes distorted following a gross failure to meet its aspirations, which makes it unclear how far it should lower them or whether it has the capability to change its policies so as to improve its performance. Sometimes, 'corporate depression' is the sequel to corporate euphoria – here I am using 'depression' in a mentalistic more than a financial sense – but more usually it seems to be a characteristic of 'sleeper' companies that have suddenly woken up to the dire positions into which they have allowed themselves to slip. Whereas in the euphoric firm an excess of confidence leads to insufficiently careful project appraisal and planning, and hence to a crisis; in a depressed firm confidence and morale collapse, exacerbating an existing crisis. Usually the thrusting attitudes of managers in euphoric firms are accompanied with sufficiently open minds so that they experience a great deal as a consequence, being driven to change their planning procedures, organisational structures and product lines; and, after a plateau of consolidation, they head off again to achieve yet greater targets. In the absence of careful therapy (for example, from management consultants), the same cannot usually be said of a firm with a depressed personality.

In normal circumstances, a failure to meet aspirations will provoke a search for alternatives, before sights are lowered. Depressed *individuals* characteristicaly do not behave like this. Instead, dogma of a decidedly negative kind displaces any attempt at constructive criticism or investigation of alternative hypotheses. Therapy involves getting such a person to become a 'scientist' again: 'the patient learns to make a distinction between "thinking" and "believing", i.e. simply because he thinks something does not, *ipso facto*, mean he should believe it' (Beck (1964), p. 569). In the absence of such therapy, a depressed person continues to suffer from a variety of distorted cognitions that support a personal lack of self-esteem:

(1) Selective abstraction: the tendency to ignore relevant information and form conclusions on the basis of isolated details;
(2) Arbitrary inference: the tendency to reach conclusions without supportive evidence;
(3) Overgeneralisation: the extraction of a belief as a principle for action from an experience or event and applying the concept to other situations which are essentially dissimilar to the original;
(4) Magnification: the over-estimation of the significance or importance of undesirable events;
(5) All or nothing thinking: the tendency to think in absolute terms.

My research on company histories (and, indeed, my own experiences as an employee in a university suddenly told to cut its size by one third in the space of three years) leads me to contend that depression in an organisation shares these characteristics with individual depression, and hence that the necessary therapy is similar. A firm that has lost its self-esteem must be shaken, gradually, out of the belief that continued decline is inevitable, so that it becomes willing to experiment aggressively and is not overwhelmed by its environment.

The word 'gradually' in the previous sentence is significant. Therapy that seeks to produce sudden changes in attitudes is likely to have disastrous results. The reason is that a person who is under pressure is likely to be unable to develop new channels for thinking. Instead, as Kelly (1963, pp. 128–9) observes,

> he will tend to reverse himself along the dimensional lines which have already been established. If he is a client, and his therapist merely exhorts him to change himself, this will be the type of movement open to him. If the emergency is great and the pressure is intense, the movement is likely to be abortive. In that case he will show marked contrast behaviour along the major axes of his personality.

A neat corporate example of this kind of shift concerns the behaviour of the failing British Leyland subsidiary in Australia, described in Davis (1983, p. 84). The firm's last desperate gamble was the large Leyland P76 saloon. In designing this the firm went overboard trying to kill the traditional BMC problem of having a small boot. The P76 was provided with a huge boot; so large, in fact, that it could be closed on a 44 gallon drum. The thick wedge shape it necessitated made the car acquire a false reputation as being tail heavy; actually it handled very well and its real drawbacks related more to indifferent quality control and poor parking vision. The designers at Leyland Australia *did* learn from the dire sales performance of this belated attempt at meeting Australian tastes head-on, instead of by using variants of UK models. They built fifty prototype models of a stylish coupé, based on the P76 but with the cumbersome rear end removed. But it was then too late: huge losses forced the closure of the factory before the coupé could be put into production.

4.8   CONCLUSION

In this chapter I have been attempting to show that the performance levels achieved by a firm are in large part a function of its attitudes and the ways in which they are changed, or fail to change, in response to its attainments. In particular, it has been suggested that managers who ask relatively vague and undemanding questions of the world of business are likely only to receive vague feedback to serve as a focus for their problem-solving skills. They will not be prompted to seek out sources of X-inefficiency or attempt to take up organisational slack so long as they can meet their modest aspirations. Nor will they develop their skills very far.

If their markets are growing rapidly, managers of 'sleeper'

Corporate Ambitions and Learning

companies may fail to be alerted to the superior and potentially threatening performances being realised by 'thrusters', which they do not presently use as reference standards. When market growth is relatively slow and the transfer process takes place at the absolute expense of sleeper firms, their managers' eyes *may* be opened to hitherto untapped potential. But the accumulated lack of experience may be so great that by the time they wake up to the danger, it is too late for a carefully considered response. The sort of 'last ditch' innovative capability displayed in Leyland Australia's final prototypes is often absent in depressed organisations; it is almost as if they 'die in their sleep'. To create such a capability may require a fresh managerial input (as with Sir Michael Edwardes at BL), for, without it, ambitious staff in a sinking firm will often prefer to exit in favour of immediately available attractive options, instead of staying on board and risking sinking themselves as they attempt to repair the damage of past policies. The role of such 'imported' managers consists in the generation of new attitudes and confidence every bit as much as it does in choosing the product portfolio of the firm, its production technology and organisational structure.

5 The Structure of Corporate Revolutions

5.1 INTRODUCTION

This chapter is concerned with the processes whereby managers and firms come to change their core ideas about the nature of their business and how they go about it. In terms of the ideas of Lakatos, discussed in section 4.2, one could say this chapter deals with shifts in the nature of the decision-maker's research programme, that come about in the face of difficulties encountered during its implementation. When events begin to raise questions about a decision-maker's competence to predict and control a particular area of the world (in the present case, of the world of business), he has essentially four options available. He can:

(1) continue to use his existing research programme in the existing field of application, making *ad hoc* modifications and sinking further resources there in an attempt to preserve his ability to predict and control events;
(2) continue to use his existing research programme but narrow its field of application to that which it appears to be able to handle without *ad hoc* modifications;
(3) attempt to use his existing research programme in unfamiliar territory, to maintain the scale of his operations as he retreats from familiar areas;
(4) seek a new research programme that will deal with the problems his existing one cannot handle (except with the aid of *ad hoc* modifications) in its usual territory, or which will equip him for an aggressive move elsewhere.

The Structure of Corporate Revolutions

In economic terms, option (1) may be said to involve defensive investment; option (2) involves retreat and rationalisation; option (3) involves rationalisation combined with diversification; option (4), unlike the others, involves a thorough-going change of policies to permit rationalisation without retreat (consolidation), using new tools and/or institutional arrangements for controlling events, or to provide a basis for diversification.

In Lakatosian terms, options (1) and (2), if applied repeatedly, are indicative of a degenerating research programme (see Lakatos (1970), pp. 116–18). They enable the decision-maker to avoid unfamiliar ideas or fields of application but are likely ultimately to result in a crisis. With option (1), the decision-maker is contorting and patching up his set of theories and the images he sees, in order to preserve the apparent range of convenience of his set of constructs. With option (2), he is allowing his world view (and his command over resources, along with his salary and status prospects – see section 1.2) to crumble away. Described in this way, options (1) and (2) sound decidedly unattractive. But, sad to say, they are frequently chosen and only reluctantly abandoned. The emergence of revolutionary new strategies or organisational structures in firms is often painfully slow and tends to follow episodes during which managers 'pour good money after bad' instead of facing up to the fact that a mistake has been made, or that their products, production methods or organisational structures are now obsolete.

To a certain extent, such errors are explicable in terms of the complexity of the task of identifying obsolescence or the fact that one's competitors have the upper hand, even if the decision-maker tries to understand what is going on from a range of perspectives and with a long-term point of view. This much will become clear in Chapters 6 to 9. The present chapter is concerned rather more with the roles that managerial blinkering and myopia have to play in shaping the route taken on the way to a shift of core ideas.

The rest of the chapter is structured as follows. Section 5.2 is concerned with the problems with which managers have to contend in working out whether or not conditions can no longer be described as 'business as usual', so that a rethink of core ideas might be necessary. It is then possible for us to consider how their world views will affect their evaluations of possible high-level policy options in ways which may lead them into making mistakes. Sections 5.3 to 5.5 therefore discuss, with the aid of simple numerical examples, the basic myopia trap originally outlined by Lamfalussy (1961). Section

5.6 complicates the basic story by considering, after the work of Frankel (1955), the effects of uneven depreciation rates within technological systems. Section 5.7 deals with a common response of firms faced with a *persistent* competitive squeeze on their markets, as opposed to the one-off shift used in the earlier examples. This is a form of defensive investment known as the 'segment retreat strategy'. It can be fatal for a firm that chooses it. Section 5.8 attempts to ram home earlier remarks about the malleability of images of the future, in the minds of decision-makers, by considering the extraordinary case of the General Dynamics Convair 880/990 airline programme. Section 5.9 is concerned with how debates over core ideas come to be resolved in the face of clashes of managerial world views and interests. Finally, Section 5.10 is a conclusion which, though original, should not come as a surprise to readers who are familiar with Kuhn's (1970) famous book, *The Structure of Scientific Revolutions*.

5.2 BUSINESS AS USUAL?

In normal times, in business as in science, the typical decision-maker will not feel under a compulsion to trouble herself with what might be labelled 'strategic' questions. A firm that is established in business and meeting its aspirations has a legacy of prior assumptions, about the nature of technological and market conditions; about the strengths and weaknesses of its competitors; and hence about the appropriate broad policies ('recipes for success') that it should follow and/or the goals it should have. Such matters will be taken as 'commonsense knowledge', even though it may well be that many managers would actually find their firm's strategy – the 'hard core' of its corporate research programme – very difficult to articulate formally (cf. Garfinkel, 1967) and if forced to do so, might discover they had different opinions as to its content. Normally, managers will focus on their own, lower-level strategies, which define their individual operating rules within the larger organisation. They will use their own, lower level recipes for success to deal with the seemingly soluble problems thrown up during attempts to implement the current programmes of action. They will not keep asking themselves, 'Is there another way of looking at things?'

The rationale for behaving in this way is simple, though, as we shall shortly see, not *always* appreciated. It has four main elements.

Firstly, a conflict exists between short run and long run uses of managerial resources. If managers continually procrastinate about the choice of strategy, they will fail to form and test auxiliary hypotheses about the world of business, and will fail to accrue operating experience. On the other hand, however, managers who are engaged in making tactical choices about how an existing strategy might adequately be implemented cannot be devoting their attention to the consideration of possible alternative strategies. To a certain extent, a firm can overcome this conflict by hiring more managers, or by hiring the services of consultants. Both of these options are not without costs. Newly hired corporate planners or bought-in consultants will inevitably absorb resources as they attempt to discover what happens currently within the firm, while consultants may use the information they acquire, to improve the performances of rival organisations.

Secondly, resource and competitive constraints will tend to preclude the simultaneous testing of several programmes for action, or the sequential implementation of mutually exclusive strategies in quick succession to discover, 'other things equal', which one works best. Scale economies and synergy considerations militate against scaled down simultaneous tests of entirely separate strategies, even where these involve entirely different markets. Even 'hedging' strategies, of the kind mentioned in Chapter 2, will tend to involve some attempts of integration and cannot, therefore, be thought of as properly separable. To implement different strategies in rapid succession is likely to be disastrous – as well as being in no way guaranteed to show which is the best owing to the fact that the environment is changing continuously, partly as a result of other attempts to implement strategic experiments.

With any set of experimental foundations, the 'building' process must continue for some time in order for experience to accrue: markets take time to build up; a set of constructs and lower level recipes for success within a market is not something that managers can evolve, nor whose ranges of convenience they can judge, overnight. Initially, mistakes are likely to be made, before managers come to see appropriate problem dimensions or stumble upon a set of recipes that works. A firm whose response to setbacks is always to seek a new strategy will display characteristics comparable to a drifting individual suffering from an identity crisis; its inexperience in operating each strategy it tries will also mean that it seems persistently to be in difficulties. ICI, for example, seems to have fallen into this kind of trap in the 1960s. Turner (1969, p. 158) notes that

In the past, the company has had clear policy guidelines but it has tended to adhere to them for too short a time. For this reason it has often been more concerned with immediate problems than with long term principles and it has sometimes seemed to dabble uncertainly in fields where its expertise is inadequate.

Its lack of expertise was compounded by frequent personnel reshuffles that accompanied the changes of strategy. I am told, for instance, how a new research director of ICI's Mond Division complained that his research scientists were reluctant to take risks which he was encouraging them to take. One of his able section leaders then commented that the Division had had eight research directors in fourteen years, so it was not worthwhile adjusting to the ideas of any of them. Shortly after, the director in question was himself promoted to another post! To develop competence, then, managers, like scientists (including industrial scientists), must tentatively commit themselves to a set of foundations and remember that 'Rome wasn't built in a day'.

Thirdly, opportunity cost arguments will tend to favour the continued use of any core set of ideas once these have been acted upon. On top of the costs of designing alternative programmes there are the costs of evolving and learning new, lower level tactical procedures; of substituting physical capital in a world of imperfect secondhand markets; and of negotiating the changes in the firm's organisational structure.

Fourthly, there are the practical difficulties of open-minded thinking. Ideally, a manager should be able to see that any set of blinkers through which he views the world produces some degree of tunnel vision and myopia, for the world is too complex to envisage as it 'really is'; and he should recognise that a set of blinkers useful in one context may be misleading in another, so it is useful to have other sets at his disposal. In practice, remarkably few people make a habit of assuming there is no such thing as an objective universe. People and firms find it unnatural to attempt to look at problems from the standpoint of several, mutually incompatable research programmes (cf. section 3.6). A person will typically experience considerable difficulty in seeing, for example, 'himself' or 'the nature of a mistake' from several conflicting perspectives. His cognitive processes will naturally seek to minimise perceived inconsistencies. The ability to avoid inertia, by cultivating a multiperspective way of facing up to the world, *can* be acquired, given some determination and guidance (in this respect, Nolan (1981) is very helpful). But most people who attempt to obtain it find initially that its subjectivist foundations are rather unsettling.

Having initially adopted particular sets of core corporate policies and come to use particular personal sets of blinkers for looking at the world, managers will use these when deciding whether or not the state of the world is such that a major rethink is necessary. That is to say, how they construe problems or, indeed, whether they construe them at all, will depend on the theoretical frameworks they are using. Appropriate search may fail to be generated at an early enough stage because the 'real' nature of a long-run survival problem remains undetected. When managers receive information suggesting that performance is not as expected, they have to decide whether what they are looking at is a new trend or a disturbance around an existing trend; whether a little local difficulty is symptomatic of something more fundamental (cf. Malmgren, 1968).

If managers regard themselves as competent to deal with the task at hand, they will tend to experience considerable difficulty in recognising a major problem as such. As Austin Smith (1966, p. 9) puts it, 'the unexpected report of trouble, like Banquo's ghost, just doesn't fit into the scheme of things'. This is more likely to be the case the more tightly specified are the decision-maker's core images, and the more closely interconnected these are with themselves and with other subordinate images. Looking ahead to the Convair 880/990 fiasco (section 5.8), for example, we can note that the managers involved would have found it mentally very confusing to see themselves as 'competent to build and sell the most advanced airliner hitherto conceived' while simultaneously envisaging that costs might possibly get out of hand or future sales figures might be dreadful. Given their priorities to preserve particular images, it was only natural for them to twist or ignore others in a convenient way. But they would have been able to perform far better if their core images were less tightly specified – facing up to uncertainty at a high level would have permitted them to countenance broader bands of conjectures at lower levels without producing mental inconsistencies. To admit that one may possibly *not* be as good a manager as one would ideally like to be is, paradoxically, likely to enable one to make fewer mistakes.

Uncertainty as to the significance of a falsified expectation often means that it can seem justifiable to respond by applying existing programmed decision methods and waiting for more information to be generated. Instead of acting, when action *might* not be necessary, managers prefer to react (cf. Loasby, 1967b). But the consequence is that, when the underlying situation has moved beyond the range of convenience of existing policies, they are disadvantaged by being late.

The delay in concluding that a rethink is necessary compounds any delays in the processes whereby information is gathered and transmitted to top management. The larger a firm, the more relay stages there may be in its intelligence system, and so the slower it will be to react (Cyert and March, 1955). Lower-level managers who are supplying information will act as filters, in both conscious and unconscious ways (March and Simon (1958); Downs (1966)). Such managers will be expected to produce particular kinds of results and their efforts will be concentrated on the variables that have been specified and which can be measured precisely. The use of routines for dealing with these requirements will have the first claim on their time. Normally, this tendency for non-programmed activity to be driven out by programmed activity may work, but it can be catastrophic in its consequences. As Loasby (1967b, p. 248) observes,

Just as quality control inspectors may become expert at recognising common, though minor faults yet may easily miss a rare major fault by being conditioned not to look for it, so may an organisation become adept at dealing with day-to-day issues but in the process become blind to the fundamental changes which threaten to destroy its future.

Thus, by the time managers realise there is a need to engage in a strategic rethink, they may already be faced with a crisis of survival.

But the arrival of a crisis can itself make it difficult for managers to deal with the need for a new set of core ideas. Either of two extreme reactions tends to ocur and make matters worse. One response to the perception that something fundamental has gone wrong is to make the sort of extreme shift described by Kelly (see section 4.7), and move from a relative preoccupation with daily operational activities to an exclusive focus on long-run planning. This was a trap into which management at British Leyland fell prior to the arrival of Sir Michael Edwardes. As Bhaskar (1979, p. 186) notes, 'the old style management had been too preoccupied with the longer term (e.g. the LC10 medium saloon) to notice the very collapse of BL under their eyes'. Edwardes realised, quite correctly, that if short-term improvements could not be made to existing products, the company's dealer network would disintegrate before the fruits of any new strategy could provide dealers with new products to sell. More often, however, managers become so embroiled with current survival (since, unlike those at BL, they are not being eased through the crisis with government aid) that they fail to construct new strategies. After his arrival at BL, Edwardes (1983a, p. 75) realised that this was the main problem with the firm's approach to employee relations (if not to marketing and product policy): 'we were still fire-fighting, . . . running from dispute to dispute without tackling the root of the problem'. Later (p. 282) he describes how his every waking hour was absorbed with the business, even while on holiday. And this was so *despite* his awareness of the fire-fighting problem (which is analysed formally in Radner, 1975).

Many managers simply fail to appreciate it. This much is evident in the work of Carlson (1951), Bates and Sykes (1962) and Austin Smith (1966). Even if the firms in which they worked were not themselves crisis stricken, many of the executives studied by these authors acted as if they faced a crisis, yet denied they faced one. They worked very long hours; took work home; were constantly interrupted by visitors and telephone calls; and were plagued with a need to make minor decisions, which subordinates should have handled but did not, because company policies were imprecise. In the case described by Austin Smith (1966, pp. 171–2) – the now defunct Ingalls Industries – the problem arose largely because the organisation had been built up by one man, who took all the major decisions 'off the top of his head' and never laid down formal plans (cf. section 3.8). When he died, his successors had no idea where the company was supposed to be going or what was actually going on 'down the line'; and they were too loaded down with day-to-day operations to find out. The situation described by these authors is a vicious circle: failure to lay down policy led to insufficient time being available to form policy. Many managers failed to break out of it because they were convinced that conditions were temporarily abnormal and that the pressure of work would soon ease. They did not realise that their workloads would only diminish if they stopped, took stock of things, and rearranged how they used their time.

It should be noted, finally, that there is no guarantee that managers will necessarily use spare time to sit back and consider strategic issues, even if their lives are not spent embroiled in day-to-day operations. Facing up to the possibility that one's existing philosophy might be wrong (and, perhaps, that one is not very good at suggesting alternatives) is not easy at the best of times. It is something that managers can avoid by busying themselves with other things, such as a reorganisation of the company structure. As Knight (1974, p. 19) notes, in respect of this kind of behaviour at Courtaulds in the 1950s,

It is almost as if the absence of any clear sense of direction led people to an excessive preoccupation with dividing amongst the various members of the Board the responsibility for administering that which already existed.

It took an attempted takeover by ICI in 1961, and the rise to power of a new management team, who had for a long while been dissatisfied with the way the company was drifting (Knight, p. 36), to lead to a revolutionary new strategy being constructed.

5.3 The Myopia Trap

The mentalistic analysis of reasons for persistence, outlined in the previous section, is rather different from the explanation of 'defensive investment' originally proposed by Lamfalussy (1961), though both make use of sunk cost arguments. He sought to explain why firms in sectors with declining profit rates would continue to invest there, instead of undertaking aggressive 'enterprise investment' elsewhere. In his analysis, defensive investment need not involve a managerial error, yet it may still be socially undesirable owing to managers having shorter time horizons than the rest of the community. A fully informed decision-maker, expecting to retire or move elsewhere in the near future, might prefer to respond to, say, the pressure of foreign competition by rationalising existing activities (taking up slack) and patching up existing machinery or giving facelifts to outdated products, instead of investing in new capital. Lamfalussy's investigations of investment in the Belgian economy in the early post-war period led him to suppose that this practice was widespread. In the long run, it would be necessary to adopt new techniques and products, but this did not seem to be happening on a sufficiently great scale. A similar pattern was observed in the UK, in the cotton textiles industry, by Sutherland (1959) and Miles (1968). Miles also found that some firms failed to modernise, even if they had the funds to do so, because they doubted their ability to manage the new techniques and believed that investment in them would be just as likely to result in failure as would a strategy of merely patching up what they had (cf. section 4.7, on 'corporate depression').

To the extent that Lamfalussy did try to understand the phenomenon of defensive investment in terms of managerial perceptions, his emphasis was on the shortness of time horizons used in investment planning. His recognition that managers may be lured into a defensive investment policy which they will *themselves* regret is evident in his (1961, p. 158) remark that 'the likelihood of such a policy is greatly enhanced if the entrepreneur focuses his attention on the solution of current problems without much bothering about the rationality of his choice in a longer perspective' (cf. Radner, 1975). Even those managers who do think about the strategic rationality of defensive investment schemes may suffer *ex post* regret if they only look a few years into the future, and the consequences of what they do rebound against them before they move elsewhere. Lamfalussy's studies of Belgian firms led him to be pessimistic on this score. His ideas may also be useful in explaining the poor growth performance of the UK: Neild's (1964) study of investment policies in a sample of UK firms showed that two-thirds of them used as their decision criteria payback periods (commonly three, five or ten years) that implied exceedingly high required rates of return. The PEP (1965, pp. 110–19) study found it most popular among firms classified as 'sleepers'. But the alternative recommended in both studies – discounted cash flow analysis – *also* severely de-emphasises long term payoffs unless a *very* low discount rate is used, and encourages firms to make single line forecasts of highly uncertain outcomes in situations where scenario planning might be a less misleading basis for making what is inevitably a dogmatic 'leap in the dark' (cf. Williams *et al.* (1983, pp. 25–8) and sections 3.7 and 4.2).

Lamfalussy's analysis of the causes of defensive investment assigns major roles to three other features, in addition to the shortness of managerial time horizons. These are: (a) the longevity of capital equipment when it is kept in good repair; (b) the slowness with which returns may decline (for example, due to breakdowns or erratic quality levels) if equipment is not serviced regularly; (c) the low ratios of scrap values to replacement costs, that are common for capital equipment. When a decline in profitability occurs in a market, it is only profitable to scrap assets and leave that market if the scrap value of the assets is higher than the present value of the total sum of the future cash flow which they might yield if they continue to be used. (Strictly speaking, cash from the liquidation of working capital, which can be significant, should be included in the 'scrap' value, but, for simplicity, I leave it out of the examples that follow.) This possible cash flow stream will vary according to the amount spent refurbishing the assets. Depending on how the four factors interact, it may seem perfectly rational for managers not only to refuse to scrap assets which have ceased to earn normal profit rates on replacement cost values, but also to go on ploughing back depreciation allowances into this technology (see also Salter, 1966). The next two sections present examples of worthwhile and mistaken defensive investment schemes, adapted from Lamfalussy's original work. In both of these examples, the discussion proceeds as if there has been a one-off shift in the pattern of profitability and as if future returns to any strategy can be known with certainty for as far as the decision-makers choose to look into the future. Naturally, I hope that readers will remember the role of cognitive processes in determining what happens in practice, when future returns are at best conjectural.

5.4 An Example of Profitable Defensive Investment

Suppose that the normal rate of return to investment is 6 per cent a year, and that a firm is operating in an environment where a change of conditions results in its existing assets only being able to yield a net annual return, on their original value (which is the same as their replacement cost), of 3 per cent. The replacement cost of these assets given in arbitrary monetary units is 1000, but their scrap value is only 200. If the firm keeps them in first-class condition, by spending 100 annually to prevent depreciation, these assets will yield gross annual earnings of 130. Net earnings each year are thus 30 (that is, 3 per cent of 1000) in this activity, which I shall call 'activity X'. Suppose, further, that a failure to invest 100 a year in activity X results in its gross earnings falling by 30 a year, until they are nonexistent.

Let us now consider the payoffs to the following pair of possible strategies:

Strategy (1) Invest 100 in activity X at the end of each year, to preserve gross earnings from X at 130. Invest the net earnings of 30 to yield 6 per cent a year compounded.

Strategy (2) Do not invest 100 in activity X each year to prevent depreciation. Instead, invest gross earnings from X at 6 per cent a year compounded, and scrap activity X's assets for 200 when its gross prospective earnings fall below 6 per cent of 200.

Table 5.1 Returns to alternative strategies, given in arbitrary monetary units, where earnings decline is rapid in the absence of defensive investment

Year	Gross earnings on activity X Strategy (1)	Gross earnings on activity X Strategy (2)	Net earnings taken from activity X Strategy (1)	Net earnings taken from activity X Strategy (2)	Overall net earnings Strategy (1)	Overall net earnings Strategy (2)
1	130	130	30	130	30.0	130.0
2	130	100	30	100	$(30 \times 1.06) + 30 = 61.8$	$(130 \times 1.06) + 100 = 237.8$
3	130	70	30	70	$(61.8 \times 1.06) + 30 = 95.5$	$(237.8 \times 1.06) + 70 = 322.1$
4	130	40	30	40	$(95.5 \times 1.06) + 30 = 131.2$	$(322.1 \times 1.06) + 40 = 381.3$

Table 5.2 Returns to alternative strategies, given in arbitrary monetary units, where earnings decline is slow in the absence of defensive investment

Year	Gross earnings on activity Y Strategy (1a)	Gross earnings on activity Y Strategy (2a)	Net earnings taken from activity Y Strategy (1a)	Net earnings taken from activity Y Strategy (2a)	Overall net earnings Strategy (1a)	Overall net earnings Strategy (2a)
1	130	130	30	130	30.0	130.0
2	130	115	30	115	$(30 \times 1.06) + 30 = 61.8$	$(130.0 \times 1.06) + 115 = 252.8$
3	130	100	30	100	$(61.8 \times 1.06) + 30 = 95.5$	$(252.8 \times 1.06) + 100 = 368.0$
4	130	85	30	85	$(95.5 \times 1.06) + 30 = 131.2$	$(368.0 \times 1.06) + 85 = 475.1$
5	130	70	30	70	$(131.2 \times 1.06) + 30 = 169.1$	$(475.1 \times 1.06) + 70 = 573.5$
6	130	55	30	55	$(169.1 \times 1.06) + 30 = 209.3$	$(573.5 \times 1.06) + 55 = 663.0$
7	130	40	30	40	$(209.3 \times 1.06) + 30 = 251.8$	$(663.0 \times 1.06) + 40 = 742.7$
8	130	25	30	25	$(251.8 \times 1.06) + 30 = 296.9$	$(742.7 \times 1.06) + 25 = 812.3$

The net earnings paths for both strategies are shown in Table 5.1 up to the end of year 4; the choice between the strategies having to be made at the end of year 1. In year 5, under Strategy (2), the net return from activity X would fall to 10, which is only 5 per cent of the scrap value of the assets. Hence, under Strategy (2), activity X is abandoned at the end of year 4 with the assets being sold for their scrap value of 200.

At the end of year 4, the prospective returns from the two strategies (assuming no environmental change) are as follows:

Strategy (1) Activity X will continue to earn 30 a year net after year 4. Other assets accumulated by this point only amount to 131.2 and these, if invested at 6 per cent, will earn 7.87 in a year. Hence the maximum that can be taken in profits, without reducing the earning capacity of the firm's assets, is 37.87 a year.
Strategy (2) At the end of year 4, assets will total 581.3 (381.3, plus 200 from the scrapping of X). Invested at 6 per cent for a year, this would yield 34.88.

Clearly, in this case, defensive investment is the preferable strategy to adopt – so long as nothing happens to reduce the net earnings rate on activity X further below the rate available elsewhere on new investment.

5.5 AN EXAMPLE OF UNPROFITABLE DEFENSIVE INVESTMENT

In the example in this section, everything is as it was at the start of the previous section, except that gross earnings decline by only 15 per cent a year if 100 is not invested in the activity each year. To avoid confusion, I will call the activity 'Y', the defensive strategy (1a), and the exit/scrap strategy (2a).

The net earnings paths for strategies (1a) and (2a) are shown in Table 5.2, up to the end of year 8; the choice between the strategies having been made, as in the previous example, at the end of year 1. In year 9, under strategy (2a), the net earnings from activity Y would fall to 10. Therefore, under strategy (2a), activity Y is abandoned at the end of year 8 with the assets being sold for their scrap value of 200.

At the end of year 8, the prospective returns from the two strategies (assuming, once again, no environmental change) are as follows:

The Structure of Corporate Revolutions

Strategy (1a) Activity Y will continue to earn 30 a year net after year 8. Other assets accumulated by this point amount only to 296.9 and these, if invested at 6 per cent, will earn 17.8 a year. Hence the maximum that can be taken in profits, without reducing the earning capacity of the firm's assets, is 47.8 a year.

Strategy (2a) At the end of year 8, assets will total 1012.3 (812.3, plus 200 from the scrapping of Y). Invested at 6 per cent for a year this would yield 60.7.

Here, then, is a case where it is a mistake to adopt a defensive investment strategy, instead of deliberately milking the original activity until it is only fit for scrap.

Strategy (2a) actually overtakes strategy (1a) in its ability to permit earnings to be siphoned off without harming asset values, during year 5. In year 4, strategy (1a) would yield an overall return of 35.73, comprising 30 from activity Y and 5.73 (that is, 95.5 × 0.06) from the previous three years' investments in other activities; strategy (2a) would yield 34.08 in year 4 if activity Y had been scrapped at the end of year 3 (that is, (368 + 200) × 0.06 = 34.08). However, in year 5, strategy (1a) would yield 37.87, comprising 30 from activity Y and 7.87 (that is, 131.2 × 0.06) from the previous four years' investments in other activities, whereas strategy (2a) would yield 40.51 if activity Y had been scrapped at the end of year 4 (that is, (475.1 + 200) × 0.06 = 40.51). Thus although the end of year 8 is the best time to make an exit from activity Y (because, until then, the rate of return to continuing in Y is greater than 6 per cent of the scrap value of its assets), the vital thing for avoiding a mistake is that the firm's planners, at the end of year 1, should be considering relative rates of return at least four years ahead.

The numerical examples above are both static illustrations. But the risk that resources will be wasted on investment in declining markets is obviously enhanced by any cumulating effects of the transfer process which defensive managers fail to perceive. For example, the return attributable to investment in giving an existing product a facelift, when the alternative is to tear up the production track and develop an altogether new model, may appear very attractive if a static view of the market is taken, but could appear disastrous from a dynamic perspective. The 'defensive' firm fails to experience anything new because it does not change what it does or how it looks at the world; whereas those firms producing rival new products or using new production techniques may learn how to cut their costs, and customers may learn how to appreciate their products. Section 5.7 is partly based on this idea, but a more detailed discussion of the significance of such 'learning effects' is provided in Chapter 7.

5.6 THE SEQUENTIAL WEAROUT TRAP

Mistaken defensive investment decisions are particularly likely to arise when products or production processes are integrated structures; when decision-makers are wary of expanding their borrowing and are short of ready cash; and when decision-makers presume that short-run resource constraints will eventually be eased. The essential difficulty arises because components of integrated structures are prone not to wear out at identical rates. Modernisation may fail to take place if the components cannot be replaced by those of more recent vintages. About the only economist seriously to discuss this problem is Frankel (1955), in the context of an attempt to assess 'early start/premature maturity' theories of why Britain has fallen behind as an economic power since 1870. But a variant of the problem surfaces in everyday life, in the context of car ownership. The car ownership example is the easiest to follow, so it is useful to consider it first.

A car owner with an old car may be torn between, say, buying a new tyre now and keeping the car, or trading it in for a newer (or brand new) model. To replace the worn-out tyre will make a negligible impact (less than the cost of the tyre) on the secondhand value of the car, yet it has an advantage in that it seems to avoid a large run down in the person's financial reserves or unused borrowing capacity. Worried by the prospect of overcommitment, the person buys the new tyre. A few weeks later the battery fails, and the decision focus is repeated. The person is aware of having been seen by others to make a mistaken purchase of a tyre but justifies ploughing yet more money into the 'banger' by saying that 'it will be a cheaper way *overall* of getting the kind of motoring that I'm looking for – I don't require anything flash, and can afford the odd inconvenience of repairs'. Unless she has a detailed knowledge of the wearout rates of components and does work out the overall cost of what she is doing, she may fail to realise that she might be less constrained financially if she borrowed to buy a new car, instead of making payments for new parts for the old one. It is only when the pattern of repairs begins to emerge in her mind that she will begin to come round to the merits of the alternative strategy. But she will never know for sure whether the person who ends up with her old car will reap the benefits of her 'defensive investment' in it or be faced with a continuing stream of bills.

In the industrial context, the three most obvious examples of the sequential wearout barrier to modernisation concern the railway, steel and textiles industries in Britain. Of these, let us consider the steel industry. Between 1870 and 1900, the inventions of the Bessemer converter, the open hearth and electric furnaces, and the rolling mill all served to raise the optimum size of blast furnace and produce fuel-saving economies. But no single one of these changes would yield its potential reductions in costs in full except in conjunction with the others (though steelmakers could choose to build an integrated system around either the Bessemer or the open-hearth technologies). There had to be a juxtaposed grouping of coke ovens, furnaces and rolling mills, in a particular proportionate mix, in order to keep one another employed. This was difficult to reconcile with the existing unintegrated and dispersed investments of the British steel industry, or with the existing ownership pattern. In contrast to Germany and the US (which had a more concentrated ownership structure and more conveniently located prior investments), these changes had hardly begun to be absorbed in the UK by the interwar period.

The problem may be summarised as follows. When a technological change occurs, it is inappropriate to see an established firm as being in the same position, as regards modernisation, as a newcomer. Its ability to change technology is restricted by the extent to which the required changes can be married with the existing system. Ideally, it should write down its asset values and delay replacement until the existing system wears out. However, differences in wearout rates set a trap:

To replace a worn-out component of the old plant with one that fits the specifications of the new would require the discard of other components of the old plant which were still quite serviceable. On the other hand, to replace the worn-out component with a duplicate of itself would entail continued use of the old method; unless several or all of the components wore out simultaneously at a later date, the cycle would repeat itself. In these circumstances, modernisation would be indefinitely postponed (Frankel (1955), p. 302).

5.7 SEGMENT RETREAT STRATEGIES

The third kind of defensive investment trap has its roots firmly embedded in the blinkering produced by a corporate research programme (or, in Kuhnian terminology, by a corporate 'paradigm'). It is conveniently to be illustrated by the cases of the UK motorcycle industry (described in Boston Consulting Group, 1975) and the UK footwear industry. For many years, the UK motorcycle industry had led the world, but, in the 1960s, while the world market for motorcycles grew rapidly, the sales volumes of UK firms remained virtually static. Over fifteen years it steadily lost its share of the world market, mainly to Japanese producers. In 1974/75 a crisis became apparent: whereas Honda alone sold two million machines, the entire UK industry could sell only 20,000.

Japanese success was built on producing small capacity models on a large scale, using mechanised production techniques and highly specialised machinery. When these products were launched on the UK market and in other traditional markets for UK motorcycles, domestic producers found they could not make profits at a competitive price and withdrew from this segment of the market. This retreat did not involve a contraction for the UK industry since the total motorcycle market was growing very rapidly. It merely meant their value added was in terms of larger capacity machines. However, the Japanese applied to medium-size motorcycles the techniques they used in the manufacturing of 50cc machines. Again the UK industry retreated up-market, losing its share of the total market yet still filling most of its factories with work. The segment retreat strategy failed when UK producers found themselves having to compete with newly launched Japanese superbikes which, once again, were mass produced on very specialised production tracks. The UK firms could retreat no further unless they gave up production altogether. Mounting losses meant a lack of resources to develop new models to compete with the up-to-date Japanese designs and the latter gained the bulk of the spectacular growth in sales in the superbike segment. Between 1969 and 1973, the British output of motorcycles with a capacity in excess of 450cc remained roughly constant at around 30,000 units, while Japanese sales of such machines in the US increased from 27,000 to 218,000.

It appears that the UK motorcycle industry was wiped out because firms were using research programmes that led them not to ask the right kinds of questions about the problems they were facing.

Furthermore, until the Japanese started mass-producing superbikes, the UK firms had not found themselves in a situation where their paradigms could not provide seemingly suitable answers to the questions that had been asked.

The UK firms confined themselves to asking about how to maintain profitability in the short run; they did not ask about what they would need to do for long-run survival, not did they feel a need to reappraise their approach to building motorcycles. In the UK industry there was a tradition of focusing designs on engineering considerations rather than on trying initially to design products to suit low-cost mass-production methods. As a result, none of the UK models produced in the early 1970s could have been made using Japanese production techniques. Another 'hard core' idea was that UK motorcycles were necessarily of higher quality – and hence assured of long-run success – because they were almost hand-made by craftsmen using general-purpose machines. The Japanese, by contrast, found that precision engineering was best achieved by using automation and specialised machinery, thereby reducing the scope for human error. Had the UK firms used highly specific machinery to produce models in the first sector to be threatened, they would have been unable simply to use their equipment in the production of up-market models and would thus have been forced to consider more carefully their long run positions. As it was, their policy seems to have involved uprating or withdrawing products whenever their accounting systems showed them to be unprofitable. But their accounting systems were based on existing costs of production and not on the costs that might be attainable with alternative manufacturing methods and high-volume production levels. In the words of the Boston Consulting Group (1975, p. xv):

Long term commercial success depended on achieving sales volumes at least equal to the Japanese and using equally sophisticated low cost production methods. The British industry, however, limited its vision to the costs achievable with existing low volume equipment and methods, concluded that profitability was impossible, and dropped out of the segments where they were facing superior competition. The alternative would have been to push for volume during the high growth development phase of the industry.

The 'intellectual tunnel vision' (Loasby (1971), p. 868) produced by their corporate paradigms was thus fatal for their long run viability.

However, in mitigation of this, some of the firms might claim that they had seriously considered a high-volume strategy, and that they had been driven to reject it as something which would increase their vulnerability in the face of lurches in domestic macroeconomic policy – since their main market in the UK consisted of young, credit-reliant males, they were inevitably prone to be hit severely by changes in purchase tax and hire-purchase regulations during the 'stop' phase of the 'stop/go cycle' that characterised UK macroeconomic policy for the first three decades after the war. Against such a defence, one could argue that if they had looked more towards exports as a source of sales – as the Japanese had done – they would have been able to reduce the risks of being 'mugged' by such macroeconomic measures; for it was only in the early 1970s that a widespread synchronisation of macroeconomic cycles occurred in OECD countries. All too often there was a tendency to think of exports merely as a welcome addition to domestic sales and not as a core part of the market.

The UK footwear industry shows how firms with different sets of blinkers can respond very differently to increasing international competition. Here the example concerns the contrasting reactions of old-established Northamptonshire producers and the younger, geographically separated Clark's firm in Somerset, in the face of threats to their markets from southern and eastern European footwear manufacturers. The former were using a similar research programme to the motorcycle firms and decided to specialise in quality shoe production on a small scale. And like the motorcycle producers, they did not try to expand their export markets so as to obtain economies of scale in the production of a high-quality range. Many of these firms have suffered a fate similar to that which beset the motorcycle producers. Clark's, on the other hand, operated according to a research programme that was much less confining and contained a different decision algorithm. They were located well away from the traditional centres of production and traditional attitudes. When managers at Clark's were faced with a decline in profits and sales, their response was to ask, '*Why* are we being undersold by foreign producers?' They did not merely assume that the decline came *because* they were being undersold by producers with lower wage costs. The Northampton producers assumed they knew the best techniques for making shoes and hence did not search for other ways of making them; their attention was focused instead on discovering in which kinds of shoes they still had a cost advantage, *given* their method of production. By asking a different question, Clark's were able to find a way to a more secure long-term future.

They analysed their profit decline as being due to producing too many brands and, much more importantly, producing them in a far less mechanised way than their foreign rivals, even though the latter had lower labour costs. After streamlining their brands, increasing their exporting efforts and introducing more mechanised production techniques, they were able to play their foreign competitors at their own game in the market for quality shoes.

5.8 AN EXTREME EXAMPLE: THE CONVAIR 880/990 AIRLINERS

If ever there was a case of a company clinging desperately to a degenerating research programme on the basis of unbridled optimism and twisted perceptions it must be the General Dynamics Corporation. In the period 1960-2, General Dynamics wrote off some $425 million as losses in respect of its Convair 880 and 990 jet airliners. The loss on its jet-transport programme became the biggest sustained anywhere on a single project by any company. Even Ford's disastrous Edsel project a few years before had 'only' involved losses of $200 million. The processes whereby General Dynamics came to make this 'error to end all errors' are described in detail in Austin Smith (1966). These processes bear a disturbing similarity, in some respects, to those involved in the Concorde programme (which cost much more, but which were not borne by the manufacturers), though they were not compounded by political pressures for persistence, as happened in the case of Concorde. Instead of attempting to reproduce Austin Smith's blow-by-blow account of the venture, I will merely highlight some of the features that relate to what has been said so far. Other lessons from the fiasco will be considered later in the appropriate contexts.

Firstly, one should note that the dogmatic commitment to the programme was so strong that, even before things began to turn sour, Convair negotiated sales contracts which created the impression of a growing order book at the cost of greatly restricting their ability to generate future sales. The first big order, from Howard Hughes' TWA, was only achieved with the aid of a clause which prevented Convair from selling the plane to his competitors for a whole year. Hughes' desire to keep the advanced 880 from his rivals simply drove them to purchase Boeing 707s and 720s, and Douglas DC8s. The damage caused by this agreement drove Convair to make dramatic modifications to the 880, in an effort to sell it to American Airlines, the only remaining large operator not sold on rival designs. In attempting to ensure this order, Convair promised to produce, in the 990, the 'fastest airliner in the world'. Moreover, they were to deliver it at an early date, despite the fact that it was effectively a brand new aircraft with a brand new engine, by bypassing the prototype stage. In the event, the 990 was six minutes slower than American had specified for a transcontinental run and the contract was cancelled. A renegotiated contract was hastily concluded – once again at enormous cost, for it involved Convair paying an inflated trade-in price for American's old piston-engined DC6s.

Secondly, there was an extraordinary degree of flexibility in Convair's perceptions of possible sales levels and of the minimum figure at which it would be safe to proceed with the project. However, at any one moment they only seemed to keep in mind one pair of figures for market size and break even. The original projections in March 1956 were that 257 aircraft could be sold within a ten year period for over $1 billion, leaving $250 million profit. It was estimated that sales of 68 planes would break even and that, at worst, General Dynamics could only lose $50 million. The intention was to go ahead only when orders were at 60 per cent of the break even level. By May 1956 the break even figure had been raised to 74 planes, but the minimum required was dropped to 50 per cent of this, fitting the fact that forty firm orders had been achieved (ten from Delta and thirty from TWA). It was on this basis that the project was given approval, despite the onerous terms involved in securing the TWA contract. Between June and September 1956, estimates of the potential market were first raised to 342 and then dropped, after an appraisal of the European market, to 150. As Austin Smith (1966, p. 90) notes, 'These gyrations gave substance to an industry rumour that the division undertook a thoroughgoing market analysis only *after* commitment to the 880 programme!' By the time the project was abandoned, only 66 880s and 23 990s had been sold. It is hard to escape the conclusion that the desire to build the most advanced passenger airliner has such a high priority that it swamped all other considerations; and that Convair executives pushed aside worries about the effects of their highly restricting contracts with TWA and American by convincing themselves that they could cross their bridges (of, respectively, generating future sales and building the 990 without a prototype) when they came to them.

Thirdly, it is evident that the programme was carried out despite early warnings that the 880 was severely underpriced. At the time of the TWA deal, such warnings were ignored because they could not be substantiated at such an early stage – an objection which could equally have been raised against the claim that the price was adequate. A year later, cognitive fudging had to be supplemented by physical action to preserve the world views of those committed to the programme. The orders for subcontracted components (expected to account for 70 per cent of total costs) had largely been placed and an engineer in Convair's purchasing division added them up. They came to more than the total price per plane. He warned his superiors in Convair that they should abandon the project there and then and take a loss of $50 million. It is not clear whether his advice and figures ever reached the General Dynamics head office. What is known is that, when he persisted in threatening his superiors' world views in this way, he was fired, and only reinstated two years later when his judgments had been validated by events. Such a 'Procrustean' response to challenges to core constructs is precisely what is predicted in Kelly's theory of personality (see Kelly (1955), p. 510, and Earl (1983c), pp. 132–3; 172–5).

Fourthly, it appears that the 990 airliner was an outright 'double or nothing' gamble; a defensive investment, made in the hope that its success, as a *modified* 880, would make up for the mistakes made on the 880 and thereby salvage the reputations of those involved. They were prompted to consider it when the appearance of the medium-range Boeing 720 deprived them of a contract for the 880 with United Airlines. The 990 was much more than a modification, even though this was how it was presented to the Board after the contract with American was signed and sealed. It was a larger plane, built to American's specifications, around Convair's revolutionary fan jet. It thus had its own design costs and break-even level. However, the costs had been based on those of the 880, despite the fact that these were rising and open to conjecture. If everything had gone as hoped, Convair's 990 would have been an outstanding plane. But two major problems, to whose possibilities the Convair managers had largely shut their eyes, actually arose. First, the lack of a prototype meant that wing flutter problems were only discovered on the first production models, so the costs of correction were inordinately high. Secondly, its reign as the only plane with fan jet engines was unexpectedly shortlived. Pratt and Witney adapted the idea and produced the front fan engine used in the Boeing 720B. This plane did for sales of the 990 what the 720, as a rapidly concocted medium-range 707, had done for those of the 880.

5.9 The Selection of a New Strategy

It has been suggested that the normal initial response of managers to the perception of problems is to apply the conventional policies of their firm's existing research programme, as if nothing fundamental needs to be changed. Repeated attempts to do this in the face of anomalies result in either the concoction of increasingly complex, tortuous and *ad hoc* justifications for corporate behaviour, or a shrinking of the range of convenience of the firm's research programme. It is only in the face of an actual crisis of profitability that many companies will actually begin seriously to consider alternative ideas that zealots, who woke up earlier to the fundamental nature of the problem, have long since been proposing. The eventual perception of a crisis in the applicability of an existing set of core presumptions and policies is often very sudden, and takes the nature of a 'gestalt shift'. That is to say, the whole picture is seen differently, as with a mother who one day realises her son is now a man, even though he may have been protesting precisely that for a long while previously.

This pattern is well documented – as Austin Smith (1966, p. 9) observes,

Unhappily, corporate difficulties are more often the result of inaction in the face of a dangerous change than of being the hapless victim of circumstances. It's the exceptional executive who can bring himself to admit that a crisis is in the making. . . . Even fewer are the executives with the courage to take drastic action *in time*. On the contrary, case histories reveal too many instances where top management procrastinated about an emergent crisis [emphasis in original].

Further evidence of this regrettable pattern is to be found in the business history episodes described in the work of Chandler (1962; 1977), Coleman (1969), Perrow (1970), Hannah (ed.) (1976) and Church (1979). It is also implied by Downie's (1958) empirical work on the interaction between the transfer and innovation processes. Indeed, after reading about the tendency of the Courtaulds textile firm to go through such crises every quarter of a century or so, Checkland was driven to ask, in concluding his review of Coleman's (1969) history of the firm to 1945,

Is it inherent in the growth of a firm, and indeed of all great organisations, that they cannot adjust to change continuously, but must reach some critical level of vulnerability before a response is forthcoming? (Checkland (1970), pp. 559–60.)

In the light of the analysis I have proposed above, I would contend that the answer to this question should, broadly speaking, be given in the affirmative.

Precisely how new strategic programmes come to be conceived (and how they *should* be evaluated), once the need for a major rethink has been perceived, is discussed in Chapter 2 and Chapters 6 to 10. In considering the actual process whereby a choice is made between rival new proposals it is therefore convenient to assume that some managers have realised the need for a major change and have already formed their own ideas about what might be done. Let us consider what happens next.

Whether or not a manager will choose to propose a particular new set of core ideas to her colleagues, and her attitudes to the alternatives that they propose, will depend on where her own interests seem to lie. Major changes of direction will not be without adjustment costs for individual managers, while any proposal for a change in a policy conceived previously by a superior (who may control promotion) is likely to be taken by the latter as criticism, and as a challenge to her competence. However great a manager's past experience may be, there is always the risk that it will not be valid in a new context and that she will find herself out of her depth, in competitive situations which she cannot comprehend. Such anxieties may be so great that the manager's cognitive processes bias her perceptions against any major changes and, once again, inflate the prospective returns from adhering to current policies. Even a less emotional manager may fail to propose, or object to, new ideas because she expects to have retired or moved elsewhere by the time they come to fruition (see Leibenstein (1969) and, on the related problem of locating any long-term interest in government, Dell (1973)). For her to be amenable to new ideas, the costs they impose on her must be outweighed by the benefits she expects to obtain. If the benefits to the company are unlikely to be traced back to her initial advocacy of a scheme, or if for any other reason she would be surprised to receive enhanced remuneration or status, there is little point in her proposing it. It is only really guilt that will make a manager propose something in the corporate interest that threatens her own interests (see further Earl (1983c), pp. 178–84).

The pursuit of self-interest, and the tendency for managers with different ranges of experience to see things differently, will often mean that strategies will only come to be chosen after a bargaining process has taken place; after stances have been taken and votes cast. For the bargaining process not to result in acrimonious departures by defeated proponents of other strategies, the strategy selected must promise, even after any concessions have been made by its proponents, returns sufficiently great to meet the minimum acceptable targets of all of those involved. That is to say, when there are initial disagreements about the choice of a strategy, there must be some room for manoeuvre – sufficient organisational slack – to permit a climb down on either or both sides. Either the proponents of the dominant strategy may need to modify it to appease their rivals, or the latter must be prepared to make concessions, thereby losing face. If there is not a large enough all-round willingness to lose face, fragmentation will occur (see further Shackle (1949, ch. VI) and Earl (1983c, pp. 184–8)).

When the fragmentation of a management team does occur, because people are prepared to quit instead of allowing their self-images to be squeezed into an inferior mould by their rivals, the consequences for the firm in question will often be severe. In the short run, performance may be harmed while their replacements are acquiring experience. In the long run, the firm may face greater competition from firms started or joined by the departing dissidents. Herbert Austin, for example, gained his early experience as a motor manufacturer managing the Wolseley car company for the Vickers brothers, but parted company from this firm in 1905 after being criticised for clinging to an out-dated design (Church (1979), pp. 13–14). By 1926, the Wolseley company was in receivership and Austin had become so successful that he put in a bid for his old company (Church, pp. 105–6). Other examples of this kind of behaviour, and of dissidents enjoying the rewards of their vision, are to be found more recently in the US electronics industry (see Klein (1977), pp. 129–30).

How damaging a particular climb-down will be to a manager is likely to depend upon the prestige of her opponents; that is, upon their past successes. When relative positions have not become established and no set of recipes has been tried sufficiently to become trusted, the stakes are so much higher. Once one faction has gained a position of status, promotion-seeking managers may find that the most anxiety-free approach is to follow that faction, instead of attempting to beat it – one of the best ways of guaranteeing that one will *not* be promoted is to criticise the world views of those with a power to grant promotion. However, even those managers who disagree fundamentally with the opinions of the majority may 'see' the possible long run advantages of remaining a member of the team, despite their short-run loss of face. (What they see will be shaped by their cognitive processes, and they may have an even greater unconscious fear of their ability to handle resignation, than of their ability to function in the current team with shrunken prestige.) If their opinions concerning the shortcomings of the favoured strategy are correct, they will be very well placed for a rise to power when the favoured strategy begins to founder and they can say, 'I told you so.' Factors such as these will prevent the fragmentation of management teams in the face of clashes of opinion.

Accumulations of prestige, which give particular managers excessive confidence in particular kinds of strategies; which blinker them to the power of objections raised by their weaker colleagues; and which enable them to railroad their proposals into operation, can be very damaging indeed. This much is clear in the dreadful performance of the Chrysler Corporation in the late 1940s and 1950s and in the bankruptcy of Rolls Royce in 1971. In both cases engineers were too powerful. For Chrysler, this meant that pricing policy was virtually a postscript. Furthermore, as Moritz and Seaman (1981, p. 48) observe,

At a time when mechanical triumphs were steadily outshone by styling changes, past triumphs allowed the engineers to exercise their might over too many critical decisions. . . . Engineering largely determined the size, styling and content of cars, which would be presented for approval and only then submitted to the careful gaze of accountants for detailed costing. . . . "Good cost control," the engineers blithely repeated, "Lies within the draftsman's pencil."

In the case of Rolls Royce, failure resulted because of the tremendous drain imposed by the RB211 engine contract. The engine was a major technical achievement but the engineers had a far too rosy view of the ease with which it might be developed. A passage from the inspectors' report on the failure, quoted by Grant (1977, p. 96), states plainly how the disastrous decision was taken: 'the personalities on the financial side were out-gunned and out-numbered by those on the engineering side'. In the event, the accountants could indeed say to the engineers, 'We told you so', but it was by then too late.

There is a striking parallel between what I have been saying about the processes of strategy selection in large companies, and the processes whereby scientists choose to switch between research programmes and scientific disciplines fragment into rival schools of thought (see Earl, 1983a). In both cases, the returns to the choices involved are highly uncertain and there are no obviously applicable sets or ranking of criteria relevant for choosing research programmes. Differences in hard-core presuppositions of the personalities involved, even in the languages they use (see Kuhn (1970), pp. 201-4), will make it very hard for them to 'see' the significance of what their opponents are saying. And, in both cases, there will be strong career pressures making either for conformity, or for exit in favour of employment in places where people think in a similar way: it is difficult to be at ease in an environment in which other people are continually doing things, or asking one to perform tasks, at variance with one's world view. Where exit seems incompatible with meeting higher goals (such as 'paying the rent'), and where one's current position seems sufficiently secure, there are essentially two personal strategies open. One can either acquiesce uneasily in the view of the majority (cf. Marshall (1923), pp. 317-18) or one can opt for the more demanding route of attempting to instil a revolution in attitudes, so that one is given the opportunity of testing the applicability of one's research programme.

5.10 CONCLUSION

A major change in the activities in which a firm is involved, in the production techniques it uses, or (as we shall see in Ch. 9) in its organisational structure, involves changes in the 'hard core' of its corporate research programme. Usually such a change will also involve major shifts in the constructs of individual managers, for their roles, status rankings and credibility will change. Such restructuring and redefinition is not, therefore, an everyday event, even in companies where management are not so preoccupied with 'fighting fires' that they cannot see ways of releasing time for strategic thinking. On the contrary, it is something which managers will wish to avoid, for, to a greater or lesser extent, it necessarily involves them in pursuing policies in areas where their experience is lacking. Their existing experience in other areas may be invalid, but this will be difficult to judge for certain, and they may have very many prior instances of its apparent validity. Consequently, they will be loathe to make any major changes until some kind of crisis produces so great an invalidation as to swamp, in their minds, the earlier set of accumulations of evidence in favour of a particular construction of the nature of things. This will be particularly so if the admission of the invalidity of a set of core theories casts doubts on their credibility as decision-makers, and thus threatens to reduce their status and power.

Managers will differ in the times at which they perceive the need for a strategic change; in their abilities to face up to such a need; and in the possible solutions they conceive. Thus although firms may experience great difficulty in adjusting smoothly to changes in their environments, internal forces making for change will usually be building up for a long while before it takes place; and, after a new strategy has been accepted by a majority of those responsible for taking the decision, many personnel may experience great difficulty adjusting to it.

Given the way in which I have explained management and entrepreneurial activities as being entirely analogous with the activities of scientists, it seems both fitting and instructive to end this chapter by pointing out that observed patterns of processes of change in corporate strategies mirror very closely the patterns discovered by Kuhn (1970) in the history of science. If I amend the terminology accordingly, a summary of Kuhn's views on the structure of scientific revolutions (based on one in Ward (1972), pp. 33–4) may thus serve as a summary for the present analysis of long-run corporate change:

(1) A new strategy will emerge in a firm only after a pronounced failure of the problem-solving activities of the old one.
(2) A significant sign of the breakdown of a strategy is the proliferation of alternative possibilities and of methodological debates.
(3) The solution to a corporate crisis has been at least partially anticipated before, but such anticipations are ignored or swept aside in the absence of a crisis.
(4) The conceptual framework of the old strategy exerts a powerful inertial effect on the manager who uses it, and older managers usually do not absorb the concepts involved in the new strategy.
(5) The new strategy redefines a number of puzzles the firm has been facing and may generate new ones. The process of redefinition often means that adherents to old and new strategies will talk past one another.
(6) The new strategy emerges over a limited timespan. The full emergence of a corporate crisis and of a solution which attracts

significant adherents may take as long as a decade or more. Coming to terms with the new framework is also a lengthy process.

(7) Managers who succeed in making the transition from believing in the acceptability of one strategy to favouring a new one will often experience a discontinuous shift in their views of their firms and the business environment. (This shift will be rather similar to the more trivial kind of perceptual shift one experiences when looking at images designed for psychological experiments – the classic ones concern a black and white pattern, which can be seen as *either* the silhouettes of a pair of faces *or* as the shape of a white vase against a black background; and a set of lines intended to represent the edges of a transparent cube, poised in space, where it is possible to see various of its corners as being the ones nearest the onlooker. It is easy to see one of the possible perspectives at first sight in such experiments, but not everyone will see the same one first, or be able to see others without suggestions as to what they might try to see.)

I hope that, in the remaining chapters of this book, readers will not forget that this 'Kuhnian' view of discontinuities in the ability of firms to reach particular levels of attainment is not the only perspective I have provided on the problem. Within the context of a particular strategy, cycles can still occur for reasons independent of structural changes in the environment. It may be more useful to try to 'see' these in terms of the mechanistic model in section 1.6 or the euphoria/depression analysis in sections 4.6 and 4.7 – or, indeed, in terms of the three analyses combined as a single, complex whole.

6 Diversification and Rationalisation

6.1 Introduction

This chapter is concerned with the processes through which firms go when deciding which activities to internalise within their boundaries, and with the problems these processes create. Firms do not face fully specified, God-given lists of possible combinations of activities between which to choose. Corporate strategies have to be devised before such choices are made, and choices are never made between fully specified plans of action. Rather, a hierarchy of choices exists and it is useful to outline this by way of introduction, to provide a bridge from the previous chapter.

At the highest level, there are 'revolutionary strategic choices', about diversification and rationalisation, which involve fundamental shifts in the way a firm thinks about the nature of its business – for example, the decisions at Chrysler first to acquire a major European production interest and then, in the face of a crisis, to sell off these operations and abandon the European market (see Moritz and Seaman, 1981), or the decision at Courtaulds in the 1890s, again in the face of a crisis, to move into rayon production (see Coleman, 1969). These were the kinds of choice discussed in section 5.9 but, there, sets of imagined alternatives were assumed already to exist; I did not explore how they came to be devised.

At a rather lower level are what might be termed 'programmed strategic choices'. By this I mean that they are concerned with changes in the activities undertaken by the firm, that are seen as aspects of 'business as usual'. Instead of involving shifts in core ideas, these changes represent the application of tenets of the existing corporate research programme to the task of dealing with a world of business which is itself defined for the firm by these core theories and presumptions. They do not involve a fundamental re-think, even though they involve the firm in new activities, but they are choices *channelised* by a particular set of fundamental decisions arrived at in the past. It is in this sense that they are 'programmed', though it may well be that they are also programmed in the sense discussed in section 3.4 and hence do not involve a great deal of deliberative thought within the conceptual framework defined by the firm's core ideas. Corporate planners, in the business of trying to anticipate the truncation of some product lifecycles, the prospects for 'take-off' in others, and the combinations of activities thus implied for their particular firms, are *usually* operating at the level of programmed strategic choices.

At the third level are tactical choices. These concern the details of fighting the competitive battles arising in respect of *individual* activities, as a result of first- and second-level strategic choices of *sets* of activities (cf. Kay (1982), p. 52).

Just as these three levels exist in corporations, so, too, do they exist in individual managerial imaginations. At each of the three levels, the decisions involved are problem oriented. But, as was argued in Chapter 5, problems are often tackled at the wrong level. In this chapter the aim is to consider how problems are addressed when they are seen – rightly or wrongly – in strategic terms (that is, levels one and two). Section 6.2 analyses how firms come to focus on particular activities as possible targets for internalisation within their boundaries. Section 6.3 is concerned with the importance of corporate world views in shaping the way some activities that fall into focus come mistakenly to be seen as profit opportunities. Section 6.4 is a development of earlier discussions (sections 1.6 and 4.6) of 'corporate euphoria', which addresses the common problem of uncontrolled product proliferation. Rationalisation is often a belated response to the perception of this problem, but tends to bring with it yet other difficulties; these are the subject of section 6.5. Section 6.6 is a short conclusion.

6.2 Focus

In seeking to consider how firms come to focus their attention on particular strategy options, it is useful once again to devote some attention to the work of Moss (1981) – though to the analysis in Chapters 2 and 3 of his book, rather than his subsequent arguments which were criticised in section 2.5. Like other previous theorists, Moss does not make the kind of distinction I have just made between 'revolutionary' and 'programmed' kinds of strategy choice. But, unlike most, he makes much of Penrose's (1959) work on managerial learning and this is why his work meshes well with the present analysis.

Moss argues that the factors which both drive firms to create new strategies, and shape the kinds of strategies they create, can usefully be collected under two headings: 'focusing effects' and 'inducement effects'. Managerial attention comes to be focused on particular possible courses of action as a result of the past gathering together of managerial and physical resources in the firm. In particular, 'Focusing effects turn on imbalances arising from the resources and administrative structure of the firm' (Moss (1981), p. 62). That is to say, which strategy options managers see depend on factors internal to their firm. However, competitive forces outside the firm will also shape what managers are interested in doing, insofar as these external events relate to their firm's existing activities and those of its competitors. Thus Moss (1981, pp. 62–3) suggests that 'inducement effects turn on technological linkages among the production activities of different firms and forces arising from competition among firms'. However, for a competitive force to be potent, it must be seen by the firm's managers, so inducement effects are best defined as 'the result of competitive pressures and focusing effects operating conjointly' (p. 63). To appreciate fully the significance of these effects it is necessary to devote some attention to three of their elements: resources, imbalances, and (extending the discussions in section 2.4) linkages.

Resources

Any firm is a unique collection of physical and human resources, which can yield a variety of services in a production process (see Penrose (1959), pp. 24–5). Physical assets are sometimes highly specific but, frequently, they can be applied in a variety of contexts. Steel presses, for example, might be used in making car bodies, washing machines and other 'white goods', office equipment, and so on. Managerial knowledge may be applied, in many cases, to more than one kind of activity. A knowledge of assembly processes for electrical components and steel pressings, for example, might be relevant in some degree in the manufacture of cars, white goods, locomotives and typewriters.

The determinants of the volume of experience held by a firm were examined in Chapter 4. Given the significant role of Penrose's work in shaping Moss' view of the focusing process, it is timely for us to examine how she sees the nature of managerial experience (see also section 2.5). Penrose suggests (1959, p. 53) that it takes two forms. The first she calls 'objective' knowledge; that is, knowledge about the 'state of the art' in respect of technology and markets, which is, in principle, transmissible. The phrase 'in principle' is rather significant, and not merely for reasons relating to the possibility that knowledge may be withheld by opportunists. It is a mistake to believe that technological know-how is something which managers or consultants can spread easily within firms, between firms in the same economy, or between firm (or branches of firms) in different countries. Pratten (1972, p. 190) notes how this is something ignored by economists studying disparities in growth rates between countries in a world of multinational firms, and he rams his point home by reminding his readers that students who have access to the same books are by no means guaranteed to learn the same things.

Secondly, there is what Penrose regards as genuine experience: knowledge which cannot be transmitted because it actually changes the individuals involved in a subtle way and cannot be separated from them. Thus, a change in managerial knowledge, including knowledge of how the current collection of individuals can function as a working group, 'not only causes the productive opportunity of a firm to change in ways unrelated to changes in the environment, but also contributes to the uniqueness of the opportunity of each individual firm' (Penrose (1959), pp. 52–3). It may well be the case that this kind of experience precludes the strict replication or transfer of *any* industrial process (cf. Nelson and Winter (1982), pp. 117–21). The importance of 'tacit knowledge' was central to the work of the late scientist–philosopher, Michael Polanyi, and his (1958, p. 52) remarks about the scientific study of industrial processes have considerable relevance in the present context:

Great industries . . . were carrying on their activities in the manner of an art without any clear knowledge of the constituent detailed operations. When modern scientific research was applied to these traditional industries it was faced in the first place with the task of discovering what was actually going on there and how it was that it produced the goods. . . . [E]ven in the modern industries the indefinable knowledge is still an essential part of technology. I have myself watched in Hungary a new, imported machine for blowing electric lamp bulbs, the exact counterpart of which was operating successfully in Germany, failing for a whole year to produce a single flawless bulb.

In terms of the Kellian analysis in Chapters 3 and 4, we could say that managerial experience, gained in the context of a particular collection of physical resources, provides a focus because a manager will only be able to conceive of those strategies which she can visualise in terms of her existing set of constructs, or in terms of these constructs combined with new, related ones supplied by colleagues and other sources of information. (But it is important to note that new perspectives can sometimes prove a mixed blessing: as one of Shell's scenario planning pioneers, Pierre Wack (1983) has pointed out, 'originality in future studies is a pernicious value . . . because then you are focused on the two or three new things you have found, and you lose sight of the whole'.) A manager's ability to see the need for a change is also channelised by her construct system – i.e. her awareness of competitive forces, and her ability to anticipate them, is limited by her repertoire of constructs.

To the extent that their 'unique' experience is not invalid, managers in a firm may be justified in feeling that they have a head start on those in other firms, in areas of activity where this experience *seems* applicable. But Moss fails to discuss the important corollary of this point: knowledge that is valid in one area may, in the event, be hopelessly unsuited to another field which seems, on the surface, to have similarities. Unique experience may turn out not to get to the essence of a new activity and other, more general constructs used by managers may then turn out to be disastrously superficial.

Imbalances

Having initially been narrowed by the perceptual fields of its managers, corporate focusing is given greater definition by the existence of particular unused resources and bottlenecks within the firm, that come within the vision of those managers thinking about matters of strategy. So long as they are not obsolete, idle resources are indicative of a possibility that the firm possessing them may have a 'sunk cost' advantage over firms who would have to acquire them from scratch (though a firm entering a new activity on this basis may find itself in difficulties if these resources need replacing and it has no remaining advantages against rivals who are more 'experienced' in other respects, or if the resources are once again required in the original activities). Bottlenecks, on the other hand, generate idle capacity. Moss focuses mainly on idle resources and bottlenecks which *have* emerged within a firm. Often, however, one should also speak of capacity imbalances which are *expected* to emerge – though in doing so one is to some extent merging inducement effects with focusing effects, for such expectations may result from anticipations of changes in market conditions. Both physical and managerial resources may be idle. Machines may be operating below capacity or factory space unused. Managers may have finished (or be expected shortly to finish) implementing earlier schemes or may have gained greater competence in their daily operation. The question will thus arise as to what use they might next be put. Indeed, the managers themselves, in their eagerness to prove themselves worthy of greater things, may be the ones asking such questions and providing suggestions as to the answers.

The processes of learning within a firm, and changes in its environment, will tend continually to create new imbalances which will focus attention. For example, spare managerial resources may be directed to using spare physical resources to overcome a bottleneck, which may lead to other bottlenecks being encountered and other resources appearing underutilised. Indivisibilities, and the inability of management to anticipate fully the nature of the problems they are setting themselves (see also Loasby (1976), Chapter 5), compound the tendency for attempts to achieve balance to be upset by environmental changes.

Linkages Revisited

In the abstract theoretical world of neoclassical economics, with its characteristics of freely available technological and market knowledge, and perfect markets for capital and used resources, a firm need not feel, or be, constrained by its past. The real world is rather different. The presence of focusing effects means that a change of strategy – even a 'revolutionary' change – will never involve a management team in selling off *all* of a firm's assets, firing *all* personnel at lower levels, and starting with a *completely new* technology, to produce for markets in which they have never previously sold.

Focusing effects ensure that, to a greater or lesser extent, new activities taken on by a firm will have something in common, in respect of services from physical and managerial resources, with activities it has previously performed. Managers may decide to change their technology or products but keep the same group of target customers in mind; they may use their existing technological expertise but switch to producing for a different market; they may combine either or both of these strategies with a continuation of their existing activities; they may engage in backward or forward integration, to overcome actual or potential bottlenecks in supplies of inputs or demands for outputs. (In the last case, as was argued in section 2.4, the technological or market conditions may be considerably different from ones in which they have experience and the link is really between the reliability of their suppliers and customers, and the viability of existing activities.) It is, in short, quite natural for firms to try to exploit synergy in their strategic choices – even if they have never heard of the word (it is nowhere mentioned by Moss himself), nor seen Ansoff's (1968) classic normative contribution, nor thought of the possibility of trading synergy and about the hedging/synergy trade-off discussed by Kay (1982; 1984). However loosely and in ignorance of the modern literature, firms will focus on business themes that are common to, and link, activities which conventional neoclassical theorists naturally treat as separable. Firms simply do not branch out into territories that are *wholly* unrelated to what they have done before, any more than an academic scientist will switch suddenly to a wholly unrelated discipline (for example, from economics to chemistry) because she has decided her existing research programme is shrinking in its explanatory power.

In the real world, the closest that one comes to observing unfocused, fully flexible strategy choices is when studying conglomerate corporations (cf. Kay (1982), p. 30). A true conglomerate is little more than a portfolio of unintegrated companies under the ownership umbrella of a holding company. But even the management team of a holding company will not decide merely on the basis of past performances which firms they should buy or sell. Their company's results will depend on the future performances of such firms, whose projection will require special expertise. Managers of conglomerates will find their attention spans focused in respect of particular kinds of companies, related to ones in which they have previously had financial interests. Furthermore, the pure, *completely unintegrated* conglomerate firm, none of whose business activities have been selected on the basis of shared themes, is a rather rare breed. It is also one liable to extinction in the face of firms making synergistic use of business themes common to a variety of activities (even if the latter firms are, to some extent, hedging by mixing markets with shared technologies, or mixing technologies in market segments that serve similar or related customer wants).

6.3 Mistaken Focus

For any manager in search of a new strategy, the big problem consists in knowing whether or not she has preceived correctly the linkages upon which her attention has come to focus. One can make the point at an everyday level by considering how incompletely specified may be a person's belief that she 'knows how to drive' (the idea for this example comes from Nelson and Winter (1982), pp. 83–91). In the absence of extra information, this person may find herself totally confused by a new car which she has hired – as in the case of the American tourist reported to have driven a hired car around the UK for a week without engaging top gear, because her knowledge blinkered her to the fact that three-speed automatic transmissions are not the only form of power train! Furthermore, her ability to drive is also something whose bounds are affected by the weather and the behaviour of other motorists, and she may so far have not encountered driving conditions extreme enough to enable her to discover how far her competence stretches.

Very many examples could be offered to show how firms make mistakes as they focus on seemingly related activities as candidates for diversification experiments. Here, I have room for only four brief sketches. The first comes from Selznick (1957, pp. 53–4) and is succinctly contained in a quotation he takes from unpublished notes by Edward Boehm, a former vice-president of Gar Wood Industries:

> The first boats made by Gar Wood were high quality craft, made of the finest materials by master boat builders. Later, the company decided to produce a comparatively low cost speed boat for wide distribution. It developed that the entire organisation found itself unable to cope with the effort to shift commitments. Workmen and shop supervisors alike continued to be preoccupied with high quality craftsmanship. Members of the selling staff, too, could not shift emphasis from "snob appeal" to price appeal. The quality commitment was so strong that an entirely new division – operating in a separate plant hundreds of miles away and therefore recruiting from a different labour market – had to be created to do the job successfully.

Secondly, we may consider how, in the 1950s, the three giants of the UK electrical engineering industry – AEI, GEC and English

Diversification and Rationalisation

Electric – ran into difficulties as they tried to enter the explosively growing market for televisions. They failed to compete successfully with much smaller companies run by Jules Thorn and Arnold Weinstock, who had a different view of the nature of the market. The three giants were preoccupied with engineering excellence; American techniques of marketing and financial control were outside their corporate imaginations. They were, as Jones and Marriott (1970, p. 13) observe, naturally inclined to make electrical consumer durables with the kinds of precise tolerances that were necessary for heavy electrical plant for power stations. Such tolerances were unnecessary in this product; what *was* needed was an appreciation of how much the mass market was prepared to pay and of how to use mass production techniques to bring costs into line with consumer budgets. Unencumbered with engineering expertise, Arnold Weinstock 'was among the first to see that all television sets were alike and that they were fashion articles, not engineering problems' (Jones and Marriott (1970), p. 212). While Weinstock's Radio and Allied Industries boomed, AEI showed every sign of having failed to learn from its abortive venture into the production of wireless sets in the 1920s, where it was priced out of the market. On that occasion, 'The cases of each set were made by the high class furniture people, Waring and Gillow, and AEI gave up rather than adopt cases of a lower standard' (Jones and Marriott, p. 86). English Electric, meanwhile, had offered a high quality, but overly expensive set, designed by its recently acquired Marconi division. Here, Jones and Marriott (p. 179) sum up the mistake as follows:

Looked at from the standpoint of an attempt to break into domestic television, [English Electric's] purchase of Marconi was about as sensible as it would have been for Lord Nuffield to buy Rolls-Royce in order to compete with Henry Ford.

As a case study of mistaken focus, the AEI/GEC/English Electric experience with televisions anticipates many of the issues discussed in detail in Chapter 8. The upshot of what happened is well known: Weinstock's firm became part of GEC, and GEC, with Weinstock in charge, later merged with the other two giants.

The other two examples of diversification attempts, that were marred by mistaken views of the problem at hand, concerns firms in the car body pressing industry: Briggs Manufacturing, in the US (described in Miller (1963) and Loasby (1976, pp. 85–6)); and Pressed

Steel, in the UK (Loasby (1976), pp. 91–2). Briggs decided that one use of surplus pressing capacity might be in the production of steel bathtubs. This idea seemed a good one as they already had contracts with a large mail-order company to supply steel sinks. Pressed Steel saw the boom in the market for refrigerators in the late 1950s and concluded that their experience in industrial refrigeration (itself a product of their ability to use their steel fabrication expertise beyond the realm of car bodies), and ability to produce on a large scale, should enable them to make a successful entry into an industry dominated by small-scale assembly. In both cases their expectations were falsified.

Briggs discovered that bathtubs did not sell along the same channels as steel sinks, for they were installed by plumbers, not home handymen; did not sell in the absence of a complementary range of fittings; could not be given a suitable ceramic coating in the simple way that car bodies could be spray-painted; and, irony of ironies, could not be pressed using their existing presses, because of their thickness, depth and curvature. Ultimately, Briggs overcame all these problems – but to deal with the last required the purchase of new presses, leaving the original ones as idle as before. Pressed Steel's venture failed hopelessly, despite the excellence of their fridge design. They simply lacked the experience required in selling consumer durables, and failed to see how long it might take to pick up enough customer goodwill to make their automated production line viable. Their attempt to salvage the situation by handing over their entire output to John Bloom's direct selling operation collapsed with the failure of his Rolls Razor Company.

In all four cases, the schemes the managers in these companies perceived were linked to their existing activities and knowledge; but their physical and mental constructs were more limited in range than they imagined. In neither the boat-building nor the electrical engineering industries did a past record of manufacturing excellence in high value, small batch, production contexts guarantee the hoped-for advantages in 'related' low budget, mass production, market contexts. Similarly, the activities of producing and selling steel bathtubs and domestic refrigerators had less in common with producing and selling car bodies, steel sinks and industrial refrigerators than had been anticipated. But, all the same, one can see why these ventures would quite naturally come to the minds of their proponents. More successful strategies are formed in the same kind of way – that is, they are linked to the firm's prior experience and commitments.

Diversification and Rationalisation

The difference is in the validity of the experience in the contexts selected.

6.4 UNCONTROLLED PRODUCT PROLIFERATION

Some of the linkages upon which managers come to focus are, to say the least, tenuous. Not only that, but some managers allow their firms' activities to proliferate to such an extent that they experience considerable difficulty in producing corporate coherence through the exploitation of synergy potential. Two, admittedly rather extreme, examples are Guinness and Olin Mathieson. In the case of the famous Irish firm,

> A major problem was that what should have been a basically simple business, running two breweries, had got out of hand to the extent that there were more than 200 separate activities, including film-making, orchid growing and horse drawn carriages (Kay (1983), p. 59).

In the corporate revolution that took place in the year to September 1982, forty Guinness subsidiaries were sold, raising £19 million, but problems with those remaining necessitated a proviso of £25.8 million being made against losses on future sales.

The problem facing Olin Mathieson in the late 1950s was similar, but on a larger scale. As Austin Smith (1966, p. 20) notes,

> It had been manufacturing what was probably the widest assortment of products in the United States, among them industrial chemicals and agricultural chemicals, brass and aluminium, cigarette paper, cellophane, flashlight batteries, Winchester guns and Winchester-Western ammunition, hardwood flooring and lumber, antifreezes and brake fluids, explosives and powder actuated tools, nuclear fuel elements and high energy fuels, Squibb drugs and pharmaceuticals.

Such extreme diversification, within a firm not arranged as a simple holding company, could only lead to eventual management bewilderment and a corporate identity crisis of the first order, during which the company 'denegrated into a loose confederation of tribal chieftains' (Austin Smith, p. 20).

To understand how such product portfolios come to be created, it is useful to recall the discussions of managerial euphoria in section 4.6, and to tie them still more closely to the ideas of Marris and Penrose. Managers have good reasons for wanting to expand the sizes of their firms (section 1.2), but their expansionary activities are constrained by financial limitations (section 1.4) and by the finite learning capacities of management teams (sections 1.5 and 4.5). However, both of these constraints are heavily dependent on the prevailing state of expectations. Relative euphoria in financial markets can promote internal managerial confidence that is not justified. Growth is achieved at the cost of paying imperfect attention to matters of control. This point comes out clearly in comments about the financial position of Guinness made by Ernest ('Deadly Earnest') Saunders, the manager who instituted the rationalisations described above:

It was like flying through fog. . . . We had 52 accountants floating around, no one was producing monthly figures, overheads were not being properly allocated to subsidiaries, and when I asked about our debt position I was sent a note saying that we were within the arrangements agreed with our banks, who were willing to extend further facilities. I'll bet they were. (Quoted in Kay, 1983.)

The apparent confidence of the banks meant that managers felt they could safely pursue empire-building activities and neglect the task of consolidating new activities in order to release synergy. Links remained unexploited even though upon them rested the 'justifications' of diversification into new fields where other kinds of experience were lacking.

Underlying problems associated with the rapid internalisation of loosely related activities may go unrecognised for a long period, owing to (a) earnings generated by activities built up in the past on a more secure foundation; (b) the ease of obtaining external finance; (c) a belief that activities internalised by merger should at least continue to perform at their past levels (a belief that is often misguided; see Chapter 10); and (d) the difficulties of deciding when the answer to a 'question mark' activity is 'no'. Meanwhile, managers may form the misguided impression that they 'can do anything', that a detailed evaluation of synergy potential and experience requirements is unnecessary prior to decisions to branch out into new areas.

Their product lines thus become ever more exotic, with one weak link leading to an activity from which other weak links spread forth. Until failures become evident, they will not be aware of the need to develop specialised knowledge and complex construction subsystems for viewing the new activities. They become rather like the patients encountered by Kelly, who kept 'getting into trouble' with exotic adventures; for these patients, he (1955, p. 526) reports, tend to have all-inclusive or comprehensive constructs – that is, constructs under which almost anything seems to fit. Their constructs seem to come with a set of dishes, a Crackerjack prize, a horoscope, a false mustache, and a full year's subscription to *True Romance*.

They thus embark upon disastrous adventures because they do not *see* them as 'dangerous' but, rather, as things they can take in their stride without destroying their basic prediction systems.

In the cases just described, product proliferation was extreme in the sense that the firms became involved in a wild variety of markets. But the belief that 'we can do anything' is also prone to cause proliferation of a dangerous kind within single broad markets, that are divided into many segments. This is particularly the case when all the segments can be serviced from the same set of physical equipment and most work is subcontracting, in response to initial inquiries from customers. Engineering and textile firms, particularly, find it difficult to refuse orders even if they are of very low value. Turner (1969, pp. 302–3) provides some examples of the former: Tube Investments at one time had 1,000 customers under £5 and none in six figures, with no attempt being made to assess the profitability of each order; while an AEI finance director reported visiting one factory turning out two hundred different products and finding that the managers had no idea which were profitable.

British textile firms fell into this trap in the 1960s in depressed rather than euphoric circumstances, for overcapacity had appeared as a result of growing competition from imports. Many producers resorted to taking on any orders that they could get, with little appreciation that the production of small batches involved high managerial start-up, and stock-holding, costs. This problem was highlighted in a report prepared for the Wool Textile Economic Development Council (1969), which urged individual UK firms to cease being 'general practitioners' and produce standardised lines in particular well-defined areas where they possessed key advantages. This would reduce inventory and production costs and increase delivery speed, thereby permitting a higher average price. Quality and reliability would be improved too, while the simplification of the task of coordinating production would release managerial resources, which could then be directed to the task of *selling* the standardised product. The report argued that firms which rationalised in this way would remove 'more market than capacity' (1969, p. 213) and thus make the overcapacity situation even worse for the remaining 'general practitioners'. But it also recognised that such a change of behaviour would require a revolutionary shift in the ways in which firms saw themselves *vis-à-vis* their customers. They simply were not used to offering goods from stock; traditionally, they sold the *service* of providing tailor-made products. Thus they did not naturally think of taking the initiative of deciding first what to produce and then selling their products as such.

But even marketing-oriented firms can fall into this trap if their designers and stylists, who do not see themselves as cost controllers, apply an excess of differentiation to products in a segmented market. Thus, instead of producing merely an illusion of choice for their customers, using common components wherever possible, they offer an actuality of choice so large that synergy is lost unnecessarily. Possibly the most extreme case of this is that of Chrysler in the 1960s, described by Moritz and Seaman (1981, pp. 102–3). The troubles experienced by the firm in the 1950s had eventually heightened its appreciation of the importance of understanding the style-conscious car market (cf. section 5.9). But its cost control techniques were still poorly developed. This was an unfortunate mix of perspectives in a firm which, at the best of times, had a hard time enjoying the scale economies available to Ford and GM.

Chrysler made the mistake of attempting to segment the market even more than Ford and GM, while allowing its stylists to incorporate differences between segmented products that were so minute that they could not be seen without close examination (for example, faceplates on the radios of the Chrysler and the Imperial had slightly different lettering styles). Inevitably, there was a dramatic rise in the number of physically distinct parts ordered, from 12,000 in 1962 to 75,000 in 1970. In the latter year,

Chrysler was making 156 different engines, 72 different side-body lamps, 69 rear axles and 17 shapes of door handles. There were even 11 kinds of seats for Plymouth and 13 for Dodge. The cars also managed to gobble up 93 shock absorbers, though it only took 11 Delcos and 13 Monroes to service the entire fleet of cars on the road. In a supposedly high volume business, the parts factories were running off some batches that were no bigger than a thousand (Moritz and Seaman, p. 103).

Evidently, there was nothing superficial about the stylists' abilities in differentiating cars, and they had obvious incentives to keep themselves occupied with designing cars that *were* physically distinct, in order to justify their claims on the firm's resources.

Diversification and Rationalisation

The role of the Chrysler stylists was a tactical one, but it should not have been left so divorced from matters of strategy. Despite their ignorance of the details of car design processes, the strategists at Chrysler should at least have attempted to ensure that the stylists exploited common components wherever possible. After failing to ensure that competitive costs were designed into Chrysler's cars, the strategists could only see one other route to low unit costs. This was to make as many units as possible, forcing them through the factories at high pressure and then handing them over to the sales force. It will become evident in the next chapter that this 'solution' to the problem was not without its drawbacks. Eventually, rationalisation was unavoidable.

6.5 Rationalisation Problems

Whatever its form and origins, product proliferation that has got out of control is difficult to reverse. A major rationalisation, involving the sale or abandonment of many of a firm's activities and a change in the way its managers look at what they do, is an inherently 'revolutionary' activity. It involves facing up to the fact that there are limits to the activities which a firm can perform successfully, and that these limits have been overstepped. For some managers and their departments it may entail a loss of control – as their activities are sold to another corporation – or outright redundancy. Threatened parts of a firm will thus have strong interests in resisting rationalisation, and their cognitive processes will serve to heighten their feelings that their own activities should carry on much as before. Marketing staff will argue that 'good service' requires a full line; manufacturing will believe that almost any sale can be shown to make a net contribution to overheads. And, so long as accounting control mechanisms have not caught up with the spread of the company's activities, these claims will be relatively difficult to dispute.

Prior to the perception that things have indeed got out of control, piecemeal attempts may be made to cut costs by reducing staffing levels. Chrysler tried this, but in the process made its problems all the worse. Senior management were too detached from the production process to realise that the victims of the cuts were often the quality control personnel, since these were not seen as performing essential line tasks (see Moritz and Seaman (1981), p. 232). While the quality of Chrysler's cars fell, and their manufacturing costs soared, the key executives were spending a disproportionate amount of time attending to the expansion of the firm's non-automotive interests. Chrysler's defense/space activities never amounted to more than four per cent of total sales, and the firm's other auxiliary interests (real estate, chemicals, outboard motors, and so on) to even less. But that did not stop Lynn Townsend from making 'more trips to Louisiana and Cape Canaveral than he did across Detroit to the headquarters of the United Auto Workers' (Moritz and Seaman, p. 80). In such a case, it is small wonder that the established core of the firm's business can begin to come under threat from environmental change without top executives realising what is happening.

Once the basic problem of facing up to the need for rationalisation has been overcome, other problems may come to the surface. First, there is the question of whether it can be accomplished without a collapse of corporate morale occurring (cf. Turner (1969, p. 133) on rationalisation at Unilever, and Chandler (1962, p. 200) on Standard Oil, New Jersey). Managers who *have* come to see the nature of their firm's business in a new light tread a precarious pathway as they try rapidly to 'convert' their colleagues and subordinates. Instead of spreading the revolution they may merely provoke the kind of depressed reaction discussed in section 4.7.

Secondly, the presence of linkages between activities greatly complicates the task of rationalisation. British Leyland, for example, found itself in the mid 1970s in the somewhat paradoxical situation of producing too many models, making relatively incomplete use of common components within its model range (though on a less dramatic scale than Chrysler), and yet unable to close its unsuccessful mass market operations without harming its successful up-market activities. The view at BL was that Jaguar-Rover-Triumph could not be run without Austin-Morris because the dealer network would collapse in the absence of turnover from volume car sales, and because of the higher costs that would result from the loss of the (admittedly limited) component sharing advantages (see Ball (1978), p. 62). BL, like Chrysler, needed a *completely new*, slimmed-down product range in which synergy was more effectively exploited. An integrated structure of such proportions could not be created overnight. (BL's concern about preserving its dealer network makes eminent sense in the light of its earlier experience of trying to improve the network's efficacy by rationalising out the 'deadwood' dealers, for this merely let foreign firms gain a stronger foothold. However, if the component sharing problem had not existed, and if the closure of

Diversification and Rationalisation

Austin-Morris had actually taken place, this need not have spelt the end for the Jaguar-Rover-Triumph distribution network. An option implied by the discussion of Kay's work in section 2.4 would have been to attempt to trade synergy in respect of dealerships, via some form of joint franchising arrangement with, say, a Japanese firm. The political sensitivity of such an arrangement might have been sufficient to attenuate opportunism by the latter.)

The linkages complication will, of course, not be present if the excesses of diversification have been brought about by mergers on the basis of alleged synergy opportunities which have not yet been realised. Here the link is so far only in the minds of the managers involved and a de-merger will not usually rebound on the viability of those activities that are retrained. A case in point in the early 1980s is Bunzl. This firm sold off its interests in telephone call-logging, the distribution of computer software and hardware, flexible packaging manufacture in Canada, and self-adhesive labels. It also closed down its ill-fated carpeting concern, Filtrona Textile. Only the Canadian subsidiary and the labels activity were obviously related with its original pulp-based core theme – to which it has now returned, concentrating its attention on paper manufacturing and merchandising, packaging, cigarette filters and sterile medical wraps.

A third problem concerns the rationalisation of competing brands produced by a single firm for a single market segment. If several brands are merged under a single name, goodwill may be lost: customers, on finding their usual brands are not available, may easily switch to a brand made by a rival instead of adopting the new 'consolidated' brand. This was certainly the case when AEI rationalised its dispersed electric lamp operations in the period 1955 to 1960. In this attempt to remove the identity of the old constituent companies, simultaneously with cutting costs, all the old brand names, except Mazda, were dropped. The new 'whole' was less than the former, ill-knit 'sum of parts' had been; for a substantial share of the market was lost (see Jones and Marriott (1969), p. 239). In rationalisations such as this, there is also the risk that productivity will fall, owing to a reduction in the pressure of competition within the firm. Such considerations appear to have been behind the decision at Dunlop to keep the marketing and management of their Dunlop and Slazenger brands of sportsgoods distinct and competing, at a time when the group had been engaging in considerable restructuring. However, as Newman (1982, p. 57) notes, 'two brands mean two managements, two marketing operations and two sales forces – which, it could well be argued, Dunlop can currently ill afford'.

Insofar as firms can sell off activities and discontinue brands without harming remaining operations, the latter may benefit not merely from the cash that is generated, but also because of the freeing of managerial resources. Thus released, managers may be able to focus on areas in which they have a greater comparative advantage as coordinators. They may be more alert to environmental and technological change, and better able to exploit synergy. They may be putting 'their eggs in fewer baskets', but in doing so, they may be able better to defend, against the risk of 'mugging', those baskets that they retain. However, it is important not to forget that rationalisation is not *necessarily* the best path for a firm to take when a crisis follows a proliferation of the activities it internalises. Instead of bringing the number of activities down into line with the capabilities and special skills of existing managerial resources, a management team *might* usefully consider expanding its human input while retaining its existing product portfolio. Often, problems of building effective teams at high speed will preclude this as a viable option, as Penrose rightly points out. However, experience suggests that sometimes diversification attempts founder, not because the ideas were wrong in principle, but because existing managers did not delegate enough.

6.6 CONCLUSION

This chapter has presented an analysis of the evolution of the contents of product portfolios (that is, of changes in the activities carried on within the boundaries of firms) that ties together many of the themes from previous chapters into an integral structure. I have emphasised particularly the historical nature of the processes and the fact that activities tend automatically to be linked together, even if sometimes the linkages are rather questionable. The processes often lead to regrettable outcomes because experience is invalid or too superficial in seemingly related contexts, or because managers underestimate precisely how many activities they can coordinate at any one time, given their propensities to delegate. Many of these mistakes might have been avoided if managers had better appreciations of the nature of product lifecycles, for these would have alerted them to the limitations of their experience in new contexts that seemed to be related to what they had been coordinating hitherto. Others might

Diversification and Rationalisation

have been avoided with organisational structures that enabled problems to be identified more readily while leaving top management free to engage in less impulsive decisions and better informed evaluations of competing sets of proposed investment and merger activities. These matters are addressed in the next four chapters.

7 Learning Curves and Experience Curves

7.1 Introduction

In attempting to assess the upper and lower bounds of possible business events, a scenario planner might be expected to consider how her firm's cost position may evolve relative to those of her rivals. She should ask: at what rate can I expect to be able to reduce my costs if I pursue strategy X, and at what rate may my competitors be able to reduce their costs if I pursue this strategy? A failure to ask such questions may result in wasteful defensive investment in an existing market or a disastrous entry into a new market. Learning curves and experience curves are tools which may help to generate quantitative answers to questions about possible cost changes. Their use has been popularised in the last decade or so by the Boston Consulting Group (BCG) – to such an extent that they have even attracted the attention of governments (see, for example, the appendix to HMSO, 1978). But economists have tended to view with scepticism the relationships claimed to be embodied in these curves. This chapter, therefore, seeks to consider whether they are tools that it is a mistake not to use, or whether the BCG are themselves making money from the sale of a defective product.

The rest of the chapter is divided up into four main sections, followed by a concluding cautionary tale. Section 7.2 attempts to dispel some common misconceptions concerning what these curves may be thought to represent. It should be clear from Chapter 4 that learning is not something which necessarily takes place merely as a result of repetition. Section 7.3 consequently examines the extent to which learning effects are contingent upon incentive structures and employment relationships in firms. Section 7.4 is concerned with the

Learning Curves and Experience Curves

impact of the disruption of production flows on learning rates. With the determinants of the slopes of learning and experience curves thus clarified, section 7.5 considers what strategic implications these curves may have and whether or not a willingness to use them as tools in strategic planning may itself be a major source of corporate errors.

7.2 A Clarification of the Concepts

If a firm's average production costs for a particular product in one production period are lower than they were in an earlier period, this might be explained in a variety of ways:

(1) Learning by doing has taken place in respect of assembly methods, machine usage, machinery layout, teamwork coordination or average stock requirements for inputs.
(2) Superior managerial inputs have been applied from outside the earlier collection of resources involved in the production process, whose own past experience enables a productivity improvement to be instituted.
(3) Technical improvements may have been obtained from outside the system via, for example, the installation of a newer vintage of capital equipment.
(4) The scale of production could have been changed, producing either economies of scale proper – higher output rates with a constant mix of factors – or economies that partly result from a change in the mix of factors (something which the heterogeneity of different kinds of workers and machines makes very difficult to render quantitatively meaningful).
(5) The mix of the firm's output may have changed, with costs being affected because of changes in the use of linked production and marketing facilities.
(6) The product itself may have been redesigned to make it easier to assemble without error, or so that it uses fewer material inputs.
(7) Input prices may have fallen, or economies of bulk purchasing negotiated due to an increase in the rate of output.
(8) Workers may have changed their tendencies to take 'on the job leisure', or to concentrate on their tasks.
(9) A greater volume of orders may have been achieved, so that fixed factors and workers who cannot be laid off in slack periods are being used more fully.

Over the life of a product in a firm's portfolio, such period-by-period cost changes may cumulate, or be reversed. Proponents of learning curves and experience curves believe that various of these long-term changes produce statistical relationships between average costs and cumulative output *levels*. I hope it will not escape the attention of readers that not all of these sources of cost changes need bear any obvious relation to total output over a succession of production periods, even though they may relate to output *rates* in individual production periods. It is far from obvious that management consultants, who use in strategic planning the curves we are about to consider, are universally aware of this point. Bearing it in mind, let us now consider what these curves are supposed to represent.

A learning curve is a logarithmic relationship which depicts unit direct labour costs (UDLC) as a decreasing function of cumulative output. For example, suppose that the UDLC of producing the one-hundredth unit of a production run is 100 hours. If the relationship is of the kind known as an '80 per cent' curve, the UDLC of producing the two-hundredth unit will be only 80 hours: doubling the cumulative output reduces the UDLC by one-fifth. Similarly, if 400 units are eventually produced, the UDLC for the four-hundredth unit will be only 64 hours. By the time 800 units have been produced, the UDLC will have fallen to a mere 51.2 hours. Learning curves are normally supposed to be concerned mainly with the effects of increasing dexterity and the discovery by workers of quicker ways of making given kinds of final output with a particular set of capital aids. But this kind of behaviour may cease after a time, as workers begin merely to repeat experience instead of reconstruing events. Some authors also seem to regard learning curves as if they incorporate effects of changing worker attitudes (see, for example, Hartley (1969), p. 876). Thus learning curves may turn upwards if boredom sets in or if, towards the end of a production run, key workers are moved to new product lines and those that remain lose concentration as they worry about the new tasks (or redundancies) that await them. Learning curves would supposedly appear to be associated with cost reductions due to factors (1) and (8), with possible contributions from (2) and (6). But there is a possibility that effects of other factors (with the exception of (7)), which have not properly been isolated, could be responsible for a relationship which is taken to indicate that learning about the production process has taken place.

The Boston Consulting Group (1972) find the learning curve idea unnecessarily restrictive. They believe that negative functional relationships exist between *all* costs – that is, not merely direct labour costs but also capital, administrative, research and marketing costs – and accumulated output over the lifespan of a product. Furthermore, the BCG argue that although the cost reductions they depict in 'experience curves' are not usually achieved without some definite effort on the part of management, they are achievable for any product at a rate of between 20 and 30 per cent for each doubling of total output. No levelling out or upturning of experience curves is postulated by the BCG, for they see other factors as likely to swamp any failure of labour productivity continually to increase. The BCG analysis, in contrast to some views of learning curves, presumes that it is possible to obtain significant cost reductions with cumulating output in highly mechanised production complexes. In such contexts, direct labour may only be a small part of total costs. But it can nonetheless be a very large bottleneck preventing effective utilisation of such plant (cf. Hirschman (1964), p. 130), both in the start-up phase of its use and in down-time due to maintenance.

To a conventional economist, the BCG's view of 'experience' is bound to look curious. They define it as a composite measure of the effects of specialisation and learning on the shop floor and in the management hierarchy, plus investment and scale. It appears that the BCG are mixing together the effects of learning, in the contexts of successive sets of machinery and organisational structures, with cost reductions attributable to the exploitation of new techniques of larger scale production, along with bulk buying arrangements that become possible as rates of output increase. The BCG view of 'experience' looks less peculiar if it is recognised that firms often have to evolve their own techniques of production as they change the scale of their operations, and learn new skills in bargaining for supplies of inputs. They do not possess a 'book of blueprints' of the kind assumed to exist by neoclassical economists who write about firms. Thus the initial costs of successively larger scale production rigs will be affected by engineering experience gained on previous rigs, plus any bought-in expertise. This is what Baloff (1966, p. 277) calls 'cognitive learning', as opposed to the 'manual learning' stressed in the early literature on learning curves.

The fact that experience curves embody much more than simple learning effects naturally makes an economist wonder about their reality as statistical relationships between costs and experience, despite the range of examples accumulated by the BCG. Such correlations as have been observed may owe much to external events – such as changes in the prices, quality and availability of material and human inputs, or in the pressure of competition and pattern of demand (Gold (1981), p. 18) – which have combined by chance and overwhelm any cost changes associated with the reconstruction of events in the minds of managers, designers and line workers. If experience curves are not to be counted on as existing with the kinds of regularity of slope postulated by the BCG, firms may be driven to suffer unnecessarily from paranoia about the ability of their rivals to undercut them as their production rates increase. On the other hand, however, such fears may be entirely justified if their rivals are using, say, the idea of an '80 per cent experience curve' as an aspirational focus for their cost-cutting activities. If firms believe in the possibility of creating such patterns of experience, the beliefs of the BCG concerning the strategic significance of experience curves could well become self-fulfilling. With this possibility in mind, I will now turn to consider some of the difficulties firms may encounter if they attempt to force reality into conformity with BCG images.

7.3 Employment Contracts, Incentives and Experience

It should be recalled from section 2.2 that partially specified employment contracts are fundamental to the nature of a firm. Workers and managers are not required to perform *given* tasks, with given equipment and informational inputs from colleagues. It is simply too complex and costly to specify a worker's role so that all contingencies are covered and every aspect of her output rate and quality is predetermined. The idiosyncratic nature of experience enjoyed by workers during the production process makes it impossible to specify precisely what assistance they might be able to give to their colleagues as a result of learning. It also lays open the possibility that workers may perform voluntarily at higher rates than they might if they were given the same remuneration for following detailed instructions specifying what managers actually knew about the production process. However, contractual vagueness also gives workers scope for enjoying organisational slack and devoting their inquisitive activities to learning about matters other than those concerned with the production process (for example, they may gossip about everyday matters with their colleagues instead of concentrating on their work). It is by no means easy to design incentive systems to ensure that productivity levels grow at rates in keeping with targets embodied in experience curves.

Incentives to work may be provided by three main means: (a) by shaping a worker's world view in such a way that she will feel excessively guilty if she does not contribute a particular standard of performance (Earl (1983c), pp. 178–84); (b) by using supervisors to check a person's work rate against what is specified in her employment contract; and (c) by the form of remuneration offered. Here I wish to concentrate on the last two factors.

It is a mistake to believe that productivity improvements can always be achieved by increasing the level of supervision. This is the main finding of Gouldner's (1954) classic study of a gypsum mining complex in the northern United States. In this plant, a social consensus had been established in respect of absenteeism, breaches of safety regulations, tolerable rates of pilfering, and so on. A new manager arrived from another of the firm's operations, and was horrified by what he saw. His attempt to run a tighter operation by introducing closer supervision was a disaster. What happened is summarised by Gouldner (1954, pp. 160–1) as follows:

Close supervision enmeshed management in a vicious circle: the supervisor perceived the worker as unmotivated; he then carefully watched and directed him; this aroused the worker's ire and accentuated his apathy, and now the supervisor was back where he began. Close supervision did not solve his problem.

In fact, the impossibility of keeping a continual watch on even the reduced number of workers in a supervisor's charge meant that workers retaliated behind the backs of their supervisors, with even more breaches of regulations and higher rates of pilfering. Collectively they felt little guilt about doing this, for it seemed to them that the supervisors were deliberately trying to violate established norms of equality by trying to show who was the boss. By retaliating they were able to show that the supervisors did not enjoy any superiority.

To illustrate some of the difficulties of overcoming motivational problems by changing remuneration arrangements, it is useful to consider the impact on productivity levels at British Leyland of piecework schemes and the measured day-work system that followed them. In the former arrangement workers were paid according to the number of units (pieces) they produced. What they could produce was limited by their supplies of inputs and by the speed of the production track, which, in turn, was limited by the productivity of workers further down the line. This system turned out to be disastrous in two main respects. First, 'the quality of the product, despite inspection at every level, was adversely affected by the natural desire of the employees to produce at as high a rate as possible' (Arnott (1982), p. 80). Reduced direct labour costs were offset by higher warranty claims and a poor market reputation. Second, shop stewards tried to negotiate local piece rates almost weekly, to ensure that their members' bonus levels were not harmed by failures at other stages in the production process. Unofficial disputes over past production levels and bonus entitlements generated further disputes, while still others resulted from relativity disparities that emerged from the fragmented 'shop-level' bargaining pattern.

The measured day-work system was an attempt to overcome these quality and disputes problems, by using the concept of a standard performance to make fair comparisons and determine on an equitable basis the number of workers required to produce a particular output. In principle, the standard could have been expressed in terms of an initial assessment for the plant, and an agreed experience/learning rate at which the standard would be tightened as output cumulated. In practice, however, the company went *up* a negative learning curve. For example, output in the press shops of the firm's Swindon body plant fell by 25 to 30 per cent in the first month after measured day-work was introduced and then stayed at that level. The problem was not merely that management failed to agree on a plan of progressively rising productivity standards and instead converted basic piecework times *en bloc* to measured day rates as an expedient to obtain an initial agreement with the unions. It was also that the systems of measurement and control were not adequate and the removal of incentive payments thus left individual workers with the incentive to do as little as possible and blame low output levels in their sections on shortcomings elsewhere in the plant. Negotiations and disputes over standard times and labour loadings replaced negotiations and disputes over bonuses and, as new or modified machines or models were introduced, manning levels were often pushed to higher levels.

Beynon's (1978) account of the demise of British Leyland's Speke factory presents a rather different picture (seen from the workers' standpoint) of the ways in which measured day-work was a disaster for productivity. The fate of this factory was intrinsically bound up with Leyland's great hope for the US sports car market, the TR7. Other models produced at the plant had been or were to be phased out or transferred elsewhere; and, because it produced the TR7 from start to finish, Speke was an easily identifiable profit centre (cf. Chapter 9). Fear of closure meant that very tough standard output rates could be enforced by foremen, in contrast to the situation in other Leyland factories, where more fragmented production arrangements made it easier to blame other plants for poor output levels. The standard output rates were not inherently impossible to fulfil with the manning levels that had been agreed, but managerial problems meant that foremen had to use 'terror tactics' to force cars through their sections at the required rate. The impact on quality was as bad as it had been under the piecework system.

The managerial difficulties were twofold. First, they changed the specification of the TR7 almost daily in attempting to meet criticisms of the car. Before the Speke plant closed, workers had been faced with around 3000 engineering changes and so many wiring alterations that an up-to-date wiring diagram had long since ceased to exist. The second problem concerned production scheduling. This frequently caused chaos by being out of sequence. The two problems combined to ensure that workers were constantly facing surprises and an atmosphere of crisis.

Now, although learning is very much an incentive-related problem-oriented phenomenon, it should be clear from sections 4.7 and 5.2 that it is unlikely to be a feature of a persistently crisis-ridden environment. Under pressure, people contort what they see and do, or swing to opposite extremes, instead of developing new channels of thought. And this is precisely what happened at Speke. Beynon (1978, p. 500) quotes one of the workers from the body plant as follows:

"When we started on TR7, I actually saw cars . . . which had literally burst like a balloon. They'd been forced together in such a way that the welds weren't in the right position and the panels had been pushed together with a bar when they didn't fit correctly. The whole thing had been forced together [and when it was] welded together it just went buff . . . it just exploded."

In other words, managerial learning in some respects, and the failure of managers to learn sufficiently rapidly in other respects, conflicted with the need workers had for a stable working environment in which they could come to terms with what they were doing and thereby meet standard output targets without letting quality suffer in the process. Consequently, the rate at which the plant as a whole could accrue experience was attenuated.

7.4 THE EFFECTS OF DISRUPTION

High pressure production scheduling caused problems, similar to those at the Speke plant, across the other side of the Atlantic in the Chrysler Corporation in the late 1960s. This pressure was in large part a result of the firm's attempt to generate productivity levels in line with those of GM and Ford. The idea was to run plants continually and produce for a sales bank, instead of making cars in response to erratic patterns of orders and closing down production lines when orders failed to arise. Ultimately, as will be shown in section 7.6, the sales bank policy was to prove Chrysler's downfall. However, a key idea behind this policy is one that other companies have ignored at their peril. This idea was embodied in the maxim of the then chairman, Lynn Townsend, that 'You'll never learn how to build a quality car with the plant down' (Moritz and Seaman (1981), p. 101). It is the aim of this section to demonstrate that companies will have trouble creating experience curves with the kinds of slope suggested by the BCG if they cannot generate continuity in their production processes.

It is useful to draw a distinction between a lack of continuity produced by learning processes themselves, and actual breaks in production; it was the latter that Townsend was concerned to avoid. To a certain extent, I have already covered the first kind of problem in discussing the experiences at the TR7 factory. In that example turbulence was associated with product improvements and incompetent production scheduling. Organisational restructuring can also pose a barrier to learning processes. An example of this is provided in the BCG report on the British motorcycle industry (Boston Consulting Group (1975), pp. 56–7). Workers had to assemble motorcycles against a background of mergers, acquisitions, factory closures, redundancy programmes and, finally, a workers' occupation of the Meriden factory in 1973 following a threat that it was to be closed.

To illustrate the costs of breaks in production in terms of a loss of 'experience', I will take, first, the example of the Convair 880 airliner (discussed in relation to defensive investment in section 5.8); and, second, the problems of the strike-prone UK automotive industry.

Labour costs on the first Convair 880 were expected to amount to $500,000. It was assumed that the firm would be able to move down a learning curve with a slope of around '80 per cent', so that on the fortieth or fiftieth plane, labour costs would be in the region of only

$200,000. But the possibility of devious behaviour by Howard Hughes had not been taken into account when this scenario was being worked out. For a long while, Hughes had been stalling on the nature of the final configuration of the 880s that were being built for TWA. When the first four were nearly ready for delivery, Hughes' men kept them guarded and impounded in a hangar to prevent them from being despatched to TWA. He had been stalling about their specifications because he lacked the money to pay for them. Thirteen other TWA 880s were already at various stages of completion. Convair were faced with the alternative of finishing them and being prepared to sue if Hughes would not pay, or moving them from the production line into a 'boneyard', only completing them when he solved his financial problems.

A few years before, Hughes had put Boeing in a similar position. Boeing adopted the former solution and were paid for their 707s without even taking Hughes to court. Convair made the mistake of adopting the latter solution. When Hughes sorted out his financial problems the magnitude of their error become apparent. Austin Smith (1966, pp. 102–3) quotes a vice-president of General Dynamics as follows:

It took a real expert . . . to diagnose the exact state of each plane. . . . For instance, he had to work with a stack of blueprints to decide whether the wiring was nearly finished, just begun, or had to be completely changed [to incorporate additional engineering changes made in the interim]. Do you continue the wiring? Do you rip it out? Additionally there was some water damage from the months the planes had been sitting out on the field. Since the production line had been cut back, some of the trained people had been let go; others had to be retrained and all this was terribly expensive.

Since it was so unclear as to precisely which stage of production each plane had reached, they had to be finished on the field instead of being moved back on to the production line. This added even more to the production costs. The firm could only get Hughes to pay for all the excess completion costs on the four planes he had impounded and had to add most of the other excess costs to the mounting losses on the project as a whole.

The deficiencies of the British motor industry were analysed in 1975 by the Central Policy Review Staff. Their report pointed to dramatic productivity differences between UK and continental plants, even where identical capital equipment was in use – in assembly, UK labour requirements were sometimes double those on the continent for producing the same models. They highlighted four main factors in explaining why UK firms were unable to compete in cost terms with overseas rivals, despite having lower wage costs: (a) overmanning; (b) slower line speeds; (c) more frequent breakdowns in plants despite higher numbers of mechanics; (d) more losses due to disputes. Factors (a) and (b) are indicative of a managerial failure to negotiate the kinds of cost reductions experienced by their competitors. Factors (c) and (d) indicate a lack of learning by the parties involved, despite repeated experiences of failure (cf. the end of section 4.2), but they may also have made changes in respect of line speeds and manning levels harder to achieve by making it difficult for workers to keep up their concentration levels. The disruption in production flows certainly harmed the UK components industry, making it almost impossible for firms to plan the production of components: they were faced with monthly variances of 20 per cent or more in their production rates, while their continental counterparts rarely faced variances of more than 5 per cent (Central Policy Review Staff (1975), p. 98). This harmed their efficiency and caused supply problems for the motor manufacturers, with the result that the latter had either to keep several days or even weeks of stocks as an insurance measure (raising costs against the Japanese producers who work with only a few hours' worth of stocks), or to face further production losses (cf. also section 11.4).

The obvious moral of the arguments and examples in this and the previous section is that those scenario writers who make use of learning curves and experience curves in strategic planning should include in their scenarios not merely the possible consequences of their colleagues and members of rival firms being able to *manage* movements along '70 per cent' or '80 per cent' curves, but also the possibility of either their own or rival management teams being unable to prevent rising or stagnant real costs, despite continuing cumulations of output. Learning curves and experience curves, like demand curves, are potentially dangerous tools if conceived of merely as lines on graphs and not as conjectural channels of what might be possible. I have yet to see them depicted in the latter way.

7.5 Strategy Implications

In one of the first published papers on learning curves, Andress (1954) identified four ways in which they might be used:

Learning Curves and Experience Curves

(1) *In pricing decisions*. For example, when an aircraft manufacturer is trying to obtain orders for more of a particular plane which it has already produced for an airforce or airline.

(2) *In decisions about component sourcing*. For example, suppose that a firm has been subcontracting some of its component supplies during the peak of its product's life cycle, and that sales have now entered the decline phase. Should it end its subcontracting arrangement or cut its own production? Although they have only produced during the peak of sales, the subcontractors may be potentially more efficient. If both firms' learning curves are extrapolated (assuming it is safe to do so), the subcontractors may seem able to produce the rest of the run of components more cheaply. Whether or not this is the case will depend on the total number of extra parts required before the product is phased out. If the decline in sales is very rapid, it is more likely for the firm to find it worthwhile to abandon the subcontracting arrangement and produce the components itself on the basis of its greater accumulated experience.

(3) *In production planning*. By extrapolating the learning curve which it has established, or which it expects to be able to establish, a firm may be able to forecast output rates from a constant workforce, or predict necessary work force sizes in situations where sales are fluctuating.

(4) *In financial planning*. If a firm uses learning curve extrapolations to estimate the total cost of producing a particular volume of output to be sold at a constant price, it will also be able to work out how long it will take for costs to fall to the average level for the batch as a whole. If the analysis suggests that the initial financial drain is not viable, the firm can use the learning curve to work out the financial implications of negotiating shorter term supply contracts with successively lower unit prices (based on expected cost reductions). In this way it could enjoy a succession of short-lived financial outflows and inflows, instead of a single, unbearable initial cash flow problem.

Andress stressed that his suggestions would be most applicable in companies which do frequent major and minor design changes or produce short runs of a product at well separated intervals. This is because the logarithmic nature of the relationship means that cost reductions are at their greatest near the tops of learning curves.

The tone of the recommendations in Andress' seminal paper was tactical rather than strategic. He was usually writing as if the firms in his examples had already committed resources to particular industries, and were now considering on which terms it would be worth modifying existing kinds of contracts. In the hands of the Boston Consulting Group, however, learning curves and, more significantly, experience curves have become tools of strategic analysis.

Stripped down to its essentials, the BCG view of the strategic implications of experience curves appears to be: that 'first to market' is the only sound strategy; that a firm should never enter a market where a rival is established; that production engineering is what counts; and that novelty does not pay within an established market. Such conclusions are derived from the following kinds of reasoning. A well-managed firm should be able to move down an experience curve with a slope of 70 to 80 per cent if it chooses to enter a particular market. Firms who cannot achieve such rates of experience will, sooner or later, be squeezed, by well-managed firms, out of markets where they are presently operating. To survive in the long run, firms with poor experience rates should pull out of such markets and concentrate their resources in markets where they *are* able to achieve the necessary rates of cost reduction. In markets where a firm's experience rate can match the highest being attained, the key issue is where it stands in terms of actual and prospective market share. A bigger market share involves not merely the possibility of static economics of scale. It also means that 'experience' is accumulating at a faster rate. A well-managed firm which already has a larger market share than any other firms which can match its experience rates will, sooner or later, be able to squeeze out all other firms by virtue of its superior cost position. A well-managed firm which presently has a smaller market share should be planning to leave the market in the long run for this reason, and should be wary of falling into a defensive investment trap. A qualification to this point, emphasised by the BCG, is that an existing relatively small market share could be transformed into a relatively large one if the firm's own product is at the take off phase in its product life cycle, and its sales are expanding for reasons other than relative lowness of cost (for example, the 'pioneers/sheep' interaction described in section 1.3).

In the BCG analysis, a firm which achieves consistently poor rates of experience in a market is only likely to be able to survive there if it currently has a large market share and has been in the market for a long while. (In the early stages of the market, it may have been the 'best of a bad bunch' of competitors, but it may now face threats from better-managed interlopers – as in the cases of old established UK or US firms now facing Japanese competition.) Despite its poor experience rate, its cumulative output may be so great that it presently enjoys costs lower than 'less experienced' new rivals. It can therefore set prices low enough to impose an intolerable financial burden on them as they pick up experience. If it has a very large present market share, it *may* be able to keep a dominant cost position for a considerable time, picking up smaller amounts of experience on larger production volumes without even *having* to squeeze the interlopers. But it should recognise that its ability to achieve cost reductions is limited by its previous great cumulation of output (owing to the logarithmic nature of experience curves) as well as its managerial deficiencies, unless it can produce a discontinuous shift in its costs by changing its managerial policies. For this reason, it is likely to make sense for such a firm to impose a 'limit pricing' policy, based on its present advantageous cost position (cf. Andrews (1949) ch. 5; Earl (1983c) ch. 2), and kill off the interlopers at an early stage.

As long as its limitations are recognised, the BCG's way of using learning curves and experience curves in strategic planning is likely to reduce the incidence of corporate mistakes. But it does have important limitations. Clarke and Scanlon (1982), for example, emphasise how managers using it often fail to define market segments in appropriate ways. Brand managers are apt to define them so narrowly that their firms are bound to appear as market leaders. That is to say, they define the market in terms of their own product, despite the fact that it shares many characteristics with other products (for example, 'We have leadership of the sugar-coated crispy breakfast cereal market'). Clarke and Scanlon also emphasise that firms frequently fail to look at their market shares in a world-wide context – even if *they* dominate in their own markets, their rivals may be picking up experience more rapidly because they sell in more countries. To attain a secure position they may need to internationalise their business skills still further, and penetrate new markets.

A limitation which deserves more attention than it has so far received concerns the focus generated by the BCG analysis in the minds of managers: it concentrates thoughts on extrapolations of smooth curves that relate to costs alone. Attention is taken away from the possibility of achieving discontinuous shifts in these curves, or changes in their slopes, by bringing about rationalisations and revolutionary shifts in managerial imaginations. It is altogether too mechanistic (cf. section 1.7) and one-dimensional. Competition is not only about costs and prices. 'Non-price factors', such as design, reliability and delivery times matter too. Furthermore, experience is something which, to a certain extent, can be purchased. Would-be interlopers can observe some of the mistakes of those who have gone before; they may also be able to purchase transmissible know-how about the current 'state of the art'. Firms with dominant market shares and high experience rates should not believe their experience creates an unassailable barrier to new competition. As Porter (1980, p. 16) observes,

> The barrier can be nullified by product or process innovations leading to a substantially new technology and thereby creating an entirely new experience curve. New entrants can leapfrog the industry leaders and alight on the new experience curve, to which the leaders may be poorly positioned to jump.

Finally, we should pause to consider what might happen in an industry where several firms, of roughly equal stature in terms of experience, simultaneously sought to achieve unassailable positions by tooling up for larger and larger volumes of output without regard to their collective impact on their industry's total capacity. In 1971-2, there were signs that too many of the world's giant chemicals companies were swallowing 'hook, line and sinker the more glossy brochures of the plant salesmen or consultants' (Beck (1972), p. 287). Their tendency to treat technology as the master and not the servant, and to focus on costs instead of studying the whole business, led to too many large new plants being built. The result was that many of these plants, particularly those involved in the production of heavy organic chemicals, were forced to operate with considerable spare capacity.

7.6 Conclusion: A Cautionary Tale Concerning the Pursuit of Volume

The points raised at the end of the previous section collectively point to a need for a detailed examination of strategic complications caused by interactions between product lifecycles, experience curves and technological change. These interactions form the subject of the next chapter. But it seems appropriate to end the present chapter with a case that highlights the possible perils of pursuing production throughput regardless of other considerations. It concerns Chrysler's

Learning Curves and Experience Curves

attempts to overcome scale disadvantages against GM and Ford by producing cars continuously, ahead of customer orders (Moritz and Seaman (1981), pp. 100–8; 244–5).

Chrysler was too small and too poor to achieve 'experience' by modernisation and large scale production, so the firm's management sought to achieve 'experience' and high quality by forcing as many cars as possible through their factories. (Had Chrysler possessed the resources to opt for the former route, it would have been interesting to ask the BCG whether they would be inclined to represent the impact of such a change of scale at a point in time as the start of a new experience curve or as a move down an existing curve relating costs to cumulative output.) However, the peculiarly fashion-conscious and consumer confidence-based nature of the US car market meant that sales gyrated on a grand scale, both in total number and in terms of model and option mixes. New orders were processed very rapidly by an advanced computer system, but production continuity depended on being able to think *ahead* of the market and in being prepared to back hunches with temporary stock-building.

They were not alone in doing this: Japanese car producers have necessarily to produce ahead of dealer orders by virtue of their distance from export markets, but limitations on imports of their models into western car markets have given the Japanese firms much more of a sellers' market than Chrysler could have hoped to enjoy. And by 1967, Chrysler's output had been divided into four different price lines and 160 styling options. If customer whims bunched on options that Chrysler had not anticipated or, worse, on rival products, cars would be put into a 'sales bank'. The tast of predicting demand patterns was simply too great. Cars built up in the sales bank in huge volumes. The costs of carrying them mushroomed not only as interest rates rose but also because they required maintenance owing to vandalism and flat tyres and batteries. Furthermore, the dismal sights of Chrysler cars 'standing exposed in the cold of winter or the heat of summer hardly conjured up an image of a company dedicated to providing cars with top-quality finishes' (Moritz and Seaman (1981), p. 106). And workers could see little point to ensuring consistency in quality, for if a customer complained, she could always be given a replacement car from the sales bank; all that mattered was to get the cars out of the factory gates and thereby meet the production quotas.

Although it should have provided the dealers with instant flexibility, the sales bank policy for a time resulted in their being antagonised. The sales bank repeatedly got out of control. The first time this happened was in 1966, when it reached 66,000 cars. On this occasion, Chrysler pressurised the dealers into taking cars with an extraordinary degree of vehemence. But it did not take long before the dealers realised that Chrysler needed them more than they needed Chrysler. Instead of cooperating and attempting to sell the mix of models that had accumulated, the dealers held off until the factory offered incentives. These took the form of rebates, home furnishings, and many other gimmicks. The dealers learnt to anticipate when to expect such incentives.

Americans did not like the 1969 Chryslers, but the company kept building them and kept trying to force them on to dealers. By February 1969 the total dealer and sales bank stock amounted to 408,302 cars. With an inventory of this size, there was no alternative but to close the plants until it had been reduced. This experience ought to have spelt a lesson for Chrysler. It did not. The continuous production recipe was continued and, exactly ten years later, the new chairman, Lee Iacocca was shocked to discover the full horror of the sales bank system. His marketing vice-president requested funding for a promotion campaign for March 1979 to shift stock from a bank of nearly 100,000 cars. It was only then he realised that the sales bank/dealer incentives cycle was a way of life for the company. As a way of life, it had turned out to be practically fatal.

8 Product/Process Lifecycle Interactions

8.1 Introduction

This chapter, like Chapters 5, 6 and 7, is concerned with mistakes that firms can make as they decide whether or not to persevere in their existing markets or enter new ones. It relates directly to what has been said in these earlier chapters. In Chapter 5, I discussed defensive investment mainly in relation to production processes, only mentioning briefly that it might involve attempts to revamp existing products and thereby give them a new lease to life. To understand when defensive investment in seemingly obsolete products is worthwhile, it is necessary to analyse the processes that lead to some products becoming rendered unsatisfactory by others, which may themselves subsequently be displaced. In section 8.2, therefore, I will cease taking product lifecycles for granted, as features largely to be explained in terms of crowd behaviour by 'pioneers' and 'sheep', brought to an end by market saturation. Sales profiles only result in part from such 'epidemic-related' factors. They also depend critically on competent management in respect of pricing, and revamping policies (cf. Dhalla and Yuspeh, 1976).

The successful management of product life cycles requires a degree of flexibility which theorists tend to neglect. Firms which are successful at achieving high 'experience rates' in one phase may be hopelessly ill-suited to achieving them in later phases when different skills are required. Section 8.3 thus considers how skill requirements change and why adjustment is often exceedingly difficult. Section 8.4 examines the implications of rapid movements through successive phases of product lifecycles for a firm's organisational structure. Section 8.5 is a brief conclusion.

8.2 Preferences, Prices and Product Obsolescence

In Chapter 3, managerial decision processes were analysed as being either menu/recipe-based and highly programmed, or as priority-based and deliberative. It was argued that managers are forced to think in these ways because it is too complicated and/or time consuming for them to perform detailed evaluations of the expected values of multiattribute options in the manner normally assumed in economic theory. Discounted cash flow analysis of expected revenues and costs (in the common numeraire of money) is about as close as it is possible for managers to come to the approach assumed in mainstream theory, but in practice clashes of opinions about forecasts of costs and revenues often make it difficult to use. In everyday decision-making, the different characteristics of products are not nearly so obviously open to comparison in common units, so the pressure to think according to menus/recipes or priorities is all the greater. To understand how one product can displace another, it is necessary to consider how the new product comes to dominate in the customer's mind. In this section, I propose to examine this issue only in respect of the deliberative, priority-based view of choice. This is not only for reasons of space but also because the kinds of recipes used for choice may vary considerably between different categories of goods, and this makes attempts to generalise seem prone to superficiality.

A product may be displaced because its former or would-be first time purchasers find it 'too expensive' when seen against a newly available or newly perceived product. Some readers may think this statement so obvious that it warrants no further explanation. These readers should, however, pause and consider how a product's price enters into an analysis of choice in terms of priorities. In *The Economic Imagination*, I argued that the price of a product can affect its chances of selection in several distinct ways. The first is where the decision-maker is uncertain about what the product has to offer and uses price as an index of quality when forming her image of it. This happens most obviously during programmed decisions, but it can also be important where priorities are being used in evaluation. However, it is not likely to lie behind refusals to purchase on grounds of excessive cost: if a rival product has appeared at a lower price and the consumer is uncertain about its quality, she is more likely to presume it will be a poor performer and continue to favour the more expensive option.

Secondly, a product's price may determine whether or not it survives an initial *budgeting* filter and goes on to be given a detailed evaluation in terms of its non-price characteristics. Consumers, like managers, choose budget plans to break up otherwise unmanageable problems into separate, smaller tasks. A budget plan will normally comprise a mixture of fully specified decisions about some categories of expenditure, and, for each of the others, a budget range (minimum expenditure likely to be necessary/maximum tolerable expenditure). The plan will also include a sequence for attending to the rival expenditure categories. Rival budget plans will be evaluated, just as if they were individual concrete commodities for ultimate consumption, in either programmed or deliberative ways. Once a plan has been chosen, a product will be excluded from consideration if its price exceeds the upper limit of the relevant budget range – unless, that is, there is something about it which implies, or which a marketing campaign can use to imply, that the consumer's budget *plan* is wrong, given her priorities, and that she should rethink her budget ranges. The rejection of a product on grounds of excessive cost may therefore reflect a reduction in consumer budgets, rather than any change in its price or the attributes it offers *relative* to its close substitutes.

Thirdly, price may be used as a tie-breaking criterion where more than one product within the decision-maker's budget range appears to offer satisfactory levels of performance in respect of all the characteristics she has in mind. In this situation, a change of behaviour in favour of a cheaper brand may reflect either of three things: (a) a cut in price of an existing product, which now wins the tie-break when previously it did not; (b) an improvement in an existing cheaper brand, so that it now meets all of her relevant priorities, and the tie-break of cheapness is brought into operation; (c) a cheaper new product, adequate in terms of all the relevant priority targets, has been introduced.

Now, it may be the case that the decision-maker will not automatically use cheapness as a tie-breaking characteristic when two or more products seem adequate. Instead, she may ask herself 'What other characteristics do these products have to offer, that I ought to consider paying to obtain?' If she does this; if she perceives other potentially relevant attributes; and if she then uses the justification that the options she rejects are 'too expensive', it may strike a conventional theorist that something has gone wrong with our priority-based analysis of choice. Such a theorist would be likely to argue that the decision-maker has effectively performed some kind of simultaneous weighing up of price and additional non-price characteristics, on the way to discovering the *total* worth of each of the rival schemes. But this behaviour can also be seen as being entirely consistent with the priority idea.

From the standpoint of the priority analysis, the very fact that the decision-maker is driven to ask herself, in effect, 'Have I forgotten anything?' is to be seen as implying that she has not been able to arrive at a decision without first working out what priorities she should have and how, at this point in time, she should rank them. It must not be under-estimated how different this view is from the orthodox one. In the orthodox view, the chooser's set of desired product attributes is fixed and so are their relative weights; 'making up one's mind', on this view, involves averaging out good and bad points using these weights. In the behavioural analysis, 'making up one's mind' has a more literal meaning – the decision-maker is not merely trying to form images of her options, she is also forming the *precise* mould she is going to ask them to fit. When she is faced with a tie and is able to add 'new' attributes to her list, she is not obliged to rank them any more highly than a particular ability 'to keep money aside for other presently unspecified uses', despite the fact that her initial budget commitment led her to be prepared to spend *more* than she actually does. At the time of her initial budget commitment, she did not know that she would even find *one* way of meeting all of the goals she originally had in mind in the category, or precisely which goals she would ultimately wish to meet. Had she known of the existence of a single product that would meet a predetermined set of goals at a 'cheap enough' price, she would not have needed to make a relatively imprecise budget commitment. She would have been able to specify her choice there and then. So, when a person says 'I decided not to buy product X in the end, despite the extra features it offered, because I didn't think they were worth the money', I am suggesting that she decides she *ranks* 'keeping my options open' above the other, more tightly specified goals which she otherwise might have satisfied. She *does not average* out the various scores of her options in respect of her goals.

Where sales are lost because a product or brand is 'too expensive', the 'obvious' remedy is to cut the price. Yet the elasticity of demand may not be high enough to make a price cut viable. This is particularly likely in an oligopolistic context (where a change in the conditions of a tie-break contest would result in such a dramatic turnround in market shares that retaliation would be provoked), or where variable costs are a relatively high proportion of total costs (as is the case in assembly industries, such as the car industry, discussed in Shaw and Sutton (1976), pp. 130–41). In such contexts, the alternative policy implied by the priority analysis is to discover which product/brand attributes are not commonly included in the lists of priorities that choosers naturally call to mind, and then modify the product/brand in question by removing these features, leaving them available only as options. With costs cut by downgrading the product specification, a price cut may now prove profitable, and may become increasingly so as extra sales volumes generate 'experience'-based cost reductions.

The idea of downgrading a brand, to cater to the requirements of a market not heavily populated with connoisseurs of the particular kind of product, will be hard for many quality-conscious firms to accept. Conventional analyses of choice will lead them to suppose that extra features will compensate for a higher price. The behavioural analysis of choice in terms of priorities points to the possibility that price considerations – either initially, at the budgeting stage, or subsequently at the tie-break/'money for a rainy day' stage – may completely swamp some quality considerations. If the behavioural analysis is correct, firms that ignore it may make mistaken assessments of the lifecycle sales profiles of their products, relative to particular pricing policies. Many firms in the video cassette recorder market, for example, were slow to spot that most consumers have decided that they do not want machines with complex memory facilities, only simple machines to overcome timetable clashes and play prerecorded cassettes. While these firms focused on complex technological possibilities as the market exploded, the Sanyo company captured a very large proportion of the 'sheep' by producing a simple model at a low price.

A product/brand may also be rejected on non-price grounds, where previously it has seemed acceptable. The priority-based analysis of decision-making points towards the following five non-price explanations of product obsolescence. Firstly, an upward revision of customer budget ranges as a result of, particularly, rising affluence, leads to decision-makers adding to their agendas of possible options higher grade products/brands. These may enable them to meet all the aspirations served previously by the product/brand they had favoured, and more besides. The death of the Model-T Ford may be understood in this way: the American public grew to be able to afford more than basic motorised transportation; they wanted style, protection against the weather, and individuality.

Secondly, a product/brand offering the prospect of meeting further priority goals may be introduced at a price within the existing budget ranges of increasingly sophisticated consumers. For example, British motorcycle producers failed to make electric starting a standard feature, but newly imported Japanese models could offer electric starting without having to be priced at a higher level.

A third effect may be brought about by social interaction amongst consumers. People who initially continue to buy the fading product, because it meets a priority which the new rival fails to attain, may come to re-rank their priorities after observing the fortunes of others who have already switched. In the motorcycle example, some UK consumers may have resisted Japanese machines at first because they were foreign, but later may have come to rank the desire to 'avoid a "kick-start"' above the desire to 'avoid a foreign product'. Such a revision of constructs would become easier the more people generally were seeming to suffer no compunction about buying an imported product.

Fourthly, a product which previously has enjoyed healthy sales may lose its position because it suffers a lapse in performance in respect of a highly ranked attribute. The CPRS (1975) report on the British motor industry, for example, noted that, of a sample of 16,000 new car buyers in the period mid-1973 to mid-1974,

> Almost 30 per cent of people considering buying British cars decided *not* to do so because of unacceptable delivery dates. . . . *Long delivery times rank second only to price as a reason for not buying a particular model.* . . . [Furthermore] almost 30 per cent of people buying a British car had not received delivery within six weeks of placing the order, compared with under 10 per cent for buyers of foreign cars (CPRS (1975), p. 95, emphasis in original).

This situation arose mainly through the disruption of production and poor productivity levels in the UK. In the two years immediately preceding the CPRS survey, difficulties in obtaining UK manufactured cars had been compounded by a dramatic expansion of demand resulting from the Heath/Barber reflation. Thus, in 1971–4, a consumer who accorded a high priority to having a brand new car 'there and then' would have been driven to reject many UK models on the ground of non-availability, regardless of how well they performed in terms of other, lower priority targets. Such a consumer would only have waited for the delivery of a home-produced car in order to attain higher ranking goals (for example, 'someone like me doesn't let the UK down by buying foreign products') that more immediately available models failed to meet. And her willingness to wait would have tended to erode as she observed her neighbours enjoying the conspicuous consumption of imported cars while offering seemingly reasonable justifications for their 'unpatriotic' behaviour.

Fifth, and finally, decision-makers may become aware that, even though newly available rival products in the same price range may not offer extra attributes, they will be able to achieve higher attainments in respect of some goals if they purchase them. If products previously purchased were merely adequate in respect of the original set of aspirations, rising aspiration levels engendered for high-priority product attributes will present impenetrable filters against them when a rebuy is necessary. Product obsolescence may thus be caused because a new model *sets new standards* of feasible attainments in respect of existing goals, even though it has nothing fundamentally new to offer in terms of attributes.

Defensive product/brand investments may involve either a new sales campaign or a revamping of the same basic commodity. The priority-based, non-compensatory analysis of choice implies that such investments will be mistaken if they do not either: (a) remedy the perceived deficiencies of the product/brand in the eyes of typical consumers; (b) bring about a re-ranking of priorities and/or a revision of aspirations conducive to the rejection of the threatening commodity; or (c) permit a profitable cut in price by repositioning the product/brand in a new, lower budget market segment where it can still dominate in non-price terms. Many firms are likely instead to try to improve still further the performance of their products/brands in respect of attributes where they already overfulfil aspirations, instead of attempting to bring about the changes just described. It may seem quite natural to concentrate on what one is best at doing, but the analysis suggests that, in this context, this is a mistake. The only exception is where such a policy causes customer preferences to shift in a suitable way, by drawing attention to the 'importance' of these hitherto relatively low-ranking attributes. Normally, however, the secret is to build a 'good all-rounder'. If a product fails at a high-priority test it is removed from further consideration *regardless* of how well it performs in other, less important respects.

It seems fitting to conclude this section by considering briefly a classic business error made by an 'aggressive' investor in a rapidly evolving market – indeed, by someone who originally appeared to have a grasp of how to generate an exploding sales volume in a new market. It relates in some ways to Ford's defensive behaviour with the Model-T, for it concerns William Morris' attempt to bring to the UK public the first £100 new car (described in detail in Overy (1976), pp. 45–50). Morris' original recipe for success was built around being the first UK producer seriously to attempt to exploit economies of scale. Like Ford, he found, in the late 1920s, that this recipe no longer kept him ahead of the rest of the field. Other manufacturers copied his techniques and, increasingly, vehicle demand was affected by a preference for variety and fashion. He needed a new recipe.

With the 'Empire' Oxford, Morris tried a more up-market approach, but went too far. He painfully discovered that there was a maximum price beyond which a volume car was not viable. The advent of the 1930s recession made the need for a new recipe all the more imperative, for 'Morris was in the unfortunate position of dealing mainly with small popularly priced cars that were less likely to be bought by a second-time purchaser as buyers moved up market but were now too large or too expensive for first-time buyers during a time of economic uncertainty' (Overy (1976), p. 47). Morris' attempt to expand his sales by moving further down-market was a disaster: he discovered that there was also a minimum price below which a volume car was not viable. The original Morris Minor would only sell to those buyers with a maximum budget of £100 who insisted on having a brand new car. Morris had mistakenly focused on the changing pattern of new cars available and had overlooked the secondhand market. For £15–20, the first time buyer could obtain a three- or four-year-old secondhand Morris that, in respect of everything but newness, had much more to offer than the basic Morris Minor.

8.3 Changing Skill Requirements Through Product Lifecycles

The difficulties faced by Ford and Morris in the car market in the late 1920s resulted in part from a lack of marketing competence. The maturing of the market, and the widening of the income band of consumers able to enter it, meant that the market fragmented into a number of relatively distinct price segments. In these segments, non-price competition came to be important and it was then necessary to focus on lifecycles of individual products rather than on market growth trends as a whole. This pattern, requiring a change of focus from cost reduction and price competition, to marketing and design for non-price competition, is an aspect of product lifecycles which is not peculiar to the car market. But it is one as apt to be overlooked today by modern proponents of experience curve analyses of corporate strategy, as it was by Ford and Morris in the 1920s. Managers with construct systems well-suited to cost reduction over long production runs may be totally unable to see how to handle frequent model redesigns, even once they have seen the need to cater for an increasingly discriminating and fickle market. After long periods of moving down, say, '80 per cent experience curves', they may find their unit costs rising with further cumulations of output (cf. Abernathy and Wayne, 1974).

It is useful to continue with the cases of Morris and Ford while illustrating this contention. The difficulties faced by Morris after 1927 did not arise merely from the difficulties the firm had in understanding the form of consumer preferences. The firm also suffered from an 'alarming lack of experience in the design shops' (Overy (1976), p. 50). Before the advent of the fashion/design-conscious market, it did not matter much that Morris preferred gradually to adapt existing models instead of creating new ones. The cars made before 1927 had, in a sense, designed themselves. Supposedly 'new' models did not differ greatly from their immediate predecessors. However, Morris' reluctance to let the drawing office start with a clean sheet of paper proved very costly once competition came to focus on product differentiation. With shorter model lifespans, the car designs and production arrangements had to be right at the start of a run; if the line had to be stopped to accommodate modifications, time would be lost to competitors with new designs in the pipeline. Morris' policy of adaptation as problems arose meant that all too often development and production were merged together. This failure to think ahead often caused minor defects to appear in finished models, raising costs still further. A lack of experience in design engineering thus proved a bottleneck against the acquisition and exploitation of further production experience – rather as happened fifty years later with the TR7 (see section 7.4).

Similar problems, inhibiting successful innovative product differentiation, were faced at Ford. But there, these difficulties were compounded by the fact that, not only had Henry Ford encouraged the development of a highly integrated, one-dimensional way of looking at the business of making and selling cars, he had also created an integrated production process that was specific to the Model-T. The assembly lines, foundries and machine shops were not suited to the Model-A, still less to the annual replacement of entire ranges of products. During the eighteen-month changeover, Ford lost $200 million and laid off 60,000 workers in Detroit; 15,000 machine tools had to be replaced and another 25,000 had totally to be rebuilt. Yet, as Selznick (1957, p. 110) notes, 'even this did not bring about the changes in orientation, with attendant upward revisions in the status of sales and public relations activities, that were required. Only after World War II was a reorganisation in depth completed.'

Morris and Ford were both fortunate that they did not additionally have to cope with a different production process on top of the new design and marketing requirements. Their basic expertise concerning production-line assembly was still relevant. Many of their competitors had long since been forced into liquidation because they had failed correctly to match the physical techniques of production with the developments in the product market. This problem of matching product and process lifecycles has been highlighted by Hayes and Wheelwright (1979a; 1979b) and the next paragraph draws heavily on their (1979a) work.

In the early stages of a market's growth, or in the context of prototypes and custom-built products, the production process that is usually ideal is a jumbled flow or job shop process, using general-purpose machinery. An obvious example is the workshop of the commercial printer, able to handle one-off orders of a wide variety of kinds of printing work. With market growth, and increasing standardisation of product technologies, a degree of specialisation becomes worthwhile. At this point, batch production is likely to be appropriate and, even though products may, to some extent, still be built-to-order, they are likely to use some common components. Once a market grows beyond a certain point, the pace of work can profitably be speeded up by connecting various operations of a batch production process with a moving assembly line. A modern heavy machinery or locomotive manufacturer is unlikely to make large enough volumes of any particular model to justify moving from the batch process to assembly line stage, but a volume manufacturer of cars would be unlikely to survive without making such a move (or, in the case of a late entrant, without starting by using the assembly-line process). Extremely large volumes, with nearly complete standardisation of the product, may permit a fourth kind of production technology, the continuous flow process. Obvious examples of this ultimate stage of specialisation are sugar and oil refinery operations and food processing, but the Model-T Ford could *almost* be thought of in these terms.

The further a firm moves from the job shop in the direction of continuous flow methods of production, the lower its unit costs for a *given* item may be, but the more vulnerable it is to the sudden death of the item as a viable commodity. A firm which focuses on production experience curves when working out its strategy will be under a strong temptation to move further in the direction of the continuous flow process than it might if it appreciated also the possible shortness of products' lifecycles. This seems to have happened in the case of the US vacuum tubes industry in the 1950s. After several decades of viability, the vacuum tube was rendered obsolete by the transistor. This much was rapidly perceived by firms in the industry, but they responded by tooling up rapidly for high volume, low price outputs. At such an early stage in the lifecycle of transistors as a whole, this was a mistake. Individual transistor designs were rapidly being outmoded with the rush of technical progress. The vacuum-tube manufacturers would have done much better to limit their initial commitment to batch production of higher priced transistors for specialised markets (for example, aerospace), where compactness and high performance commanded a premium price, and where it was essential for users to be ahead of the rest of the field. Their high volume production experience was not yet relevant to the new market (cf. Utterback, 1979).

At the other extreme, as we have already seen in the case of the UK motorcycle industry, a failure to move far enough *away* from the job shop end of the process spectrum, as the product lifecycle takes off, can also be fatal. Flexibility cannot be achieved without cost any more than can integration; but the costs of flexibility and integration are different. In the former case, they relate to current input demands; in the latter, to the resources required for change.

8.4 Changing Organisational Requirements Through the Cycles

Shifts of emphasis between research and development, marketing and production will affect the balance of power within a firm. This may lead to considerable tension, for managerial world views will be under threat. On the one hand, there will be pressure from change from those whose empires will be likely to grow, and who are confident of their ability to cope with the new situations. On the other, there will be resistance from anxious personnel, who do not relish giving up their familiar, comfortable environments and possibly discovering the bounds of their competence via embarrassing errors, or whose relative standing will be diminished.

Turner's (1971) work on the early history of British Leyland provides a good illustration of this problem, as well as indicating that a firm's sales profile depends not merely on the position in their lifecycles that its markets have reached, but also on the ways in which its products are marketed. In describing the rise of Donald (later Lord) Stokes, Turner (1971, p. 25) notes that

> Traditionally the company had been dominated by company men: salesmen were told what they had to sell and at what price it was to be sold. Here, suddenly, was a man who came along and told them that he had signed a contract in Cuba or Iran and wanted 1000 trucks or buses. The production bosses did not always relish the transformation, particularly when Stokes promised things the company could not deliver.

Particularly resented were Stokes' youth and his talent for personal publicity; so much so that, 'at one stage, the company's public relations department was told to make sure personal publicity for Stokes was kept to a minimum' (Turner (1971), p. 24). But this could not stop him from rising to the head of the company – though in the long run this was not necessarily to the firm's advantage, for the business of making and selling cars for a high-volume market has rather different skill rquirements from the business of selling batches of commercial vehicles.

With the working through of product and process lifecycles, the degree of bureaucratisation in a firm will, or rather, should, change. This much is evident from the empirical work of the 'contingency' school of organisation theorists, particularly Burns and Stalker (1961) and Woodward (1965). The former distinguished between 'mechanistic' and 'organic' forms of organisation. In a mechanistic organisation, roles, responsibility and reporting relationships are closely specified. This works effectively in a stable environment, for people 'know their places'; much more can be taken for granted; and high-level decision-makers do not find themselves overwhelmed by a mass of claims for attention from lower-level people who have

Product/Process Lifecycle Interactions

bypassed normal hierarchical channels of communication. When the environment changes, the organic form of organisation will normally be more effective. At any level in the hierarchy, informational cross-flows may take place directly, instead of having first to be relayed to, and from, a higher level. High-level managers, too, may obtain more rapid feedback (though at the risk of becoming overloaded with information) if lower level personnel are prepared to bypass intermediate officials who might delay or altogether block the transmission of certain kinds of information. Lower-level employees may also be more prepared to promote innovations and advance criticisms if their roles are loosely specified and it is not commonsense knowledge that they 'do what they are told' or 'it is more than their jobs are worth' to violate established procedures. Burns and Stalker found that the structures of companies that were reluctant to change adhered most closely to the mechanistic form of organisation. Successful innovators were those firms where managers' jobs were more or less self-defined. Changes were easier to handle because they did not require the negotiation of new sets of formal roles to replace existing ones.

Woodward's (1965) work can be related directly to that of Hayes and Wheelwright (though the latter, surprisingly, make no attempt to do so). She focused on the same four kinds of process forms: unit (job shop), batch, assembly line, and continuous production. A definite pattern emerged in her empirical work, relating this spectrum of production technologies to the degree of organisational formalism. Well-specified formal relationships between organisation members were appropriate for large batch and assembly-line technologies, but, at each end of the spectrum, they seemed to be detrimental to success. Financially successful firms were those that conformed to the median organisation form for their technological category.

It is not hard to see why this should be the case. In a job shop, the custom-built nature of the product, be it a prototype for another section of the company, or a single, unique order, involves direct contact between the user and the makers, so that it can be 'tuned' to suit the user's requirements. The scale of operations is small enough for everyone to have a good idea of the entire production process. Getting things done successfully thus depends on someone being able to exert leadership not by occupying a dominant position in a written-down, hierarchical sense, but by having, and being able to articulate, a better overall view of what is going on in respect of the job at hand. With large batch and assembly-line processes it becomes impossible for line managers and operatives to have an intimate knowledge of the entire production task. To hold the flow of production together, therefore, successful firms resorted to impersonal rules of control, subdividing and ranking functions (though at the risks of alienating workers through the rigidity of their tasks and lowness of their status, and of making changes costly to negotiate). With continuous flow technologies, the worker/manager distinction is usually less obvious owing to the need quickly to spot or be able to deal with unpredictable changes. In an oil refinery, for example, so much has been worked out in advance by research and development that little should go wrong, but so much has been invested that, when it does, the need for immediate feedback is paramount. There is no sense in having a rigid hierarchy if the refinery can blow up while permission to act is being sought; everyone involved in the production process may be thought of, therefore, as a 'clock watcher in a white coat'.

8.5 Conclusion

The cycles of product and process innovations that tend to follow an initial attempt to open up a market involve a complex series of changes in the nature and mix of skills required of firms. In the increasingly technological business environment of today, these cycles must often be managed very rapidly. In such cases, as Hayes and Wheelwright (1979b, p. 131) note,

> the same people who managed the introduction of the new product may be called upon to manage its evolution into a commodity item. The type of production process, level of capital intensity, marketing skills, distribution channels, in fact the whole personality of the company must undergo profound change in the space of a relatively few years.

A company which attempts to manage the move from small-volume to large-scale production, instead of selling its expertise to another firm which has experience of the latter (albeit in the context of another product), may thus find itself heading for a kind of corporate 'nervous breakdown'. Firms deeply engrossed with the business of trying to keep up in the race to sell in a particular market may fail to realise how the required mix of design/marketing/production/organisation skills is changing. Consequently, they may be severely

Product/Process Lifecycle Interactions

shaken by their inability to cope, which seems a sign of failure despite early successes. They may completely overlook the possibility that they could still be doing very well if they had stayed in the business of invention and small-scale production.

But there is, equally, no guarantee that a large-volume producer will succeed if it waits till the market begins to mature and then enters on the basis of experience accumulated on *another* product (cf. the case of Pressed Steel, discussed in section 6.3). Difficulties in obtaining or absorbing information from the experiences of earlier entrants to the market may mean that the firm's experience curve starts too high, with too shallow a slope, and that sales pick up so slowly, due to a poor marketing/design policy being compounded by a high cost-based price, that 'experience' (in the BCG sense) fails to accumulate.

9 Strategy and Organisational Structure

9.1 Introduction

In section 8.4, I drew attention to the significance of the mechanistic/organic spectrum in organisational structuring. But there is a further organisational dimension to be considered, and it is one which, following the initial contribution of Chandler (1962), has attracted considerable interest amongst behavioural economists. This is what might be termed the 'divisionalisation' dimension, concerning the question of whether a firm should be divided up according to its functions (sales, R and D, finance, production, purchasing, and so on) or according to its products (for example, in a pulp-based diversified firm: newsprint, paper merchandising, packaging, cigarette filters, and so on) and/or regional interests, or even according to a mix of functional, product and regional divisions. The relative merits of the various forms are often imperfectly analysed even by academic theorists, so it is hardly surprising to find companies ending up choosing structures that are poorly matched with their strategic choices of product portfolios. In this chapter I propose to explore errors of divisionalisation, both in practice and in relation to the limitations of the existing theoretical literature.

The rest of the chapter is divided up as follows. Section 9.2 outlines Chandler's original thesis concerning the evolving relationship between strategy and structure. Section 9.3 considers the deficiencies attributed to the functional form of organisation and the advantages that are claimed for product/regional divisionalisation. Section 9.4, following Kay (1982; 1984), throws something of a spanner into the arguments in favour of the product/regionally based form, by considering the complications caused by synergy links. Further

Strategy and Organisational Structure

problems of control in decentralised firms are raised in section 9.5, while section 9.6 is a short conclusion.

9.2 CHANDLER'S THESIS

Chandler's (1962) business history classic, *Strategy and Structure: Chapters in the History of the American Industrial Enterprise*, is in many ways the work that provided the idea for the Kuhnian analysis of the structure of corporate revolutions in Chapter 5. Chandler identified a cyclical interaction in firms between strategic and organisational concerns, which he divided into the following four 'chapters':

(1) The initial expansion and accumulation of resources.
(2) Rationalisation of the use of resources and the development of an integrated functionally-based organisational structure.
(3) Expansion into new markets and activities in an attempt to ensure the continuing full employment of corporate resources.
(4) The development of a new multidivisional, product/regionally based structure to facilitate the continuing mobilisation of resources in the face of both changing short-term market demands and long-term market trends.

His suggestion, then, is that changes in organisational structure *follow* changes in strategy, instead of being contemporaneous with them. Strategic changes that involve a broadening of product market or regional horizons cause operating and administrative problems. Zealots propose major changes in organisational structure as a remedy, but their ideas are initially faced with strong hostility. Only in the face of a continuously deteriorating corporate performance are the restructuring proposals eventually and reluctantly adopted. These changes of orientation frequently coincide with generational changes of management. That is to say, restructuring is brought about by ascendent profit-minded efficiency experts who succeed, or displace in a crisis, the original far-sighted entrepreneurs who had focused excessively on market prospects.

Since the first companies to make the switch from a function- to a product-based form of divisionalisation – du Pont Chemicals and General Motors – had to do so in the absence of prior recommendations from organisation theorists, it is hardly surprising that their structural revolutions arose out of problems caused by strategic shifts. Top managers at du Pont were justifiably surprised in 1919, when it became apparent that their new paints activities were performing very badly against competitors with smaller access to scale economies and modern technology. They were forced to conclude that they had an internal, organisational problem, for their rivals had no secret processes, no patents that prevented du Pont from using the best method of manufacture, and no advantage in the purchase of raw materials. A sub-committee was appointed to look for internal measures that might improve performance. It concluded that a product-based, multidivisional structure should be adopted, but could not explain precisely why this might help cure the firm's ills. Consequently, it took a further period of decline before the change could be agreed. Initially, the committee's proposals were vetoed by the President, Irénée du Pont. And, as Chandler (1962, p. 100) notes,

> Irénée had strong justification for his position. The old ways had, until very recently, worked exceptionally well. Any professional writer or expert on organisation of that day would have endorsed his views completely, as, indeed, did many men in the company, including both his brothers, Pierre and Lammot. Moreover, as President, he, not the men proposing them, would have to carry responsibility for these fundamental changes.

The pioneering firms described in Chandler's book enjoyed considerable success once they had taken the plunge and adopted the new structure. Since their changes were not closely guarded secrets, it would be natural to expect that subsequently other large firms would make a practice of coupling together their strategic and operating decisions. All too frequently, however, structure has continued to follow strategy. Firms still tend only to shift their attention to matters of internal organisation after having travelled so far down a pathway of diversification that the inadequacies of their existing structure have helped to generate a crisis. It is then that they call in management consultants and are surprised to be told that an organisational restructuring could well improve their efficiency, both in respect of their existing activities and in relation to the long-run allocation of their resources. Indeed, Reader's (1981, pp. 309–18) description of the post-euphoria restructuring at Bowater bears an almost uncanny resemblance to Chandler's account of events at du Pont and General Motors over forty years before. So, too, do the descriptions by Jones and Marriot (1970, pp. 201–6) and Turner (1969, pp. 143–8) of organisational changes at, respectively, GEC and ICI. And these are by no means the only such cases.

Strategy and Organisational Structure

In part, the tendency of top decision-makers to focus on opportunities in the market, rather than matters of internal organisation, may be explained in terms of 'blindness' due to the absence of well-developed organisational dimensions in their managerial imaginations (cf. section 3.2). A more significant factor, however, may be the prevalence of programmed strategic decision-making in response to corporate imbalances (cf. sections 6.1 and 6.2). Thus although a series of minor, problem solving diversification decisions might eventually sum to a fundamental shift of balance in a firm's activities, its managers would not be aware of this since they had not consciously taken a major decision concerning the 'corporate whole'. They would not, therefore, be prompted to consider the organisational impact of their policies so long as the financial returns were satisfactory.

9.3 U-Form Problems and M-Form Advantages

Largely as a result of subsequent work by Williamson (1970; 1975), the two main organisational forms discussed by Chandler have come to be known as U-form (Unitary) and M-form (Multidivisional). Williamson has made a major contribution to the analysis of why the replacement of the former (function-based) by the latter (product- or region-based) should affect corporate performance and this section draws heavily on his work. Readers may find it useful first to consider the simple diagrammatic representations in Figure 9.1. It should be apparent that the M-form structure is effectively a collection of miniature U-form companies, each of whose chief executives is subordinate to a higher level body, the general office. It therefore appears initially as though the M-form structure involves an extra layer of managers and could in consequence prove a more costly means of coordination. However, in practice, the M-form structure often permits the elimination of some levels of management; for each of the 'minifunctions' (for example, the separate sales sections in divisions X, Y and Z) is administratively less demanding than the individual giant functional sections in the U-form arrangement. Furthermore, by having a number of chief executives – one for each product group or region – in the M-form structure reduces the demands on any single individual's information processing capabilities and thus facilitates improved decision-making. Divisional chief executives in M-form firms focus on the coordination of, and prospects for, a limited range of activities. The responsibility for overall direction rests with 'ivory tower' strategic planners in the general office, who have no day-to-day operating role. In the U-form structure, by contrast, the chief executive has to coordinate daily operations as well as thinking about strategy in respect of a variety of current and potential activities; she is much more likely to end up 'fire-fighting', or to involve heads of functional departments in the processes of strategic planning.

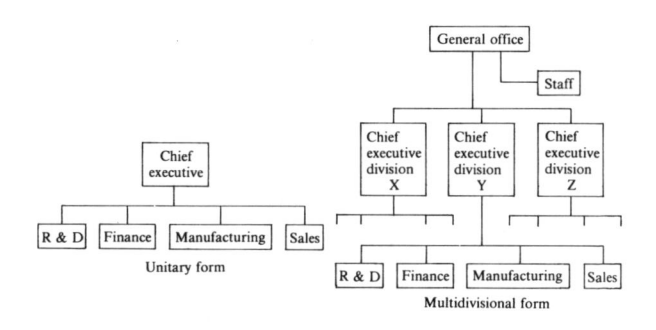

Figure 9.1   Organisational Structures

It is not merely through a greater specialisation of tasks that the M-form arrangement may improve corporate performance. It also changes the incentives facing would-be opportunists. In the U-form structure, the competition for corporate resources is between the heads of functions, who have strong incentives to overemphasise their own departments' roles in the production process. They are not interested in corporate performance except insofar as it bears on their chances of maintaining or increasing their departmental budgets; it will therefore be rational for them to bias forecasts of their capabilities and resource requirements (see Lowe and Shaw (1968) for evidence of this). Furthermore, since difficulties in assessing pay-offs to expenditure on information-based functions often mean that budgets are based on past precedents, success in obtaining an inflated budget in one year will help further a department's interests in subsequent years. To these conscious tendencies towards bias, one must add the effects of unconscious cognitive factors (see March and Simon (1958), pp. 152–3). Department heads will have been promoted from the ranks of their own subordinates in many cases and will continue to spend the bulk of their working time associating with them, particularly if there is a geographical separation between functions. Such interchanges, between people with similar world views, will be mutually reinforcing.

For these reasons, chief executives in U-form organisations will be plagued with infighting, either between all individual functions or amongst subcoalitions of functions. At GEC, such hostility was actually *encouraged* quite deliberately in the interwar period, in the belief that both factory managers and sales personnel should be seen to be making profits independently. As a result, the firm's distribution system was faced with monopolistic transfer prices charged by its factories. Production managers despised the sales staff and the latter did not see their roles as involving the provision of feedback to the former about market undercurrents. In the cartelised interwar atmosphere this system appeared to be adequate, but after 1945 GEC's wholesaling branches faced competition from general electrical wholesalers, who carried the stocks of many manufacturers, and from the showrooms of electricity boards. The separation of sales and production was a serious drawback in a faster moving world where consumers were faced with a much larger choice and could be increasingly fickle. GEC's products were more expensive and less up to date than those offered by new competitors. Furthermore, the firm kept a remarkably high stock level – about half of its turnover – owing to the fact that its factories and wholesale branches both held stocks (see Jones and Marriott (1970), pp. 201–3). Instead of cooperating, the separate functions blamed each other for the firm's lack-lustre performance.

In the M-form structure, by contrast, the general office can examine the records of divisions as if they were separate companies. Separation means that one division cannot blame another for its poor performance level. Failing products can thus be identified more readily, for they will be less prone to protection within individual functions via some form of cross-subsidisation. Functional cooperation is encouraged within divisions by the possibility that a poor divisional performance will result in the general office diverting resources elsewhere. Cooperation is also promoted on a greater scale between workers and managers. The former will be less likely to resist attempts to close down internal divisional supply sources in favour of the use of cheaper bought-in supplies, or to object to labour-saving technical changes. From the managerial standpoint, then, regional or product-based divisionalisations are a useful device for breaking any company-wide worker solidarity, by setting against each other workers performing similar functions in different divisions.

The existence of a specialist group of corporate planners in the general office does not, of course, guarantee that divisional heads cannot obtain resources for unwarranted 'pet projects' by dressing them up, on the basis of their specialist knowledge, as, say, 'technologically imperative investments'. However, these divisional heads should be aware that they cannot safely press for such investments very frequently without destroying their own credibility. In the long run, the general office will be able to detect the detrimental effects on the performances of divisions that are *more than usually* indulgent in this respect (it is still relative, not absolute, performance that counts).

In summary, one can say that a change from a U-form to an M-form organisational structure may be expected to improve corporate performance; firstly, by reducing information overload and the number of relay levels through which information must pass, and, secondly, by attenuating opportunistic tendencies to indulge in non profit-seeking behaviour. Lower level interests, or imbalances due to a preponderance of one kind of functional outlook (cf. section 5.9), are less able to distort strategic choices; for since the general office personnel have no operating commitments, they can dispassionately propose to withdraw from unprofitable markets or regions. That M-form companies do in practice tend to have superior profit performances is confirmed for the US and Britain in empirical work (see Armour and Teece (1978), Steer and Cable (1978), Teece (1981) and Thompson (1981)). However, in West Germany the gains from multidivisional organisation are much attenuated. In fact, the empirical estimates by Cable and Dirrheimer 'point to a reduction in profitability for some years following reorganisation, with no clear sign of an eventual upturn' (1983, p. 60). They suggest that these findings should not be interpreted as refuting the M-form hypothesis in general, for the structure of the West German economy is culturally and institutionally different from the US and Britain, with high levels of owner-control and a heavy involvement of banks in strategy formation.

9.4 THE INDECOMPOSABILITY PROBLEM

Perceptive readers, who have kept in mind the arguments of sections 2.4 and 6.2, will realise that I have been painting an unduly rosy

Strategy and Organisational Structure

picture of the advantages of M-form structure. For I have ignored synergy links between activities and presumed that a corporate whole can be thought of as a *decomposable* structure, as something which is simply the aggregate of its parts. My treatment of M-form structures in section 9.3 rather presented strategic choices as simple acts of portfolio choice concerning resource allocation among natural division decision units. But the mechanisms of strategy formation will ensure that it is natural for firms *not* to be fully decomposable. Attempts to introduce an M-form structure which ignore this fact may thus result in a disastrous loss of synergy.

In the 1950s and early 1960s, Unilever, as a multinational, multiproduct corporation divided into national units, suffered dearly in this way. As Turner (1969, p. 132) notes, each of the national units sought

to market a wide range of products and each of them concentrat[ed] on what would profit them rather than Unilever as a whole. They were hopelessly ill-fitted to cope with giant American companies like Proctor and Gamble, which did not recognise national boundaries and which were marketing only one group of products. Proctor and Gamble made Unilever look cumbersome – "it could turn Tide pink round the world overnight", said a Unilever director enviously, "we couldn't move like that"; with a more limited range of products it was also able to concentrate its promotional effort.

In September 1966, after five years of resistance from regional managers, product coordinators with executive power were appointed to develop overall strategies for partially separable product groups – for meat, toilet preparations, detergents, chemicals, frozen and convenience foods, margarine and edible fats. An inherently imperfectly decomposable organisation was thus decomposed in another way, with the hope of producing a greater, though still partial, sense of unity.

The indecomposability of modern corporations becomes obvious when one tries to identify possible examples: this is the age of the 'world car'; of product ranges that seek to exploit sales synergy and common physical components; of chemical companies such as ICI where, to quote Turner (1969, p. 152) once more,

No less than fifty per cent of the business of Heavy Organic Chemicals is with other divisions of the company; Dyestuffs supplies Fibres with all its nylon polymer; while Agricultural Division supplies Nobel with ammonia,

The Corporate Imagination

Dyestuffs with ammonia and nitric acid for nylon polymer and Fibres with methanol for 'Terylene'.

However, obvious as these examples make the problem seem, it is only with the work of Kay (1982, 1984) that ways of dealing with it have come to be examined in detail. Most texts hitherto have ignored Williamson's (1971, p. 357; 1975, pp. 138–40) passing comments about the decomposability dimension and have assumed that divisionalisation is a simple task.

Since the problem is essentially concerned with deciding on the boundaries of miniature firms-within-a-firm, the analysis suggested by Kay is not unnaturally similar to that in Chapter 2, which was used to analyse the choices of the *outer* boundaries of a firm. Thus internal boundaries should be drawn with a view of minimising: (a) the number of necessary exchanges of information; and (b) the risks of opportunistic behaviour by divisions as part of attempts to harm other divisions in order to enhance their own claims on corporate resources.

In his first attempt to apply this idea, Kay (1982, pp. 64–71) suggests that, where a single functional link exists between products, it may make sense to create a separate function (for example, a centralised R and D section, or sales division) whose role is to provide the relevant service for the miniature 'firms' within the larger whole. Competition is still encouraged between the product divisions dependent on the service provided by separate function, though there is some risk of opportunism against the former by the latter. However, subject to this risk, there will be synergy gains from concentrating specialists together. This analysis fits in well with Turner's (1969, p. 245) observations on performance in the UK multiple retailing sector. He notes how Debenhams' loss of ground to Marks and Spencer in the 1960s seems partly attributable to its slowness to introduce a centralised purchasing department, and that 'even a business like Great Universal Stores, with groups of shops in different sectors of the retail trade, has gathered together all its purchasing under the wing of a Merchandising Corporation'. As a counter to opportunism, this wing of GUS includes among its directors the chairmen of all the retailing divisions.

Where a firm has followed a hybrid strategy, using different combinations of linkages in overlapping groups of products, matters are much more problematical – indeed so much so that, in these cases, Kay (1982, p. 69) originally did not attempt to reach any general conclusions. However, with his latest work, Kay (1984, ch. 6) has begun to make some headway by extending his (1982, pp. 45–6) arguments about the situations in which internalisation is necessary in order to achieve synergy gains. Synergy may be tradable if the gains from trade are such that neither side has much to gain and little to lose by behaving with opportunism. If the pattern of gains and losses amongst the product or regional divisions of a company is such as to preclude strong leverage potential, then there is no need to handle the indecomposability problem by moving in the direction of a mixed structure of the kind discussed in the previous paragraph. Instead, product or regionally based divisions may trade services and inputs with each other according to their relative advantages in providing them, charging competitive extra-market, intrafirm transfer prices as they do so (cf. Turner (1969, p. 152) on the use of this approach within ICI). And, should they squabble too much, the general office can threaten to relieve them of their synergy-yielding activities, thereby to move back in the direction of a U-form structure.

It seems fitting to end this section with a discussion of how British Leyland, as a large, relatively indecomposable firm, attempted to use a mixed U-form/M-form structure – what might be called an MU or Mixed Up form – and ended up combining 'most of the disadvantages of both centralised and decentralised organisations with few of the advantages of either' (Ryder (1975), p. 45). BL's basic structure at the time of the Ryder Report is shown in Figure 9.2. It is evident that it is partly a U-form organisation, in the sense that it has functional divisions – body and assembly, power and transmission, and the international division, one of whose tasks was BL's overseas marketing – and partly an M-form organisation, in the sense that it has product-based divisions – trucks and buses, three separate car divisions, and special products.

In this structure, the role of the managing director was a major source of difficulty. His task was not that of a strategic planner in his own right, though nor was it clear that he, rather than the chief executive, bore responsibility for the day-to-day operations of the corporation. The corporate staffs, who were controlled by fifteen executives, were not analogous to a general office. Rather, their duty was to assist the managing director with the immense task of coordinating activities within the car business, and between the car business and BL's other activities. Thus the managing director had a total of twenty-nine people reporting to him: fourteen divisional

The Corporate Imagination

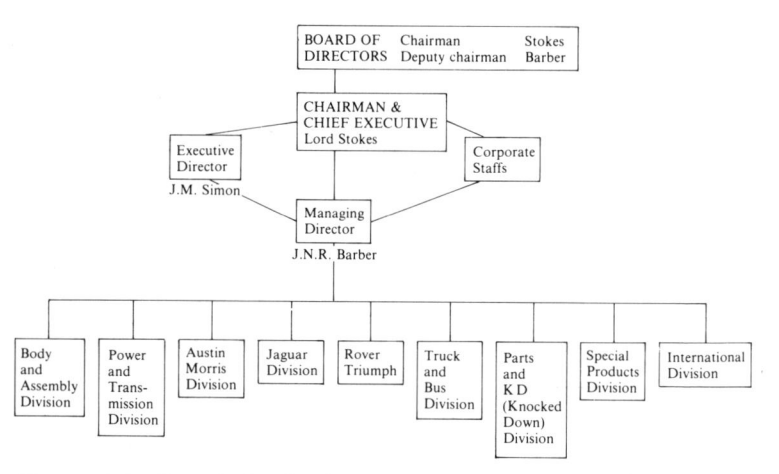

```
                    BOARD OF      Chairman          Stokes
                    DIRECTORS     Deputy chairman   Barber

                    CHAIRMAN &
                    CHIEF EXECUTIVE
        Executive   Lord Stokes              Corporate
        Director                             Staffs
        J.M. Simon
                    Managing
                    Director
                    J.N.R. Barber

Body      Power     Austin   Jaguar   Rover     Truck    Parts     Special   International
and       and       Morris   Division Triumph   and      and       Products  Division
Assembly  Trans-    Division          Bus       KD       Division
Division  mission                     Division  (Knocked
          Division                              Down)
                                                Division
```

Figure 9.2 British Leyland Motor Corporation: Basic Structure, November 1974.

directors (the lack of a head at the International Division meant that the six heads of the various international sub-operations reported instead) plus fifteen staff executives.

According to Ryder (1975, p. 45), this curious arrangement of divisions versus central staff, and functions versus products, resulted in, amongst other things,

(i) poor integration of, and coordination between, the product planning, engineering, manufacturing and marketing of cars;
(ii) lengthy discussions in committees and other, less formal groups, which delayed decisions;
(iii) the undermining of the authority and responsibility of the divisional management simultaneously with a failure to bring them under control.

Ryder's proposals for change were broadly M-form in nature. Staff at the corporate level were to be reduced and confined to the development of future plans, auditing, the monitoring of performance, and public relations. There would be just four large units: BL Cars, BL Trucks and Buses, BL International, BL Special Products. These plans were later modified somewhat by Sir Michael Edwardes, but he stuck to the idea that the organisation should not be functionally based, despite activity linkages. By March 1983 the firm was divided into six main components: Austin-Rover, Jaguar Cars, Unipart (spares), Land Rover UK (four wheel drive vehicles and vans), Leyland Vehicles (buses and trucks) and Land Rover-Leyland International Holdings.

9.5 Problems of Control in Decentralised Firms

Indecomposability is far from being the only factor that makes it difficult to adhere in practice to simple M-form organisational structures. But these other complications, that form the subject of the present section, tend similarly to receive little attention in conventional texts. In considering them, it is useful to divide the analysis into a series of subsections.

(i) The Independence of the General Office

A great virtue claimed for the M-form structure is the supposed non-involvement of corporate planners and strategic decision-makers at the head office in divisional operations. Advocacy and administration are supposed to be separated. In practice, however, pure, 'ivory tower' strategic decision-makers are rather uncommon. When a firm is being structured along M-form lines, it is often difficult to prevent directors, whose new roles formally do not mix planning and operating functions, from meddling in day-to-day divisional affairs. Delegation requires courage. It is quite common, in fact, for members of the general office of an M-form company also to be *formally* designated as heads of operating divisions. As such, they can hardly be expected to be as dispassionate about axing failing operations as the analysis of the 'pure' M-form structure might lead one to expect. But when care is *not* taken precisely to define the tasks of top managers or the roles of head and divisional offices, the distinction between operating and policy decisions is apt to become blurred (cf. section 5.2). The possibility that the firm will lack a coherent overall strategy is thus enhanced.

UK firms have, partly as a result of their relatively smaller sizes, been more prone to blur the distinction between the advocacy and choice of investment strategies, and their administration. This much is evident in the work of Channon (1973). But even in a firm as large as BL, one finds top executives involved in resource allocation at a number of levels. In the revised structure left behind by Sir Michael

Edwardes at BL in 1983, for example, the board included as executive directors two men who were each responsible for coordinating three of the six divisions: Mr David Andrews was group chief executive of the Land Rover–Leyland commercial vehicles section; Mr Ray Horrocks was group chief executive of the cars section. Neither could interfere with the operations of each other's groups of companies. However, they were also chairmen and/or chief executives of some of the companies within their respective groups. Thus they both participated in resource allocation at three levels: between cars and commercial vehicle groups, within commercial vehicles or cars groups, and within Land River UK and Land Rover–Leyland International Holdings (Mr Andrews) or within Austin Rover Group Holdings (Mr Horrocks).

The arguments of Alford (1976, pp. 52–7) lead one to suppose, further, that the informational and resource requirements of strategic planning activities make it almost inevitable that general offices should be tied to some extent to operating divisions. Alford points out that planners at head office are heavily dependent upon information transmitted by the divisions in respect of day-to-day operations, and upon the divisions' own explanations of trends and discontinuities in their attainment levels. Since the planners cannot be expected to be experts on all aspects of the firm's operations, they will also frequently need to seek advice from managers in the divisions, who, despite interdivisional competitive pressures, may not be completely disinterested parties. If the planners do not believe what they hear, they must make their own guesses or use up resources in the creation of a watchdog secondary intelligence system and groups of general office advisors. Furthermore, the planners themselves will frequently have been promoted from divisions (and, previously, to divisional boards from functions within divisions). Consequently they will find it easier to see merits in cases made by their old divisions in favour of investments in particular new products or production techniques. And they will naturally feel uncomfortable about strategic moves that threaten to shift the balance of the firm's operations away from their familiar territory. It is indeed difficult for any planner to be truly dispassionate in a world of incomplete and dispersed knowledge. However, as we shall shortly see, this is not necessarily a bad thing.

(ii) Incentives and Risk Taking
In most textbook comparisons of U-form and M-form structures,

the general office of the latter is said, with a note of approval, to perform the disciplinary function that the dispersion of shareholder interests prevents the external capital market from performing. Thus the general office is an 'internal capital market'. However, writers of such texts rarely pause to consider that M-form planners might have some failings similar to those attributed to external capital markets as resource allocating mechanisms. It is often said, for example, that outside sources of finance are reluctant to take risks with potentially pathbreaking new ideas, whose prospects of success seem doubtful, yet whose initial thirst for resources is unquestionable. A consequence may be that such research programmes can only be put into practice within existing firms, on the basis of a dogmatic belief in their potential (cf. section 4.2) and internally generated funds, over whose allocation the external capital market has little control. 'Ivory tower' planners might behave just like an external capital market if they were presented with similar radical proposals by divisional managers and lacked any prior divisional allegiances.

Consider, as an example of a high-risk project requiring a considerable resource commitment, the technically challenging programme to develop the float-glass process, undertaken so successfully by Pilkington Brothers. As Littler and Pearson (1972, p. 113) note, it 'might have been abandoned if a high ranking Pilkington had not identified with the project and if the company had not been privately owned and therefore free from outside scrutiny'. Had this firm been a mere division operating according to the ideal M-form model, the strict monitoring of this initially resource-thirsty scheme could have resulted in its premature termination by a dispassionate general office.

This scenario raises a major question about the desirability of having a fully independent general office and of separating planning totally from operating tasks. To be sure, there are many cases where a more detailed examination of a proposed programme by an 'outside' supplier of finance would have precluded serious errors by causing perceived uncertainty to be increased (cf. section 3.6). However, ivory tower planners, by virtue of their remoteness from the day-to-day realities of their firm's operations, may be unduly sceptical about radical new proposals put forward by divisional chief executives; yet for the same reason, they may *themselves* become overly optimistic about the ability of a division to manage certain activities.

The case for an 'impure M-form' is further heightened by the fact that the very detachment of a body of 'ruthlessly dispassionate' strategists from the divisions may lead to the latter covertly to indulge in *more* risky activities in desperate attempts to guarantee their survival. Austin Smith (1966, p. 14), for example, notes how General Electric 'made the fatal error of putting the managers of the [heavy electrical] apparatus group under heavy pressure to produce profits, without keeping itself fully informed about just how they were producing those profits.' The upshot was that the company was charged with collusive tendering in the electrical conspiracy anti-trust cases of 1960–1.

Organisational designers thus face a dilemma. On the one hand, it seems that if a planner has an operating role, her loyalties will be divided between her division and the company as a whole. On the other hand, however, any lost impartiality *may* be overwhelmed by a greater awareness of possible pitfalls that a manager with an operating role can bring to the planning table. Face to face contact is important. At planning meetings, a manager with such a dual role can be made to submit much more directly to clarificatory requests from colleagues about the activities of her divisions. Figures supplied by a distant divisional chief executive may conceal things that a worried planner/divisional head reveals merely by her disposition at a meeting.

(iii) The Relative Sizes of the Divisions

The foregoing arguments concerning the separation of the divisions from the general office, and the nature of incentives in an M-form company, are relevant to understanding how the Convair Division of General Dynamics managed to accumulate huge losses on the 880/990 airliners (see sections 5.8 and 7.4). But so, too, is the disproportionate size of the Division. For it produced other aircraft besides the 880/990, yet its subordinate divisions could only communicate with the General Dynamics New York general office (which employed a mere two hundred staff, including secretaries) via the group headquarters in San Diego. For a considerable period, therefore, the disasters associated with the 880/990 could be kept concealed within the pages of the divisional operating statements. The M-form control mechanism failed. The Convair Division was big enough in its own right to have all the tendencies towards the cross-subsidisation of misconceived projects, that one normally associates with U-form enterprises. But not until nine-figure losses had mounted was the decision taken to split Convair into several, more manageable divisions, so that never again could divisional managers press ahead with a single project to the point where it could threaten the existence of the entire company.

Lopsided structures have also been known to cause difficulties because of the distortions they produce in respect of focusing. One big problem attracts attention more readily than does a diverse collection of small problems with possibly greater overall potential payoffs to their solution; for it is easier to spell out the implications of a single big failure. This, surely, is why governments step in when a firm the size of BL or Chrysler founders, yet neglect to consider whether or not resources might be better used to prop up and revitalise a multitude of small businesses employing similar numbers of people. And corporate planners tend to fall into the same trap: the Ryder report on BL, for example, notes that 'The Truck and Bus Division and the International operations have suffered from the concentration of effort and resources at headquarters on the coordination of UK car operations' (1975, p. 45). It perhaps needs to be added that this tendency is not inherently at odds with the suggestion, made in section 6.5 in respect of Chrysler, that excessive executive focusing, on the start-up problems of new, and as yet relatively *minor*, activities may delay the discovery that matters have been going astray in a major area of a firm's activities. If planners sometimes come down from their ivory towers to perform an operating function, and if they only attend to their planning and operating tasks sequentially (cf. section 3.5), we should not be surprised to find them making both kinds of mistakes of focus during their careers.

9.6 Conclusion

Management consultancy firms, when they have not been propounding the virtues of strategies that take account of learning effects, have often sold M-form organisational structures as panaceas for their client companies' ills. In this chapter, I have attempted to show that M-form structures have limitations as well as advantages. In some cases a U-form structure or a mixed U-form/M-form arrangement (though *not* one of the kind adopted at BL prior to the Ryder report) may be essential for reasons of indecomposability. But I would like to conclude these discussions with some thread-tying remarks about organisational balance.

The arguments at the end of section 9.5 concerning focus seem to imply that an M-form company should seek to have divisions of roughly equal sizes, in order properly to spread the attention of planners. The case for a balanced structure appears to be heightened where an 'impure-M-form' structure is in use, in which divisional chief executives play a planning role and serve on boards that approve internal allocations of investment resources. For otherwise there is the risk that one division's point of view will predominate (cf. section 5.9). Where indecomposability means that, if a mixed-form is to be avoided without a loss of synergy occurring, trade must take place between the divisions of an M-form grouping, leverage considerations may also dictate that divisions should not be of greatly differing sizes. However, it is in the nature of the processes of strategy formation and market evolution that continuous corporate balance will normally be impossible to achieve. New activities will usually take some time to build up, unless they are ready-made units acquired through merger. Such activities grow like buds on existing organisational branches. Tensions are bound to build up, if existing divisions do not grow at identical rates owing to their differing performances and diversification prospects. But the personnel of a division that becomes disproportionately large will not welcome proposals to divide it into several, smaller divisions. This will be particularly so in cases where it would be difficult to achieve a balance of possible leverage in the trading of synergy between the proposed divisions. Thus, even once an M-form structure of some kind has been adopted, rationalisations that redraw the boundaries of a firm's organisational elements will naturally continue to follow strategy.

10 Disappointing Corporate Marriages

10.1 INTRODUCTION

The major contributory role of mergers and acquisitions in the evolution of giant companies in OECD countries is well documented (see, for example, Meeks and Whittington (1975); Reid (1976); Hughes and Singh (1980)). So, too, is the tendency for the use of such growth mechanisms to be followed by, at best, neutral or, at worse, deteriorating trends in financial performance (see Reid (1968); Meeks (1977); Cowling *et al.* (1980); and Mueller (ed.) (1980)). The only countries typically at odds with this depressing picture are Japan (Ikeda and Doi, 1983) and West Germany (Cable *et al.*, 1980) where, possibly as a result of the effects of their distinctive institutional frameworks on managerial behaviour, profit performances appear to improve following corporate marriages. Much less well documented are the reasons why such marriages so frequently fail to result in the kinds of financial performances promised by their instigators. This chapter is an attempt at least partially to redress the balance. It is divided into five main parts, followed by a conclusion. Section 10.2 considers reasons for mergers that arise from earlier discussions concerning the processes and problems of strategy formation. Section 10.3 examines the possibility that, in a world of opportunism and information impactedness, buying a company may have a lot in common with buying a used car: bargains are not always what they seem to be. Section 10.4 is concerned with the lack of pre-planning that accompanies many corporate marriages. Sections 10.5 and 10.6 deal with problems that are easily overlooked in such 'whirlwind romances'; respectively, the complexity inherent in attempts to create a rationalised and integrated structure, and the difficulties that can arise due to clashes of 'personality' between the merging firms.

10.2 STRATEGIC MERGERS

A merger between two companies, or the acquisition of one company by another, is a boundary change that permits diversification without necessarily involving the creation of new assets. Managers can enter what are, for them, 'new' markets without having to wrest market shares from other firms by means of price and non-price competition. They do not have to wait for learning advantages to build up, nor do they have necessarily to design a complex new organisational structure (an acquired firm may simply become a division of an existing M-form structure). In other respects, however, mergers are or should be thought of as a normal aspect of 'revolutionary' or 'programmed' strategy formation. It should therefore be possible to analyse merger activity on the basis of earlier arguments concerning focusing and inducement effects, transactions costs, opportunism, synergy and hedging. In doing so we may distinguish five different reasons for merging.

(1) *To facilitate rationalisation and prevent 'weak selling' in a market suffering from chronic overcapacity.* The 'market' alternatives to this way of preventing depressed prices are either for strong firms to bribe desperate, weaker enterprises not to undercut them to get orders, or for some form of collusive tendering to be arranged. Both are likely to fall foul of anti-trust policies and/or be prone to breakdown due to opportunism. In a fragmented industry, the transactions costs of arranging and policing such agreements would clearly be nontrivial; but in a concentrated industry, with firms of roughly equal sizes, legal restraints pose a bigger barrier both to the use of this means of coordination *and*, frequently, to merger as a way out of the problem (cf. Richardson (1969) on contradictions in UK competition policy in respect of the heavy electrical plant industry).

But firms which consider merger as a solution to an overcapacity problem may do well also to consider the possibility of taking measures to put themselves in a 'strong selling' position. By adopting the kinds of policies discussed in relation to the UK wool textiles industry in section 6.4, firms may be able to drive the weak sellers out of the market without undergoing the managerial and redundancy costs of first internalising them and then rationalising them out of existence.

(2) *To facilitate the exploitation of synergy and thereby ameliorate*

Disappointing Corporate Marriages

resource imbalance problems. The merger between Leyland and British Motor Holdings in 1968, to form the British Leyland Motor Company, is an example of a marriage based on this kind of thinking. It was prompted in large part by the Industrial Reorganisation Corporation, which saw severe weaknesses in BMH in respect of product planning and marketing (cf. section 4.3). An obvious solution was an injection of managerial talent in this area and Donald Stokes' reputation at Leyland was second to none. Stokes, too, saw a complementarity of interests. Davis (1970, pp. 99–100) quotes him as saying that

> To succeed, we [Leyland] had to sell more lorries and more motor cars. We hadn't got the production capacity to do that. Therefore we had to find some one who had the capacity. . . . We were up against the Americans who were bigger, and to match the Americans, the Germans, the Italians and the Japanese we had to have something of comparable size. There were two possibilities. One was to expand rapidly ourselves, which would have been physically impossible. Alternatively, we could have tried to find a suitable partner.

Neither Stokes, the IRC, nor the less enthusiastic BMH directors seem to have devoted attention to the possibility that synergy might be traded via some form of cooperative agreement. It is only in the 1980s that extra-marital corporate relationships have become popular in this industry (for examples, see Mariti and Smiley, 1983).

Like many a marriage partner, Stokes and his Leyland colleagues were soon to find that they lacked the experience and nerve required properly to exploit the hoped-for complementarities. Turner (1971) notes how these managers were appalled and bewildered by the complexity, inertia and sheer size of BMH's operations. BMH's most able executive, J.R. Edwards, who had begun the task of finding economies and restructuring the firm's management in the two years before the merger (see Turner (1971), pp. 123–4), had been lost in the battle between BMH and Leyland. Stokes himself seems to have had a personal ambition to effect the necessary changes without widespread shopfloor redundancies. He wanted to 'combine benevolence with bigness' (Turner (1971), p. 180) and had been concerned by the public storm that had arisen when Arnold Weinstock closed the large AEI telecommunications plant at Woolwich following the GEC/AEI merger in 1967. High manning levels and inefficient production practices thus remained at British Leyland. Furthermore, sales synergy proved impossible to realise, as Stokes' magic as a salesman did not transfer between markets. The face-to-face task of selling batches of commercial vehicles to public authorities or Third World governments was altogether different from the arm's length task of selling cars to a dispersed mass market of fashion-conscious private users: Leyland's attempt to compete in the super-mini class was a failure because the Allegro 'was a mechanically uncouth styling disaster; [a] piggy little saloon [that] could never sell against chic and functional hatchbacks like the Renault 5 and VW Golf' (Williams *et al.* (1983), p. 240). To be sure, Stokes realised that BMH had failed to produce a conventional saloon for the growing company car market, but the attempt then to do so with the Marina was also a failure, since he and his colleagues were unable to identify the requirements of this market with sufficient rapidity or precision (cf. section 4.3).

(3) *To facilitate capital restructuring or to take advantage of taxation legislation.* This rationale for merger is really a variant of (2), since it essentially involves the exploitation of financial synergy which cannot be traded for institutional reasons. Such mergers are common where governments treat debenture and equity capital differently for tax purposes; where they permit loss-making companies to carry forward allowances against future corporation tax payments; or where they allow divisional profits and losses to offset each other (see Steiner (1975, ch. 4) on US experience, and Prais (1976, ch. 5) on the UK). The immediate resource costs of a merger that involves Company A issuing new debentures to exchange for equities in Company B are clearly minimal, but the long-term complications can easily be neglected in the process: in general, corporate boundary changes will not have neutral effects on behaviour. The acquisition of a *loss*-making firm for tax reasons is an inherently risky business. For example, the Talcott National Corporation, a New York financial concern, were indeed lucky when, in March 1974, the Federal Reserve vetoed a merger with the Franklin National Bank of New York, that had been planned as a means of using Franklin's tax loss carry-forward. Talcott were not aware of the extreme precariousness of Franklin's position. On 8 October 1974 the Franklin Bank became the largest bank failure in American history (see Spero, 1980).

(4) *To overcome supplier or customer unreliability or to create the prospect of such unreliability for one's competitors.* A neat example of both of these aspects of vertical integration by merger concerns the behaviour in the 1950s of some of the firms later to become

constituents of British Leyland. In 1953 Standard-Triumph were alarmed to discover that BMC had taken over the Fisher-Ludlow car body company, Standard's long-time suppliers (Turner (1971), pp. 39–40). Until 1959 BMC traded bodies with Standard but then, just as bodies were required for the new Triumph Herald, they refused to extend the synergistic arrangement. Since the other major body supplier, Pressed Steel, also claimed to be too busy, Standard had to obtain body panels from a variety of smaller subcontractors. The contracts failed to specify fully the necessary tolerances and the early Heralds consequently leaked very badly whenever it rained. Standard then became obsessed with reducing its dependence on outside suppliers (cf. Section 4.2 on similar behaviour at Bowater) and rapidly concluded a number of acquisitions, some of which turned out to be 'white elephants'. And, having also recently experienced trouble from a major shareholder – Massey-Ferguson – Standard's management opted to pay for these companies with cash instead of through a share exchange. This rundown in Standard's liquidity increased the firm's vulnerability in the 1960 macroeconomic squeeze, leaving it ripe for takeover by Leyland in 1961 (Turner (1971), pp. 51–4). On this earlier occasion, Stokes *was* ruthless in making cuts, and three hundred Standard executives were sacked within a few weeks.

(5) *To facilitate rapid product portfolio hedging at a time of increasing technical and environmental uncertainty.* Unlike type (2) mergers, this form of diversification involves a deliberate attempt to move into activities where synergy links with existing activities are less concentrated. By acquiring another company, a management team that is afraid of 'putting all its eggs in one basket' can acquire another 'basket' of relatively loosely related 'eggs'. The risk of a fatal 'mugging' is reduced but the risk of inexperience and increased costs against non-hedging competitors is increased. As an example of the perils of hedging in this way, it is useful to consider the problems encountered by Sperry Univac when it acquired Varian Data Machines in June 1977, in an attempt to reduce its dependence on 'mainframe' computers by moving into the very different world of commercial 'mini' computers. Univac's inexperience in the 'mini' business and the arm's-length nature of the original evaluation meant that it failed to identify major problems with VDM's manufacturing plans and capabilities until a year after the takeover. Essentially, VDM's trouble was that it could not manage the move from building

custom-designed products for individual clients, to batch production on an increasingly large scale. VDM's new designs were difficult to manufacture and were rushed into production before development had been completed. Poor quality continually disrupted the flow of output (cf. sections 7.3 and 8.3). To overcome these difficulties, Univac had to supply top-level managerial resource inputs, as well as extra funds for R and D and to enable the original VDM factory in California to be gutted and rebuilt. With many executives working a seven-day week, the problems were largely overcome by March 1979. But this rapid turn round had cost $30 million to bring about (see further, *Financial Times*, 2 June 1980).

10.3 'BARGAIN' PURCHASES

Differences in belief about the values of companies are central to merger activity: if managers are not indifferent between bringing about corporate growth through the purchase of new capital assets, through the purchase of non-controlling holdings in existing companies, or through the acquisition of controlling interests in existing companies, then share prices must be failing for some reason to reflect the managers' own subjective valuations of companies they decide to acquire. Following Alberts (1966, pp. 273–80) we may distinguish between five kinds of perceived bargains that give rise to mergers.

(1) Forecast bargains – where managers believe the market has taken insufficient account of the possibiliy of realising synergy through merger or where they believe the market is unduly pessimistic about a potential takeover victim's prospects.
(2) Cost of capital bargains – where managers believe that the market undervalues small, relatively undiversified firms on the general principle that 'small is risky'.
(3) Mismanagement bargains – where managers believe the market has taken insufficient account of prospects for improving performance by taking up slack in potential takeover victims.
(4) Tax bargains – where managers believe the market has underestimated the scope for releasing financial synergy.
(5) Negotiation bargains – where shares in a firm are not normally traded and raiding managers can take advantage of differences of opinion in a face-to-face sale (for example, when a family business is sold by its retiring owner).

Disappointing Corporate Marriages

In so far as a company is successful in identifying bargains, it may be able to achieve accelerated growth through a phenomenon termed by Meeks and Whittington (1975) as the 'chain letter effect'. By taking over firms on relatively favourable terms, the company improves its own price/earnings ratio, and hence its share price, which means that it can effect further acquisitions through share exchanges on favourable terms, boosting its price/earnings ratio again, and so on.

But the company which seeks to make a bargain purchase has two hurdles facing it, prior to the task of properly consummating the marriage to prove the market wrong: first, it must identify a genuine bargain; second, it must get the 'bargain' at a bargain price in the face of rival bids.

As we saw in the case of the Univac/VDM takeover, inexperience can lead to misappraisals. But at least in this case the Univac management were not faced with the kinds of problems arising from asset-stripping that befall some purchasers of 'used' companies. Precisely such a case has been reported by one of its casualties, Michael Hope (1976). He had once been a director of the Crittall-Hope metal window manufacturing company, formed in 1965 by the merger of two old-established family firms following the break-up of the Standard Metal Window Price Agreement. A financial merger allowed the two companies to agree common selling prices without them falling foul of the 1962 Restrictive Practices Act, even though they continued to trade separately to avoid brand rationalisation problems of the kind discussed in section 6.5. Thereby they sought to maintain the fragile price level of the metal window trade during downturns in the building industry.

In 1968, Crittall-Hope was taken over by Slater Walker Securities. To be sure, the latter did remove much slack as they sold off assets and fired staff, but they also curtailed the firm's product development and investment activities and sold off most of its overseas operations, through which it had hedged against the vagaries of the building trade. This did wonders for Crittall-Hope's short-term balance sheet. Then, in 1971, Slater merged the firm with another company in its portfolio: a quite dissimilar engineering business called Butterley Engineering. This served further to conceal Crittall-Hope's real position and the firm was sold in 1974 to Norcross, another conglomerate. As Hope (1976, p. 177) wryly comments,

> It is . . . interesting that when Norcross had completed their takeover they announced the window business of Crittall-Hope was then running at a loss.

Under the old management this had not happened to Crittall or to Hope's, either separately or together, since the days of the great slump in the early 1930s.

By such means Slater Walker enjoyed the benefits of the chain letter effect – until, that is, the firm foundered in the mid-1970s property market crash.

In attempting to fend off Slater Walker's original advances, Hope's company had tried unsuccessfully to interest more suitable marriage partners in the idea of making better proposals. This is a common ploy, but rival bids frequently emerge anyway, in the wake of publicity caused by an initial attempt at takeover. It is often difficult to exploit information about a bargain without passing the idea to someone else, with the result the price of the assets in question rises. The merger game then becomes rather like poker, for managers become torn between letting the victim go to a rival or ending up paying 'over the odds'. The publicity surrounding such bidding inevitably enhances the personal element and the pressure to avoid being seen to make a mistake. This is precisely the kind of situation in which a manager's cognitive processes may twist his perceptions in a dangerous way (cf. sections 3.7 and 5.8).

In the US in the late 1970s, acquirers were typically paying 50–75 per cent above the recent market prices of their victims. This fact becomes more disturbing when one notes that many of these deals were financed with debenture issues and cash, in contrast to the tendency in the UK for acquisitions to be conducted largely on the basis of share exchanges. In 1981, the price/earnings ratio of the 100 largest US mergers was 18.6, implying that if nothing happened to the victim's performance the return would be barely over 5 per cent a year. At the time, the prime borrowing rate stood at 15 per cent. These figures come from Thackeray (1982) and it is difficult to disagree with his suspicion that 'after the wedding the groom has many a sleepless night wondering if he can meet the mortgage' (p. 84).

It is also difficult to face up to the facts when a bargain is found to be a 'lemon'. As Wallace (1966, p. 168) observes,

Rather than liquidate the new company and perhaps ruin their reputations and jeopardise the possibility of successful acquisitions in the future, managements are likely to divert time and energy that could better be spent on their main business to a prolonged clean-up of the new company.

Disappointing Corporate Marriages

An obvious example of this concerns Guinness' attempt to diversify out of brewing in the 1960s through the purchase of a pharmaceutical firm called Crookes Laboratories (possibly on the vague expectation that it might discover more about brewing chemistry for its main business). The latter firm had been performing increasingly poorly as its range of products lost touch with trends in home medication. After a decade of attempting to restructure the company with the aid of considerable financial injections, Guinness finally admitted defeat and sold it to the Boots pharmaceuticals group (see, further, Bhaskar (1972) and, on Guinness' more recent experiences in respect of diversification, section 6.4).

10.4 Whirlwind Romances

In introducing cognitive aspects into the analysis of corporate marriages, I am clearly moving away from the idea that merger activity is a result of dispassionate 'crystal ball gazing' where the relative merits of internal growth and mergers are carefully assessed. That it is appropriate to make such a move is clearly indicated by Newbould's (1970) detailed case study investigation of 38 mergers. His findings mesh well with Davis' (1970, p. 16) coining of the phrase 'golf course merger', to indicate that many corporate marriages arise out of casual conversations between managers, rather than from a carefully conducted search for suitable partners in the light of perceived strategic problems. Once the seed of the idea has been planted during the game of golf, managerial hearts rule over heads and the motto 'I want it' blocks out any consideration of the possibility that their snap judgments might be fallible.

In 35 of his 38 cases, Newbould found that alternative marriage partners were not considered at all. Nor was internal growth considered formally or informally in the majority of cases. Furthermore, the *whole* analysis – strategic, financial and industrial – was frequently compressed into a period of only eight weeks or less. After the merger, none of the firms planned to use techniques or production scales which would not have been possible had they remained 'single', and there was little search for synergy: in 21 cases no action at all was taken to close plant; in 25 cases no assets were disposed of; redundancies at executive and sub-executive level were similarly absent; in 23 cases no extra sales were gained and, of the few which did better, this was usually the result merely of the adoption of

The Corporate Imagination

a better selling technique. Generally it seemed that such improvements as were obtained could have been achieved within 'single' companies through hiring a new chief executive or calling in consultants.

We appear to have a picture of whirlwind romances that result in marriages which are barely consummated, a picture sharply at odds both with the Marris/Penrose view of merger activity presented in section 1.5, which emphasises its role in overcoming internal barriers to growth, and with the synergy arguments in section 2.4. But Newbould's attempt to explain his findings fits in well with our discussions about corporate fears of 'mugging'. It has four main elements:

(1) The desire to merge arises from an increase in uncertainty in the environment of the firm;
(2) Heightened uncertainty is a result of other mergers and of changes in business conditions with which firms are used to coping;
(3) Mergers are carried through if (a) potential partners, also keen on marriage, are available and identified, and (b) if the firms feel able and willing to handle them without an excessive risk that they will suffer indigestion problems;
(4) The ability and desire to merge depends on the degree of uncertainty and the number of other mergers being handled; for the more mergers there are the more uncertainty there will be in the environment, but there will eventually come a point when corporate indigestion becomes commonplace and forces consolidation – hence 'merger waves'.

Mergers, like marriages between individuals, thus owe much to crowd behaviour amongst entities that do not wish to be left socially isolated in a complex and turbulent world; they are essentially defensive devices. Size usually permits greater security, for it can bring:

(1) A reduction in the number of management teams in rival firms who can carry out a 'mugging' through a takeover raid;
(2) Increased penetration of individual markets;
(3) More markets;
(4) A wider product range;
(5) Control of suppliers and customers or intermediaries;
(6) Increased ability to raise long-term capital;
(7) Increased ability to pressurise banks;
(8) Increased importance to government policy makers.

Attack may therefore be the best form of defence when uncertainty increases, particularly if it indicates to other management teams that one will not lightly submit to a predatory takeover (see Kuehn (1975) for evidence). But some management teams may prefer to take 'suicidal' steps to lose their independence in order to enjoy a more secure 'life after death' within a bigger group.

To the extent that mergers do have defensive underpinnings, their prospective results may be difficult to express in financial terms – a fact which may explain the absence of 'correct appraisal techniques' (Newbould (1970), p. 95). Such underpinnings should also leave us none too surprised when, in terms of profitability, the merged whole is no greater than the sum of its parts, particularly if no integration attempts are made. But they do not obviously help to explain why the whole often seems to be *less* than the sum of its parts (Meeks, 1977), even when the management team of an acquiring firm are not diverted from their main activities by a 'bargain' that has turned out to be a 'lemon'.

10.5 Integration Problems

Merger activity will not improve corporate performance unless some moves are made in the direction of integration and rationalisation – except, perhaps, where internalisation by itself attenuates incentives to behave with opportunism. We have seen from Newbould's work that many marriages were not arranged with this in mind; but the sheer pace of growth by merger also makes it difficult to see how top managers could find much time away from the business of negotiating new mergers, in order properly to oversee or carry out activities aimed at making their past corporate marriages work. (According to Meeks (1977, p. 7), the average member of the top one hundred UK companies ranked in terms of their ability to grow by acquisition was practically doubling its size every two years in the period 1964–71, managing an annual growth rate of 28.6 per cent through acquisitions and an overall growth rate of 37.2 per cent.)

But, ultimately, a severe bout of corporate indigestion usually brings such merger mania to a temporary halt and forces attempts at integration. Deteriorating performance may be explained in several ways. First, slack may tend to increase when a relatively small firm, used to operating with a tight financial constraint, is accorded relatively generous budgetary allowances by head office (cf. Wallace

(1966), p. 171). Second, the very fear of a rationalisation programme may have the perverse effect of causing lower level concealments of ways of improving performance. The firm ceases to move down its experience curves at the same rates as before and suffers a profits squeeze as its rivals continue to achieve experience-based cost reductions. When cost savings are sought, lower level personnel can then attempt to preserve their positions by suddenly 'discovering' ways of reducing their costs. Until they acquire some appreciation of the operating conditions in their newly acquired divisions, head office planners will be poorly placed to assess what is going on; hence they will tend to perform badly as an internal capital market – even if they are not preoccupied with yet more merger ideas (cf. section 9.5). Furthermore, in attempting to deal with such control problems, planners at head office may allow the size of their corporate staffs (particularly auditors) to grow, with a concomitant increase in paper work. Finally, where a vertical merger has been instituted to attenuate possible supplier opportunism, supplying divisions may feel more, not less, inclined to behave with guile to suit their own goals, for now they have a captive market.

Once attempts at rationalisation and integration are embarked upon, many managers are greatly surprised by the complexity of their tasks (even if they do not encounter the kinds of personality clashes discussed in the next section). Using the example of an attempt to make a marriage of machine tool companies work, Pratten (1972, pp. 95–6) suggests that the rationalisation timetable may be as follows: (a) two years to establish a unified accounting system to allocate design and development costs to appropriate new products; (b) as much as four years from the date of the takeover to design and develop new products, and assemble or retrain a labour force that can deal with the technological requirements of their manufacture; and (c) it may take even longer to consolidate the new management team and win back any lost customer confidence. Pratten suggests that a full reform may take as long as ten years to effect, particularly if the transition period traverses a recession during which profits are further squeezed.

A major reason why the process takes so long is that many of the decisions involved are non-routine ones, that emerge either out of an unexpected failure of resources and salary systems to 'match' easily, or in the processes of creating a new organisational structure and negotiating its implementation. Wallace (1966, p. 173) provides a rare attempt to assess the complexity of the latter. The consolidation

Disappointing Corporate Marriages

of two regional sales forces in an American firm involved thirty-five major steps and over two hundred substeps, yet dealt with only one hundred staff. To extend it nationwide required 150 major steps and over 2,000 substeps. Wallace estimates that completely to integrate an acquisition of any size into a large corporation more than 2,000 major steps and 10,000 non-routine decisions may be necessary. Furthermore, the complexity of the overall problem is greatly enhanced by the fact that the sequence of many of these steps is critical. It is therefore not surprising to find that Wallace advises managers to wait and learn – to find out how their acquisitions tick, how their key people operate – before upsetting anything. This point leads us directly to the next section, for it relates to the 'culture' and expectations of the marriage partners.

10.6 Corporate Personality Clashes

It is a major theme of this book that each company has its own personality, comprising sets of procedures, knowledge and expectations formed in the light of particular sets of constructs – blinkers through which it sees the world. A firm's corporate imagination means that the normal turnover of personnel will not fundamentally affect its behaviour in the short run, yet newly-arrived staff will usually suffer from 'culture shock' until they learn how the firm thinks and acts. But sometimes, differences in world view are so fundamental that learning is either protracted or impossible; people remain at cross purposes instead of developing a proper relationship.

Bearing this theme in mind, we may enhance our understanding of corporate marital problems by turning briefly to examine the findings of social psychologists who have studied close relationships between individuals (see Duck (1983) for an excellent survey). As regards the creation of successful friendships, communication skills, not physical attractiveness (for corporations, read 'physical assets'), have been found to play the most important role. In relation to the creation of successful marriages, it has been emphasised how important it is for couples to realise that the real job of courtship consists in negotiating and working out how the future marriage will be performed. For as Duck (1983, pp. 100–1) observes,

> Complex relationships like marriage involve not only the mutual affection and commitment of both partners, but also their ability to mesh their

behaviour satisfactorily in matters like housekeeping, providing and decision-making. . . . Such activities cannot be left to chance and do not simply fall into place if a couple is deeply in love.

This seems obvious when it is written down, yet marital problems seem to be strongly associated with a lack of congruence between the partners' expectations or between their beliefs about their respective marital roles.

The same seems to be true in the case of corporate marriages (cf. Wallace (1966) and Kitching (1967)); for, owing to the barriers to premarital exchanges of information and the tendency for the courtship phase to be compressed, the corporate marriage contract is rarely specified in much detail. Furthermore, an outright takeover as opposed to an agreed merger is hardly the basis for mutual trust that will help keep the relationship going after a stormy honeymoon. Typically, there is uncertainty about the future roles of the respective parties, and they have different accounting conventions, rules of thumb and ways of looking at the world. Often, it is not clear when or where attempts at rationalisation will be made. Sometimes, it is not even obvious who has taken over whom.

In such situations, it requires very firm, yet understanding, leadership if some degree of unity is to be developed. Where this is absent, the marriage partners tend to live under the same roof (a holding company), but treat each other with suspicion and fear, and/or bicker continually about resource allocation – sometimes to such an extent that communication between them all but breaks down. An excellent example of such a stormy marriage concerns the missile producing firms within the British Aircraft Corporation, prior to the formation of the BAC Guided Weapons Division in 1963. When BAC was formed in 1960, rivalry between Bristol and English Electric was intense, owing to the fact that they were producing two similar weapon systems while talk at the Defence Ministry was of market contraction. Bristol took the view that their real competitors were the Americans and it was a distracting nuisance also to have to face competition from English Electric. Since many of the engineers had been involved with their respective projects for many years, their emotional commitments were intense. In the absence of any clear nomination of a BAC Executive with real responsibility for guided weapons, meetings between representatives of Bristol and English Electric were protracted, acrimonious and achieved little (see Adams (1976), ch. 6).

Disappointing Corporate Marriages

For an example of a marriage that was not properly worked out well over *twenty* years (as opposed to a mere three years in the BAC case), we may consider AEI, formed in 1928 by the merger of British Thomson–Houston and Metrovick. During this long period the component companies each acted as if the other did not exist, and organisation did not move beyond the holding company stage. BTH and Metrovick each independently invented the jet engine and then failed to make a commercial success of it despite their head starts. They kept separate bank accounts even when the surplus of one almost exactly matched the deficit of the other (which was forced to borrow externally); while dithering by the AEI directors about which of their divisions should get major orders sometimes meant that the orders were lost altogether. But so long as the electrical engineering market boomed, the forces of resistance could overwhelm the logic in favour of integration (see Jones and Marriott (1970), pp. 248–59).

Much of the same lack of esprit de corps and common practice was also to be found in BMH and Leyland even *prior* to their union in 1968, for both consisted of companies with completely different operational styles. The formation of British Leyland was yet another marriage in a rapid succession of incompletely digested mergers of automotive firms with increasingly split personalities. It seems a particularly useful example with which to end this section, for here we may note that the disastrous 'MU-form' of organisational structure discussed in section 9.4 was a direct result of these clashes of philosophy. Some managers were in favour of working towards full integration but others strove to preserve the independence of the original corporate elements. For nearly six years little was done. But then a compromise emerged: as we have seen, it involved the worst of both worlds.

10.7 Conclusion

Writing some time before the recent quantitative studies of merger, and before the new analyses of corporate strategies and structure, Wallace (1966, p. 178) came to the conclusion that mistakes in merger activity fall into 'a pattern of sheer failure to apply to aquisitions the same basic management principles of setting objectives, planning, exercising control, and exercising leadership that are applied routinely in other business situations'. I see little need to challenge his conclusion today, except to say that he is perhaps guilty of overestimating managerial rationality in other spheres. Like people in everyday life, companies seem prone to become overwhelmed by passion and fail to consider carefully what they are doing, or the alternatives, before embarking on marriage.

It is easy to see why managers pursue active policies of growth by merger, in a world where remuneration and status depend much more on size than profitability and where sheer size also seems the best protection against takeover by their rivals. And there is some evidence that managers who indulge repeatedly in merger activity become less prone to making bad marriages (see Allan (1966), p. 107). But the problems of making a corporate marriage work seem rather to imply that, from *society's* standpoint, internal growth with brand new assets may be better than attempts to integrate one, at least partially obsolete, system with another. Internal growth may seem too slow from the managerial point of view, yet it represents an immediate addition to national assets and not just a change of boundaries between institutions. With this point in mind, I will now turn to consider the broader implications of behavioural economics for public policy.

11 Implications for Government Policy

11.1 Introduction

The crisis conditions that have characterised much of British and American capitalism in the late 1970s and early 1980s are not wholly attributable to defective corporate decision-making. To be sure, they have more than a little to do with rises in the cost of energy (which exacerbated the process of cost-push inflation and, via the initially limited abilities of OPEC countries to spend their extra incomes, led to a rise in the world savings ratio and to fruitless attempts by oil importers to deflate themselves out of balance of payments difficulties); with, in the UK, a period in which the exchange rate appreciated as North Sea Oil came on stream; and with the pursuit of monetarist policies of deflation. These crisis conditions have occurred despite continuing advances in productivity levels (some of which are the result of successful searches induced by the crisis itself). In large part, however, they *are* the result of poor competitive performances by many UK and US companies relative to overseas producers. Rising productivity has been accompanied by growing *structural* inefficiency in UK and US manufacturing sectors, which has manifested itself in increasing import penetration and the loss of overseas markets. This 'inefficiency' is a cause for concern to the extent that these manufacturing sectors are the major sources of foreign exchange earnings in these countries. Falling net exports of manufactured goods imply a reduced ability to meet essential import requirements (that is, in the UK in particular, imports of food and raw materials). Unemployment resulting from the collapse of the manufacturing sectors cannot then be mopped up by an expansion of aggregate demand because this will tend to leak overseas and cause a foreign exchange crisis.

The Corporate Imagination

Ajit Singh (1977, p. 134), in one of the first investigations of this 'de-industrialisation' problem in the UK context, summed up his findings as follows:

> The evidence suggests a structural disequilibrium, whereby the trading position of the manufacturing sector in the world economy continues to deteriorate, in spite of increasing cost and price competitiveness. De-industrialisation is a symptom or a consequence of this 'inefficiency' or of disequilibrium, rather than its cause; this disequilibrium needs to be corrected if the manufacturing sector is not to decline further.

It is a major intention of this chapter to see what insights the behavioural analysis of corporate growth and decline can offer towards the solution of this fundamental problem.

The chapter is structured as follows. Section 11.2 considers the implications for Singh's analysis of the presence of various forms of slack in the corporate economy. In the light of this discussion, sections 11.3 and 11.4 look at the interactions between aspects of macroeconomic policy (particularly in respect of the balance of payments and inflation) and the responses of corporate policy-makers. section 11.5 is concerned with the economics of regional rejuvenation, while section 11.6 offers some suggestions on the role that merger policy can play in arresting industrial decline. the penultimate section, 11.7, investigates a topic that advocates of direct intervention in investment have rarely paused to consider, namely, the behavioural problems of a 'National Enterprise Board'. Finally, section 11.8 concludes the book by considering, outside the context of the de-industrialisation problem, why policy-makers should be concerned with corporate decline at all, if other firms are rising to employ the resources released through closures.

11.2 CUMULATIVE CAUSATION AND SLACK

Even before the imposition of deflationary monetarist policies, Singh (and his Cambridge colleagues Kaldor (1978) and Godley (1979)) viewed the prospects for the UK economy, in the absence of positive intervention in respect of industry and trade policy, with great pessimism. Their gloomy predictions were, and remain, heavily influenced by Gunnar Myrdal's (1957) theory of cumulative causation. This 'vicious circle' approach to growth and stagnation was

Implications for Government Policy

originally developed in the context of under-developed countries. The suggestion was that low income levels leave no margin for saving, so nothing can be invested to raise production; hence income levels will remain low unless aid can be provided from external sources. Adapted to the context of the growth of firms, it shares a good deal with the 'transfer process' part of Downie's (1958) analysis of the competitive process, which was discussed in section 1.7. If a country's manufacturing firms, for whatever initial reasons, fall behind in terms of relative size and hence profitability, they will decline further, due to a reduced ability to develop new products or install new, cost-reducing production techniques. The solution suggested by the Cambridge school involves: the protection of the firms' domestic markets by import controls; reflation to encourage investment; and/or an injection of funds, possibly even nationalisation, by the government if private capital markets are deterred, by poor present performance, from supplying any additional funds necessary to aid rejuvenation. In the absence of such measures, a firm or industry, or, indeed, an entire economy, caught in a vicious circle of decline, will be squeezed out of existence.

If a government insists on allowing 'market forces' to generate a solution to the problem of economic decline, some prospect of salvation appears, at first sight, to be provided via the labour and foreign exchange markets. Relatively slow growth, or even cuts, in real wages can restore profit margins. A depreciating exchange rate can fulfil much the same role. But, as Singh (1977, pp. 119–20) observes,

> whether market forces can restore equilibrium depends crucially on the nature and adequacy of the response of entrepreneurs in bringing about the required changes in productive structure, as well as the magnitude of the relevant elasticities for exports and imports, and in a dynamic world on the speed of these adjustments.

Some evidence that his objection is well founded is provided by Kaldor's (1978, ch. 6) work, which shows that Britain and America continued to lose out in world markets to the rising industrial power of Germany and Japan, despite drastic alterations of the appropriate kind in the real exchange rates between them.

But there are two possible weaknesses in the cumulative causation hypothesis which a behavioural economist finds worthy of more serious study than do its proponents. Firstly, it largely neglects the possibility of a sufficiently powerful 'innovation process' – that is, the eventual uptake of various forms of organisational slack by threatened firms – which will swamp the transfer process and bring about, unaided, a recovery. Secondly, the policy analysis pays little attention to the possibility that measures of intervention will have harmful effects on the responses of threatened firms. The arguments of Bauer (1971), a well-known critic of Myrdal's views on the economics of poor countries, may be generalised to encompass industrial policy issues. Bauer's thesis is that *some* slack must exist in under-developed countries, because the rich nations, themselves, were once in a similar position yet managed to break out of the vicious circle of poverty. Whether or not such an escape occurs depends to a considerable extent on motivation, upon social and cultural factors. If this motivation is not present already it is far from clear that the introduction of an easier environment will improve productivity: it may even make it worse.

But it must be said that it could be as dangerous uncritically to accept Bauer's analysis as it is dogmatically to pin faith in the cumulative causation hypothesis. While countries such as Uruguay have stagnated behind tariff barriers, it is also the case that the rise of Japan (as Singh (1979, pp. 217–18) emphasises) has involved an aggressive State industrial policy and controls over trade flows. And there is an obvious difference between instilling a competitive atmosphere whilst avoiding industrial 'feather-bedding', and the 1979–81 Thatcherite policy in the UK of allowing interest rates and the exchange rate both to rise. Sometimes protection and state aid have been associated with improved growth and successful decision-making; but not always. Sometimes, in the face of adversity, companies have achieved remarkable turnrounds from their own resources; but not always.

That the evidence in this area is so mixed probably owes a lot to the fact that slack in an economic system has a dual property. It provides, first, some capacity by which a firm may be able to attempt a recovery. The competitive system cannot function without it. Hirschman (1970) has emphasised that a taut economy, of the kind implicitly assumed in neoclassical economics, leaves no room for error. In such a system temporary lapses would always be fatal and the competitive process would always liquidate faltering firms instead of stimulating some of them, at least, to do something better. It is thus fortunate that the ignorance and complexity which drive firms into error should also generate a buffer against the consequences of error. But slack also provides room for avoiding necessary changes. For example, financial reserves *may* be used to re-equip a business and place it on a stronger footing, but they may also be used to support loss-making activities and foolhardy defensive investment projects. The very nature of X-inefficiency and, even more so, organisational slack makes them impossible to quantify, for they owe their existence to ignorance and information impactedness. One can never know, therefore, whether enough slack exists within a particular firm to permit a recovery from decay, nor can one predict with much confidence what use a firm will make of it. For this reason, the subjective perspective inherent in behavioural economics has been misconstrued by some economists as leaving its practitioners with nothing constructive to say about policy, but with plenty to criticise in the recommendations of others.

To the extent that the Cambridge pessimists have recognised the possible adverse motivational effects of their policy recommendations, they have countered them by saying that, within a protective fence of import controls, competition between firms would be a sufficiently powerful force to ensure industrial efficiency and dynamism. With a buoyant home market, the transfer and innovation processes would work between domestic firms, rather than between domestic firms and overseas rivals to the detriment of the former. Where sectors actually did display inertia and inefficiency, policy-makers would be recommended to apply the sorts of remedies suggested by Holland (1975): a major firm (or firms) in the laggard industry would be nationalised and given a large dose of investment; it would then be run as an aggressive market leader and a continued failure of the privately run firms to innovate would result in their market shares being transferred to the more dynamic state-run enterprise. From a behavioural standpoint, this threat (or, if necessary, actuality) of state entrepreneurship, as an addition to an import controls/reflation policy, makes much more sense than a simple policy of expanding demand behind a protective fence of tariffs or quotas – so long as there are not inherent problems involved in state entrepreneurship. (Whether or not this is the case will be discussed in section 11.7.) The complete package of the Left, that is to say, is more appealing than a subset which refers only to trade policy.

In the absence of the implementation of the entire 'Left strategy', it seems likely that import controls will be introduced as a result of industrial lobbying by particular sectors; as an *ad hoc* series of unwilling responses and not as a coherent programme. Policy-makers acquiescing to such pressures, but fearful of the possibility that such aid as they provide will be used merely as a cushion against change, could do well to make market protection conditional on the sector in question having furnished them with a plan of action to revitalise the ailing firms, and a timetable for implementation. At least there would then be a point of reference against which performance could be assessed, though it should be remembered that *ex post* appraisals of schemes have a tendency to be neglected, due to the misguided belief that a decision taken is a decision implemented.

11.3 BALANCE OF PAYMENTS POLICY AND CORPORATE REJUVENATION

Four policy measures are available to a government that wishes to alter the international competitive conditions faced by its domestic producers, but does not wish to do so by outright subsidies. They are: currency depreciation; import tariffs; import quotas; and 'red tape' (for example, the requirement made by the French government in 1982 that imported VCRs must be routed to Poitiers for customs clearance). They differ in their likely effects on inflation, on speculative behaviour in currency markets, and in the degree to which they might provoke retaliation. In this section, however, I am concerned chiefly with the different implications the different policies might have for corporate behaviour; I will not be looking at how workers will respond in wage demands or how currency speculators and other governments might react. Such issues have been discussed in detail in Hare (1980) and CEPG (1976–80) and they remain controversial.

Of the four measures, a sustained currency depreciation is the only one that generates a stimulus (which firms may, of course, fail to see) to export more. A currency depreciation will make overseas marketing attempts more attractive by raising profit margins on any given volume of sales. (Suppose the exchange parity of Sterling falls from £1 = $2.00 to £1 = $1.50. A $100 profit margin previously worth £50 on a potential sale is now worth £66.67 to a UK firm.) This should at least encourage 'non-price' competition as a means of expanding overseas markets, even if, for oligopolistic reasons, firms would not expect to be able to increase penetration there by aggressive price cutting. But such responses as are forthcoming will not occur overnight. It takes time to establish foreign sales networks and design appropriate overseas marketing policies. This point is easily forgotten by policy-makers who focus the attention on macroeconomic aggregates with little consideration for underlying microeconomic behaviour. Greater export efforts are unlikely to be made if experience tells firms that currency depreciations are not sustained in real terms, because workers, seeing higher import prices, demand compensating wage increases which have to be passed on in higher prices.

On the import side, currency depreciations and tariffs are assumed in traditional analyses to work by their effects on relative prices. However, if price *is* a powerful factor in buyer decision processes, then both of these policy measures are unlikely to lead to *relative* price changes in domestic markets. Oligopolistic considerations militate against such behaviour (see Holmes, 1978). Where importers have been imposing a squeeze on domestic firms by a policy of aggressive price leadership, they can raise their prices to maintain their profit margins with some confidence that the domestic firms will be only too eager to follow. Where importers have not found aggressive price leadership worthwhile, the more likely result is that prices stay the same; domestic producers are strong enough to call the tune. Importers will either take reduced margins and domestic producers will gain nothing, or the prospect of reduced margins will be so unattractive that some importers will abandon the market and part of their former share of it will be picked up by domestic firms.

If, as Stout (1977) has argued in the UK context, the poor performance of domestic firms arises from poor 'non-price' competitiveness, the route by which currency depreciations or tariffs may benefit them is more complex than traditional analysis has recognised. In terms of the analysis in section 7.2, a firm which sells at a 'competitive' price, yet which is uncompetitive in 'non-price' terms, is a firm which, despite offering products within appropriate consumer budget ranges, achieves few sales because its products actually do not survive far enough down customer priority filtering processes for price to be brought to bear in their favour as a tie-breaker. Such a firm finds that the advice of Posner (1978, p. 51) – 'if you cannot sell good things, sell cheap things' – is not very helpful, unless trade conditions are changed to such an extent that it can successfully reposition its products 'down market' in lower budget ranges in export markets and/or imported substitutes are pushed out of the budget ranges of domestic consumers. The Cambridge advocates of import controls have been careful to argue that these will not threaten real wages, because their policy package includes demand-expanding tax cuts to ensure that domestic recovery is not achieved by exporting unemployment to the rest of the world, for this would be bound to provoke retaliation. But the behavioural view of choice implies that, if the import controls work in price terms (and the same argument will apply to a devaluation as to tariffs), real wages have *necessarily* to be affected to bring about quantity shifts where domestic firms are uncompetitive in 'non-price' terms.

Where 'non-price' aspects of choice predominate, importers who are already highly competitive in non-price terms can maintain their profit margins in the face of tariffs or currency depreciations, by raising their prices. They will not frighten away their customers so long as the price increases do not take their products out of their would-be buyers' budget ranges. Domestic firms, that are being squeezed because of the poor 'non-price' competitiveness of their products, will be foolish not to follow such price increases if previously their products were price competitive. If the bulk of what they *do* succeed in selling is sold to the minority of people who make low non-price demands of what they buy and thus need to use price as a tie-breaker, these firms will not lose out so long as they maintain the price differential, and they will, meanwhile, enjoy higher profit margins. In the short run, therefore, there would be price increases instead of rises in sales and employment by domestic firms – in sharp contrast to the predictions of the orthodox analysis. In the short run, output and employment will only rise in the 'non-price context' insofar as the currency depreciation or tariff measures are accompanied by an expansion of aggregate demand. Indeed, in the absence of such a reflation, it is possible in the extreme 'non-price context' for the currency depreciation or tariff measures actually to have a depressing effect on employment and output – if prices of imported goods rise and domestic products follow suit, real purchasing power in the economy has fallen. In the presence of such a reflation, the 'non-price' analysis implies that price-based measures to control the balance of payments situation will not be effective as devices to contain the extra demand within the domestic economy. The qualification that adds some comfort to this comment is that the higher profit margins in domestic firms would permit them to make more investment and hence, one would hope, improve their non-price performances in the long run. But it is also important to remember that foreign rivals will, in the meantime, continue to move down their learning curves and domestic customers will have more time to learn from each other about the properties of imported products in early stages of their lifecycles (cf. sections 1.3 and 8.2).

Life is evidently not as simple as proponents of currency depreciations and import tariffs would have us believe. The greater is the importance of aggressive price leadership by foreign firms or of 'non-price' dimensions of choice processes, the more inflationary these measures will tend to be. The 'non-price' complication raises grave doubts, too, about their efficacy as means of stopping a balance of payments haemorrhage. Quotas and 'red tape' appear to be rather more promising policy tools in these contexts: it seems natural to apply 'non-price' measures to deal with 'non-price' problems. If the physical quantities coming to the economy are restricted, many consumers will effectively find that imported products with superior 'non-price' properties – except, that is, in respect of delivery – have been removed from their agendas of feasible options. They can either try to bid them away from other buyers by offering higher prices, or go without for the present and join the waiting lists for the imported items or buy domestic substitutes and fail to meet some of their 'non-price' aspirations.

To the extent that importers raise their prices as a rationing device, the earlier arguments about the case for domestic firms following apply once more. If customers are forced to queue or lower their aspirations and buy the domestic products, the domestic producers will benefit as follows. Disgruntled would-be purchasers of imported goods, who can no longer get what they want immediately, will be more likely to make use of what Hirschman (1970) calls the 'voice' signal; that is, they will complain to domestic producers about the inadequacy of their products in a way which they would not have felt necessary to do if they had the easy option of 'exit' via the purchase of an acceptable import. But the greater exercise of 'voice' does not guarantee a response by domestic firms: insofar as their sales are rising as people lower their aspirations and switch to their products, the incentive to improve their non-price performances has been removed.

11.4 Price Controls and Inflation

Behavioural analysis leads to the view that the control of inflation is a necessary prerequisite for successful corporate performances, and that measures to control it can themselves play a role in improving efficiency. The aim of this section is to provide a justification for this contention; not to provide a behavioural analysis of the inflationary process. For such an analysis readers should see the work of Baxter (1980) and Tylecote (1981).

Inflation adds to economic uncertainty and raises transactions costs. This results in a redistribution of effort by decision-makers, since profit now depends much less on satisfying customers (see Leijonhufvud, 1977). Uncertainty about the rate of inflation leads to uncertainty about interest rates and exchange rates, and about government policy. This in itself may be enough to make some firms hold back from investing and thereby remove demand from the system. Katona's (1976) work shows that consumers, too, cut back their expenditure on durables as these inflation-induced uncertainties affect their confidence. As inflation accelerates, its cross-sectional variance increases (Evans, 1980), adding to uncertainty. Longer term relative price dynamics become harder to assess, making it more difficult for firms trying to decide in which markets to invest. Deaton (1977) argues that confusion about relative prices also causes consumers to postpone expenditure: because they do not trade in all markets on a regular basis they can muddle together relative and absolute price movements and successively decide that items in different markets have got 'too expensive' to buy compared with those offered in other markets.

Inflation can also cause existing rules of thumb to become obsolete, with very expensive consequences. The 'inflation-accounting' controversy of the past decade (surveyed in Kay, 1977) owes its origins to the difficulties firms faced as a result of continuing to make depreciation provisions on an historic cost basis. Managers whose formative years were those of fixed exchange rates and the low, steady inflation rates of the 1950s and early 1960s are likely to be poorly equipped to cope when inflation accelerates and activities require the exercise of skill in speculating about price movements that are increasingly erratic. The demise of Laker Airways, the banking failures of the mid 1970s (see Dow and Earl (1982), chs 11 and 12), and the £32.5 million loss made by the Rowntree-Mackintosh cocoa buyer in forward selling on the cocoa futures market in 1973 (see Grant (1977), pp. 94–5) all serve as witness to this contention.

The uncertainties associated with inflation lead to the shortening of the periods during which conracts run, and consequently to rising transactions costs. For example, if inter-country inflation rates vary in an erratic manner, there may be gains to be made from switching supply sources as they do so, but this would be precluded by long-term

Implications for Government Policy

supply contracts. To use a series of short-term contracts will involve greater negotiation costs but these may be swamped by the benefits of supply flexibility. Shortened supply deals, however, exacerbate the uncertainties facing suppliers. To remove such uncertainty by offering a more favourable supply price for a long-term contract is costly; it may be better to engage in forward integration to secure captive customers (though such a strategy is obviously at odds with the desire to reduce risks associated with sectoral shifts of demand by ultimate consumers, and these are precisely the risks which the relative price uncertainty may be making harder to assess).

The most significant shortening of contracts to occur in times of inflation is probably that which occurs in respect of wages. The more frequently wages have to be renegotiated, the more frequently one would expect production to be disrupted by strike action. In markets where 'non-price' aspects of competition are important, a failure of supply to materialise as a result of strike action may have very harmful long-run consequences in respect of customer goodwill. People explore alternative supply sources which otherwise they would have ignored and are pleasantly surprised: an obvious example of this happening is found in the context of the 1980 strike at the British Steel Corporation, which led many long-standing customers to desert for good when they discovered that imported steel was (and had for a long time previously been) cheaper as well as more reliable in terms of delivery. The periods when a strike is looming on the horizon, and afterwards, will be characterised by poor productivity. Disrupted concentration and processes of learning are antithetical (see section 7.4); the former may result in reduced rates of production or standards of quality. Workers can hardly be expected to concentrate properly when their minds are troubled by anxieties concerning how they might cope with a strike, even if, in the event, it does not materialise. Methods of reducing inflation which do not founder in a growing tide of industrial unrest may thus contribute greatly to improvements in the competitive positions of firms in a previously inflation-prone economy.

Attempts to control inflation by reducing aggregate demand are misplaced insofar as inflation arises from the cost side. If they appear to work, they do so only by frightening workers into being less militant (as falling sales lead firms to declare redundancies), and by reducing import costs (as the monetary squeeze is associated, via higher interest rates, with exchange rate appreciation). If such policies work largely by the fear mechanism, they are likely to fail when, following their apparent success, the squeeze is relaxed – unless something has happened in the meantime to raise productivity and enable firms to meet their employees' real wage aspirations. Firms which survive a deflationary squeeze *may* emerge 'leaner and fitter' (to use Margaret Thatcher's phrase) as a result of being induced to search for ways of reducing costs and going, as a result, through a 'corporate paradigm shift', of the kind discussed in previous chapters. But there are other ways of simultaneously attempting to control inflation and improve efficiency, which do not entail such a great risk that the cure will kill patient via a squeeze on profitability and investment.

In Tylecote's (1981) behavioural/Post Kynesian analysis, inflation is depicted as being best understood from the cost side, with due attention being given to oligopolistic and socio-psychological factors. To control it, institutional measures are more appropriate than a monetary squeeze. Among these measures may be included price and income controls, though it is important not to regard them as a panacea. Price controls are necessary to make acceptable restrictions on the rate of growth of money incomes and/or on union bargaining power. However, as Shaw (1980) points out, price controls can also be designed as devices to induce firms to search for ways of cutting unit input requirements. Provided they take account of the time it takes to discover and implement cost savings, and the varying potential among firms for achieving them, they can fulfil this role without weakening the position of firms against their overseas rivals.

The implementation of price controls in the UK between 1967 and 1979 involved some attempt to use them as means to promote industrial efficiency. However, as Shaw's paper shows, the measures were often rather ineptly designed. For example, the Price Code (1973–7) allowed only a proportion of increased labour costs to be passed on in higher prices, but insisted that cost reductions had to be passed on in full in reduced prices. Firms which succeeded in making cost savings would find themselves worse off than before, since their profit margins could not be increased in percentage terms; that is, any cost reduction reduced the absolute profit margin. Furthermore, up to 1976, allowable costs were calculated on an historic cost accounting basis and as a result prices could not be increased as fast as real costs. The lesson seems to be that prices and incomes policies, which are often to be thrown together in haste, have a tendency to miss important interconnections and ramifications (just as do corporate strategies that are formed in such circumstances). But this

Implications for Government Policy

neither indicates that they are inherently prone to fail, nor that they are better left out of institutionalist anti-inflation policy packages.

11.5 THE ROLE OF REGIONAL POLICY

The geographical impact of de-industrialisation, and of structural changes generally, is uneven. When multi-branch firms face difficulties, their peripheral branches are typically the ones to be singled out for closure. Any integration of operations in large production units necessarily favours location where markets are concentrated, unless government policies succeed in overcoming the disadvantages of remoteness. Sheer distance from head office often means that peripheral branches may be neglected when investment proposals are being considered. Under-investment then results in their operations being made candidates for closure on the ground of poor productivity. The distance factor may also permit the survival, for a long period, of productivity-dampening work practices, that only come to light when organisational control procedures are re-examined because a crisis is threatening the firm as a whole. Such work practices may be deeply entrenched in worker world views in the peripheral units. From the standpoint of managers at head office, this may make it seem that retreat, involving the transfer of production to nearer centres more used to change, is the easiest option to handle.

Once in decline, regions can begin to suffer from the ravages of the cumulative causation mechanism (see Kaldor (1970), but recall also section 11.2): the contraction of production leads to the failure of local ancilliary firms and thus to rising costs; the quality of the workforce declines; the infrastructure falls into decay as the revenue of the local authorities contracts. A regional problem is like a scaled-down version of the problem of national de-industrialisation: a depressed area is essentially one that suffers from a local balance of payments deficit due to structural inefficiency. As in the national context, the existence of slack may enable a recovery in the absence of positive state intervention (though, in this age of nation-wide wage bargaining, there are strong institutional barriers to the adjustment of relative wages, whatever may be the 'slack' earnings that individual workers might be prepared to forego to guarantee continued employment); but it may also be taken up in the process of avoiding fundamental changes rather than doing something constructive to ensure long-term viability. Similarly, cushioning policies, though they *may* reverse cumulative regional decline, may also have adverse motivational effects in established enterprises. From the behavioural standpoint, then, there is more to be said for regional policies which bring in new firms and new activities, than for those which merely support established, but threatened, activities, *even if* the latter appear viable in other parts of the country.

Some insights on how the former kinds of policy might operate are to be found in the work of Loasby (1967a, 1973), whose later ideas have been used frequently throughout this book – indeed, many of Loasby's theoretical contributions seem to have originated directly from his case study investigations of managerial decision processes at work in the context of relocation choices. Fundamental to his analysis is the idea that decisions to relocate activities arise from attempts to solve major problems that cannot be dealt with in the existing premises; they do not occur as a result of firms continually scanning alternative possibilities. The stimulus to relocation thus comes not from the depressed area, whatever the incentives it has to offer, but from within the prosperous area. Since stimuli often concern the difficulties of coping with buoyant demand in existing premises, it is essential that regional policies should not be allowed to lapse during economic upturns. Politicians will probably find regional problems most pressing and conspicuous during the start of an overall economic downturn when regional unemployment rates exceed sensitive threshold figures (for example 10 per cent; 15 per cent). But the regional problem will be easier to solve in the upturn, when its symptoms are less obvious.

The mere fact that a firm perceives its existing location to be inadequate does not guarantee that it will consider the incentives available in depressed regions (for example, capital or labour subsidies). Decision-makers are looking for something that is satisfactory rather than optimal. There are many possible locations that they might consider and appraisal is not without its own costs. It is likely, therefore (and borne out by Loasby's empirical work), that firms will tend to engage in some form of sequential search when working out where to relocate. Initially they will consider a small batch of nearby sites, since these will threaten to cause the least disturbance to the workforce and existing supply or distribution arrangements. If none of these sites seem satisfactory, a new batch, somewhat further afield, will be investigated. The widening of the net ceases on the discovery of the first acceptable solution. Consequently, there is the possibility that, despite 'attractive' incentives to locate in a peripheral area, firms will be blind to the existence of potentially satisfactory sites outside the prosperous core area, and continue to locate within the latter.

In a world of corporate near-sightedness and tunnel vision, incentives may need to be accompanied by positive inducements to move. A behavioural economist will naturally be broadly sympathetic to the use that has been made of 'Industrial Development Certificates' as a tool of regional policy in the UK: for all but the smallest sites, firms cannot construct new operations outside designated 'Development Areas' unless they have been granted an IDC, and, when regional policy is active, these are not made freely available. Firms are thus forced to widen their search horizons. In the chronic recession since 1974, however, relatively little use has been made of this tool: firms have been able to threaten not to invest at all if they are prevented from investing where they would freely choose to go.

In the previous section it was suggested that measures designed primarily to help bring inflation under control may also serve as tools for improving industrial productivity. Loasby's work casts regional policy in a similar role. While discussing his investigations of the locational behaviour of firms in the Birmingham area, he noted (1967a, p. 41) that

> Many firms reported examples of increased efficiency which could clearly have been achieved in the old location, but which resulted from the pressure to rethink that was created by the pressure to move. This does not imply that these firms were badly managed. Decisions are made when problems are recognised, and the recognition of problems is far from automatic. Thus, that a decision to move to a new site stimulates such recognition is an important argument for encouraging these decisions.

He then went on to show how several firms worked out transport cost schedules which actually reduced the costs of reaching customers close to the *original* sites. Previously, the very proximity of these customers had seemed to allow the firms the luxury of not even bothering to schedule deliveries at all. It was only when they were forced to give up this luxury that they discovered how expensive it had been.

Particularly dramatic cost reductions, perhaps even swamping the value of regional subsidies that have accompanied a shift of location, are likely when a firm moves to a distant, greenfield site, with a fresh workforce, because the enforced restructuring of its corporate imagination is so great. Earlier, in section 6.3, I mentioned the case of Gar Wood Industries: this firm was only able successfully to mass-produce boats once it had relocated production in an area where the workforce were not obsessed with high-quality craftsmanship. An even greater corporate revolution is evident in Loasby's (1973) study of how the W.H. Smith retail chain coped with moving its main warehouse base from central London to Swindon New Town. Such examples point to the conclusion that regional policy may serve to help reduce the rate of de-industrialisation, and not merely help to spread its blight in a more equitable manner.

11.6 Merger Policy

Politicians and their economic advisors, who are not familiar with the kind of analysis of corporate behaviour proposed in this book, have simplistic views of merger activity, which often lead to errors of policy. In the UK in 1966, for example, the Wilson goverment set up the Industrial Reorganisation Corporation to encourage the rationalisation of some sectors of industry into larger corporate entities (see Young with Lowe, 1974). 'Shot-gun weddings' of firms were brought about in the belief that 'big is best' in an increasingly competitive world-based market system. But little thought was given to the personality problems from which the component parts of the new giant enterprises were suffering, or to potential clashes of corporate world view that might lead to strains within such marriages. A product of this approach to policy was British Leyland, whose problems have been referred to frequently in previous chapters.

Despite the passage of time and advances in economic analyses of corporate strategy issues, thinking about merger policies remains muddle-headed. As Kay (1984) notes,

> The Reagan administration in its first year has advocated the market system as the ideal system of economic organisation and encouraged merger to achieve economies and an advantageous international competitive position. [But] these are inconsistent policies since merger involves *replacing* the potential domain over which market exchange can operate with corporate systems [emphasis in original].

The policy proposals of many members of the Left contain the reverse analysis. It is argued that the market does not work effectively and that merger should be discouraged since industrial concentration

Implications for Government Policy

threatens consumer welfare. Once again, the ideas are inconsistent. Mindful of these difficulties in conventional approaches to merger activity, this section presents a behavioural perspective on the subject – but it comes to no simple conclusions.

In the increasingly turbulent environment of modern business life, a government 'merger commission' should seek to promote those mergers which reduce the risk of domestic firms becoming the victims of fatal technological or market 'muggings' by overseas rivals, and to prevent those mergers which increase such risks. In effect, the role for such a body should be to serve as a watchdog over the possibility of domestic firms making strategic mistakes. To say this appears at first sight to run counter to the normal presumption of the Left, that merger policy is a means of safeguarding consumers against the power of big business. But the nature of the modern business environment seems to be such that the protection of consumers entails taking measures to ensure, first of all, that they have jobs. Someone who lacks purchasing power can hardly be said to constitute a potential victim of persuasive advertising or restricted choices of supply outlets. In the long run, as we have seen, companies with apparent monopoly holds on their markets are usually displaced by rivals who have met the challenge posed by their attractive profit positions. Thus, if industrial concentration rises as a result of merger activity, it is simplistic to see the merger as undesirable because it confers a particular *current* market share on domestic producers. In the long run, what is more significant for domestic welfare is whether or not the merger leads to the development of an organisational structure that is poorly equipped to survive a threat to its survival from overseas producers. Having said this, however, I would be the first to concede that it is no easy task to identify which mergers will be strategically desirable in the long run and which will thereby promote structural efficiency and continuing employment for the domestic workforce.

At first sight, mergers which involve vertical integration seem to conflict with any desire to produce a disaster-proof industrial sector. The dangers inherent in such an enterprise have been highlighted by Kay (1984) as follows:

[Vertical integration] increases . . . dependence on a single product and may create a cumbersome and conservative system. Vertically integrated systems typically are difficult to change or redirect; the sheer size of the vertically integrated set of operations frequently means that any attempts at diversification are likely to be regarded as peripheral or marginal in the corporate strategies with attendant prospects for being ignored or mismanaged. Also, once the decline phase of the product lifecycle is entered, there is also the danger that the large capital commitment required simply to stay in a vertically integrated business will soak up the increasingly scarce funds available from internal and external sources, inhibiting the diversification escape route.

But there will often be situations in which vertical integration by merger seems, in the short run at least, to enhance the survival prospects of firms. Loasby (1976, p. 75), for example, notes that 'Courtaulds bought up customers in the hope of improving their sales and thus their demand for Courtauld's fibres'. It is also arguable that the inroads made by foreign firms into the UK car market in the past decade would have been far less dramatic had domestic car producers actually owned their dealerships instead of merely arranging franchising agreements with them. Lack of suitable premises would certainly have held up the establishment of importer dealerships for quite some time. On the one hand, then, vertical integration can promote corporate inertia, but, on the other hand, it may for a time enable a firm to earn greater profits by reducing transactions costs arising from the possibility of inertia, incompetence and opportunism in the firms with which it deals.

Horizontal integration, of the kind that the Industrial Reorganisation Corporation was trying to promote when it brought British Leyland into existence, is also not without its difficulties as a method of securing survival in a turbulent environment. If the merged unit rationalises its product range, it *may* be able to cut its costs and emerge stronger than before (but recall section 6.5). But it is far from obvious that a corporate marriage is necessary for such a result to be achieved. A merger commission should consider very carefully the possibility that rationalisation could be more successfully achieved via some kind of cooperation between the firms in question. British Leyland at one point might have merged with Honda but instead the Triumph Acclaim/Honda Ballade project was agreed upon, and it has proved to be very successful. One might wonder, in the light of it, whether or not the performance of the UK car industry would have been stronger had British Motor Holdings and Leyland engaged in similar cooperative projects, instead of merging. For these companies, more desirable mergers might well have been ones which took them out of dependence on the automotive market. (Suppose BMH had instead merged with Weinstock's GEC and the latter had

Implications for Government Policy

instituted the sort of shake-up that, in the event, it brought about at AEI. Such an arrangement would not only have reduced the costs of Austin and Morris cars and removed the dependence of the combined operation on either automative or electrical market themes; it might also have led to better cars and cheaper electrical goods being produced as a result of a re-examination of the use of electrical gadgetry in the former and consequent exploitation of this possible synergy link. There is, of course, no guarantee that things would have worked in this way, but it is instructive to speculate on possible outcomes.)

Conglomerate mergers between domestic firms are obvious means for hedging against the possibility of a fatal 'mugging'. Furthermore, they do not seem to pose a great short run threat to consumer welfare, except insofar as an emerging conglomerate is able to engage in predatory pricing to drive competition out of one of its markets, financing such an operation from the profits of its operations in other sectors. However, this is not to say that a merger commission should give its unqualified approval to such mergers. Once more, a case-by-case approach is to be recommended. This much should be obvious in the light of the discussions in section 6.4, which examined the consequences of the uncontrolled proliferation of activities in large conglomerate firms. In a turbulent world it is risky to focus on narrow themes in the formation of corporate strategies, but a complete lack of focus does not make for a sense of direction that might lead to a firm being able to achieve pathbreaking innovations or competitive costs. Hedging, like the search for synergy, can be carried too far. If there is one thing which the analysis in the latter part of this book makes obvious, it must be that judging how far is far enough is no easy task for decision-makers – whether in firms or as members of a merger control body.

Whatever the strategic desirability of a particular merger, it is essential that the corporate imaginations of the companies involved should not contain blind spots and philosophical predispositions that cause them to see the world in altogether different ways. Otherwise, there will be great potential for communication breakdowns and bewilderment concerning the roles the parts should be playing within the new enterprise. Any official body that is charged with investigating proposed mergers would thus do well to attempt to construct 'cognitive maps', of how the companies in question think, and then use these to see what chance there is of compatibility if a 'marriage' is allowed. This may sound an unreasonable suggestion but, if they recall section 3.2, readers should come to see that corporate world views are actually not too difficult to pin down. To be sure, the questionnaire procedure – called repertory grid technique and used in identifying how people see the world – was originally developed by Kelly (1955) in the context of his work on clinical psychology. But nowadays it is increasingly being used in industrial applications such as market research and organisational design. Case study applications of repertory grid technique being used in an organisational context play a big part in the work of Eden *et al.* (1979); for a manual explaining the mechanics of using it successfully in business applications, readers who are interested should consult Stewart and Stewart (1981).

11.7 Behavioural Problems of a 'National Enterprise Board'

Left-wing remedies for the de-industrialisation problem usually involve direct state investment in new enterprises, or the nationalisation of existing firms which would then be revitalised and run as industrial pace-setters. But proponents of such policies so far seem to have paid little attention to the questions of how a 'National Enterprise Board' (NEB), with rather more in the way of power than the body of the same name set up in the UK in 1975, might work out which activities to take into its control, and how it might then run them effectively. Decisions about whether to plunge into new activities or to sink more resources into threatened firms (in popular parlance: to attempt to restore 'lame ducks' to fitness) do not suddenly lose all their problems of complexity and strategic uncertainty merely because the decision-making role is shifted from private-sector managers to politicians and civil servants. The nationalisation of a company by an NEB is, similarly, in no way guaranteed to avoid 'marital' problems of the kind that often occur when one private-sector firm takes over another. Given that companies often make costly mistakes in these areas, it is unwise to presume that politicians and civil servants, often operating with shorter time horizons than industrial managers, are inherently likely to be more adept at coping with problems of business strategy.

Behavioural theory suggests that the success of an NEB will be heavily dependent on its frame of reference and access to resources. This will affect both *how* it appraises activities, and *which* activities it comes to consider. If the funds available for industrial subsidies and direct investment are strictly limited, along with the personnel to

Implications for Government Policy

decide upon the use of those funds, then the NEB comes closely to resemble the 'fire-fighting' model of the firm. It is likely to end up being forced by the pressure of immediate events into taking short-sighted decisions that may not add up to a coherent whole, and which would not be taken if more time were available for strategic planning. If the resources available to the NEB are limited in this way, it will have an inherent tendency towards conservatism. The imminent demise of an existing, conspicuous firm has a much greater power to arrest attention than does some, hardly-yet-imagined new idea which might have great long run potential. Once a firm is allowed to collapse, it will never be the same entity if it is revived, for the loss of particular key personnel in the intervening period when its future is in doubt will entail a wasting of its intellectual capital (one might say: corporate brain damage). New blood might, of course, be precisely what such a firm needs, but there is no guarantee that letting the organisation suffer a period in limbo will result in the voluntary departure of personnel with obsolete world views. If anything, the reverse is likely. It is this problem of imminent corporate brain damage due to unconsciousness, supplemented by political pressures, that provides such an incentive for the NEB to concentrate on preserving existing activities. And once a process of subsidisation has begun, sunk cost arguments will tend to favour continuing injections of funds, and the possibility that the NEB will be lured into a defensive investment trap is increased.

If confronted with the suggestion that a resource-constrained NEB would be predisposed in favour of investment in failing firms rather than new enterprise, members of the Left might reply by saying that the NEB should not be restricted to some pre-determined resource allocation (the initial funding of the 1975 NEB in the UK was £1000 million). Mindful of Singh's (1977) analysis of structural inefficiency defined in respect of the balance of payments position (see section 11.1) and Rowthorn and Ward's (1979) related analysis of the economics of industrial subsidies, they would probably argue as follows. The foreign exchange constraint prevents the use of conventional demand management measures as a means of solving rising unemployment, to the extent that this is structural in nature. Hence, until full employment is reached, *any* scheme of subsidy or direct investment that increases net exports is worth carrying out, provided that the short run gains are not outweighed by any short run 'crowding out' effects due to particular shortages of personnel, or long run damage to technical dynamism. And, on the basis of the

Cambridge analysis (Coutts *et al.*, 1976) of inflation in terms of workers trying to meet targets for the rate of growth in their real incomes, such schemes would be desirable regardless of their effects on monetary growth or the public sector borrowing requirement. The rise in output would permit higher real wages and hence cost-push inflationary pressure would be reduced.

Giving a free rein to the NEB, to expand its operations as far as it wished so long as net exports were not reduced, would not, however, be without some important problems. Most obvious, first of all, are those relating to motivation in the long run. Quite clearly, the private profitability criterion is not an appropriate one for the NEB to be using as it considers where to allocate resources in the social interest. In an economy suffering from a foreign exchange constraint, market prices do not properly reflect opportunity costs – *even if* there are no cases of private and social costs diverging due to pollution, which are probably best dealt with by a more appropriate government agency than an NEB. The whole point of the Rowthorn and Ward article cited in the previous paragraph was to demonstrate that an activity which makes losses in private accounting terms may be socially more desirable than one which produces the same final product in a 'profitable' manner. If workers would otherwise be unemployed, they can be used in activities which make society better off by saving imports, even if import-saving versions of the activities would be rejected by private firms because they entailed higher manning levels and 'more expensive' raw materials. The logic of allowing an NEB to invest in schemes which private enterprise would reject is obvious from this standpoint, but, from an organisational perspective, it is a recipe for possible long-run ruin. The early experiences of the UK NEB in relation to British Leyland illustrate the problem. As a major exporting and import-saving producer, BL was an obvious candidate for NEB support; but prior to the very aggressive management of Sir Michael Edwardes, the cushioning provided by such support merely enhanced existing tendencies to resist change. It is difficult to imagine an NEB, that is the tool of a staunchly socialist government, being able to adopt a highly aggressive stance in respect of workers in an overstaffed 'lame duck' whose rejuvenation it is trying to promote.

If the NEB is not subject to limited funding, there is also the problem of how the planners will work out what to do in the absence of a sufficient number of requests for assistance from the private sector, or from within the firms it nationalises. Strategies are hard enough to form *with* focusing and inducement effects to concentrate

Implications for Government Policy

the decision-maker's attention. If these effects are absent, or have been dealt with for the present, the decision-maker must either be paralysed or start a buck-shot search for new activities. The situation is rather like that facing an academic scientist when his research progamme has seemingly been so successful at generating solutions to problems that the only one left is: where next? Companies are not immune from this problem; those suffering from it are likely to have a portfolio of 'cash cows' which generate continually expanding liquid reserves that fail to be used up until a takeover occurs or the decline phase of one of the product lifecycles serves once more to give a sense of direction. (Modern-day GEC seems to fit well into this mould – see Williams *et al.* (1983, pp. 153–7).) An NEB with the great part of the economy at its disposal would seem an even more likely victim. An inability to spot market niches in new areas is likely to result in the NEB being highly conservative in outlook, just as in the finance-constrained case. And it hardly needs to be added that it is not enough merely to see an opportunity; one also needs the right product and marketing package and the ability to construct the right management team.

If politicians and civil servants are not adept at spotting market niches with long-term potential, this entrepreneurial function might be carried out by appointing from private industry project-spotters of proven ability. But there are two difficulties with this suggestion. Firstly, it seems rather strange to set up an agency, one purpose of which is to remedy the deficiency in the private sector's entrepreneurial capacity, and then staff it with private sector entrepreneurs. This sounds simply like a form of crowding out. Secondly, someone who is able to spot potential 'winners' as an executive at, say, ICI may turn out to be hopeless as a government official attempting to do this from scratch. The skill of such an executive may not lie in outright creativity, but in her ability to respond to attention-confining problems within a particular frame of reference. If she is removed from her problem-generating environment and told to come up with ideas with growth potential, she, too, may be paralysed.

11.8 CONCLUDING THOUGHTS: THE SIGNIFICANCE OF CORPORATE CRISES IN PROSPEROUS ECONOMIES

This chapter has used insights from the rest of the book to derive implications for the kinds of policy measures that may help or hinder an economy to recover from depressed conditions that result from poor international competitiveness. But long before the de-industrialisation problem was perceived – in the days of the 1950s and 1960s when, in aggregate, corporate contractions did not outweigh expansions – policy makers were reluctant to allow corporate errors to have fatal consequences. Indeed, the phrase 'lame duck' was, if anything, more popular in this period. If such prosperous times reappeared, some of the policy measures outlined in this chapter would still be relevant – the productivity-promoting inflation control or regional policies would remain useful tools even if there were no overall signs of competitive weakness. The relevance of measures to bail out failing firms is rather less obvious and it seems appropriate, therefore, to conclude this book with some reflections in this area.

As is usual in economics, one can argue about the merits of trying to revitalise ailing firms in terms of the likely costs and benefits that may be involved. Let us first consider the costs of allowing a firm to fail as a penalty for its errors. A major theme in this book has been Coase's (1937) suggestion that a firm is a device which, to economise on transaction costs, replaces market coordination with managerial coordination. The closure of a firm thus marks the end of an organisational arrangement for generating output. Managerial errors which prove fatal result in resources being returned to the market for reallocation. Managers and workers have to seek out, move to, and get to grips with, new, incompletely specified employment contracts. Those people who are assembling new activities have to seek out and assess new suppliers of factors. They have to agree manning levels with unions and discover and negotiate with potential suppliers of inputs and customers for their output. All of these activities impose costs on the parties involved. The collapse of a firm need not involve the scrapping of its physical capital; but it will render investments in particular operational procedures obsolete as well as disrupting the lifestyles of the people involved. It might therefore be worth giving serious attention to the possibility of providing assistance to enable an ailing firm to reorganise its activities, preserving its personnel and personality in broad terms, and thereby economise on the transactions and mental costs of closing it down and relocating the factors within other enterprises. The uptake of organisational slack is the normal process whereby participants in a firm economise on the costs of allowing it to disintegrate. Government support of lame ducks injects slack into a

Implications for Government Policy

context where actual and potential participants in a firm cannot collectively see or agree that it is in their interests to keep it going. Insofar as a government is able to economise on the risks of opportunism and costs of redefining the nature of a particular firm, over-riding the free working of market and organisational forces may be a good idea.

However, there is every possibility that a government which *frequently* subsidises attempts to revitalise existing firms will actually damage the economy as a whole, because it will encourage opportunistic behaviour. There may be a general preference for rising living standards in the long run, but if, at the level of the firm, there is no penalty for failing to innovate, it is not in the interests of individuals to agree to changes that may benefit everyone yet impose net costs upon themselves. But against this point might be raised the suggestion that people will be more likely to innovate if mistakes made by firms are usually prevented from having costly consequences for those involved. If the rewards for success are great, the removal of the penalties of failure will not *necessarily* lead to a lack of dynamism – particularly if there are penalties for not trying to do better. Arguably, the problem with Conservative policies towards industry in the UK has been a failure to recognise that someone considering taking a leap in the dark by trying something new is worried about coming down with a bump as well as being attracted by the possibilities of success – just as, for example, a pole vaulter will have second thoughts about trying for a gold medal if the landing mattress is removed. The Japanese economy, despite having widespread lifetime employment contracts, is full of dynamic behaviour: the social penalties a lethargic, obstructive employee will face are high and innovation is thus encouraged. In the USSR, by contrast, employment is secure but, owing to the absence of such an effective social ethos against apathy, innovation is discouraged by the fear that success in achieving higher targets will merely result in standard output levels being raised in future, and by the fear that if anything goes wrong with a new production arrangement present output requirements may not be met. One cannot, it seems, be too careful about which elements are combined in an incentives package.

On top of the somewhat open effects of 'lame duck preservation' on motivation, it is important to add two possible final dangers of such a policy. Firstly, the fact that firms are observed to be shedding resources may attract other firms to undertake investments that they

The Corporate Imagination

would not have carried out if it were necessary to bid resources away from existing enterprises. In an oligopolistic economy, firms may well be afraid that attempts to attract extra factors by offering higher rewards may lead merely to their existing users retaliating with similar offers. A moderate amount of unemployment may, somewhat paradoxically, be conducive to investment and structural change. Secondly, to the extent that corporate crises arise from sustained failures of particular corporate imaginations to match the underlying realities of their changing environments, and not as a result of what might loosely be termed 'bad luck', there is a real danger that the 'lame ducks' that are subsidised will fail to learn how to perform better and will forever need crutches. Allocating their resources afresh may not be without costs, but if their personnel are mixed in with others who think in a different way, they may at last shake off their old blinkers and be able to make a useful contribution. The problem for the policy maker, as for the management consultant, is to identify how failing firms see their worlds; how malleable such modes of thought might be; and what the reality of the business world actually is. The trouble is that the last puzzle is impossible to solve with any certainty. And when there is uncertainty, mistakes can be made.

This section, indeed, this entire closing chapter, may seem to some readers to represent a rather 'wishy-washy' approach to matters of public policy, for it lacks determinacy. The words 'may' and 'might' are used rather frequently – probably far too frequently for those with strong commitments to the politics of the Right or the Left. But such readers should beware: if they believe it is in the nature of policy aids that they should reduce uncertainty rather than highlight it, they are in danger of closing this book without having grasped one of its major themes. An insistence on single line forecasts has no general logical basis in a world where the future is undetermined and cannot be known before its time; though if such forecasts are formed on the basis of strong dogma, they *may* serve as a simple foundation for decisions that seem to be successful. If one wants to reduce the possibility that one will be unpleasantly surprised by the sequels of decisions to carry out particular policies, an attempt actively to face up to indeterminacy seems warranted. Readers who are themselves surprised by this suggestion would be well advised to turn back to sections 3.6 and 5.2; they should then realise that, throughout this book (this last chapter is no exception), I am following my own prescriptions. My 'multiple scenarios' methodology may not be

Implications for Government Policy

narrowly blinkered and deterministic, but neither does it claim that there are no bounds whatever on the behaviour of managers and corporations. Rather, it seeks to define the landscape along whose channels they may try to proceed.

Bibliography

Abernathy, W.J. and Wayne, K. (1974) 'Limits of the Learning Curve', *Harvard Business Review 52*, September, pp. 109-19.

Adams, A.R. (1976) *Good Company: The Story of the Guided Weapons Division of British Aircraft Corporation*, Stevenage, BAC.

Alberts, W.W. (1966) 'Profitability of Growth by Merger', in Alberts, W.W. and Segall, J.E. (eds) (1966) *The Corporate Merger*, Chicago, University of Chicago Press.

Alchian, A. (1950) 'Uncertainty, Evolution and Economic Theory', *Journal of Political Economy 58*, June, pp. 211-21.

Alford, B.W.E. (1976) 'The Chandler Thesis - Some General Observations', in Hannah, L. (ed.) (1976) *Management Strategy and Business Development*, London, Macmillan.

Allan, R.M., Jr. (1966) 'Expansion by Merger', in Alberts, W.W. and Segall, J.E. (eds) (1966) *The Corporate Merger*, Chicago, University of Chicago Press.

Andress, F.J. (1954) 'The Learning Curve as a Production Tool', *Harvard Business Review 32*, January, pp. 87-97.

Andrews, P.W.S. (1949) *Manufacturing Business*, London, Macmillan.

Ansoff, H.I. (1968) *Corporate Strategy*, Harmondsworth, Penguin Books.

Armour, H.O. and Teece, D.J. (1978) 'Organisational Structure and Economic Performance: A Test of the Multidivisional Hypothesis', *Bell Journal of Economics 9*, Spring, pp. 106-22.

Arnott, D. (1982) 'How to Re-Make Manufacturers: The Levitation of Longbridge', *Management Today*, November, pp. 78-84.

Austin Smith, R. (1966) *Corporations in Crisis*, New York, Anchor Books/Doubleday.

Bibliography

Axford, S. (1983) The Attitudes of Depressives: A Comparative Examination Using Beck's Questionnaires and Repertory Grid Technique, Unpublished Dissertation, University of Stirling Library.

Ball, R. (1978) 'Saving Leyland is a Job for Hercules', *Fortune*, 3 July, pp. 58–63.

Baloff, H. (1966) 'The Learning Curve: Some Controversial Issues', *Journal of Industrial Economics 14*, pp. 275–82.

Bates, J. and Sykes, A.J.M. (1962) 'Aspects of Managerial Efficiency', *Journal of Industrial Economics 10*, July, pp. 209–17.

Bauer, P.T. (1971) *Dissent on Development: Studies and Debates in Development Economics*, London, Weidenfeld and Nicolson.

Baxter, J.L. (1980) 'A General Model of Wage Determination', *Bulletin of Economic Research 32*, pp. 3–17.

Beck, A. (1964) 'Thinking and Depression', *Archives of General Psychiatry 10*, pp. 561–71.

Beck, P.W. (1972) 'Technological Advances – Help or Hindrance? An Industry View', *Chemistry and Industry*, 1 April, pp. 285–7.

Beynon, H. (1978) 'The Real Reason Why Leyland Axed Speke', *New Society*, 7 September, pp. 498–500.

Bhaskar, K. (1972) 'Three Case Studies – Guinness, Spillers and Nestles', in Samuels, J.M. (ed.) (1972) *Readings on Mergers and Takeovers*, London, Elek.

Bhaskar, K. (1979) *The Future of the UK Motor Industry*, London, Kogan Page.

Boston Consulting Group (1972) *Perspectives on Experience*, Boston, USA, Boston Consulting Group.

Boston Consulting Group (1975) *Strategy Alternatives for the British Motorcycle Industry*, House of Commons Paper 532, London, HMSO.

Brown, W.H. (1957) 'Innovation in the Machine Tool Industry', *Quarterly Journal of Economics 71*, pp. 406–25.

Burns, T. and Stalker, G.M. (1961) *The Management of Innovation*, London, Tavistock.

Cable, J.R. and Dirrheimer, M.J. (1983) 'Hierarchies and Markets: An Empirical Test of the Multidivisional Hypothesis in West Germany', *International Journal of Industrial Organization 1*, March, pp. 43–62.

Cable, J.R., Palfrey, J.P.R. and Runge, J.W. (1980) 'Federal Republic of Germany, 1962-1974', in Mueller, D.C. (ed.) (1980) *The Determinants and Effects of Mergers*, Cambridge, Mass., Oelgeschlager, Gunn & Hain.

Bibliography

Carlson, S. (1951) *Executive Behaviour* Stockholm, Strombergs.
Carter, C.F. (1954) 'A Revised Theory of Expectations', in Carter, C.F., Meredith, G.P. and Shackle, G.L.S. (eds) (1954) *Uncertainty and Business Decisions*, Liverpool, Liverpool University Press.
Casson, M.C. (1982) *The Entrepreneur: An Economic Theory*, Oxford, Martin Robertson.
Central Policy Review Staff (1975) *The Future of the British Car Industry*, London, HMSO.
CEPG (1976-80) *Economic Policy Review 2-5*, Cambridge, Department of Applied Economics.
Chandler, A.D. (1962) *Strategy and Structure: Chapters in the History of the American Industrial Enterprise*, Cambridge, Mass., MIT Press.
Chandler, A.D. (1977) *The Visible Hand: The Managerial Revolution in American Business*, Cambridge, Mass., Belknap/Harvard University Press.
Chandler, J. and Cockle, P. (1982) *Techniques of Scenario Planning*, New York, McGraw-Hill.
Channon, D.F. (1973) *The Strategy and Structure of British Enterprise*, London, Macmillan.
Checkland, S.G. (1970) 'D.C. Coleman's *Courtaulds. An Economic and Social History, Volumes I and II*: Review', *Economic History Review* (2nd series) *23*, pp. 556-60.
Church, R. (1979) *Herbert Austin: The British Motor Car Industry to 1941*, London, Europa.
Clarke, C. and Scanlon, B. (1982) 'The Quality Volume Mix', *Management Today*, June, pp. 82-6.
Coase, R.H. (1937) 'The Nature of the Firm', *Economica 4* (New Series), November, pp. 386-405.
Coleman, D.C. (1969) *Courtaulds: An Economic and Social History*, 2 volumes, Oxford, Oxford University Press.
Cosh, A.D. (1975) 'The Remuneration of Chief Executives in the UK', *Economic Journal, 85*, March, pp. 75-94.
Coutts, K., Tarling, R. and Wilkinson, F. (1976) 'Wage Bargaining and the Inflation Process', *Economic Policy Review*, No. 2, March, pp. 20-7.
Cowling, K. *et al.* (1980) *Mergers and Economic Performance*, Cambridge, Cambridge University Press.
Cyert, R.M. and George, K.D. (1969) 'Competition, Growth and Efficiency', *Economic Journal 79*, March, pp. 23-41.
Cyert, R.M. and March, J.G. (1955) 'Organizational Structure and

Bibliography

Pricing Behavior in an Oligopolistic Market', *American Economic Review 45*, March, pp. 129-39.

Cyert, R.M. and March, J.G. (1956) 'Organizational Factors in the Theory of Oligopoly', *Quarterly Journal of Economics 70*, February, pp. 440-64.

Cyert, R.M. and March, J.G. (1963) *A Behavioral Theory of the Firm*, Englewood Cliffs, N.J., Prentice-Hall.

Davis, P. (1983) 'BMC/British Leyland Down Under', *Thoroughbred and Classic Cars 10*, March, pp. 60-3; 83.

Davis, W. (1970) *Merger Mania*, London, Constable.

Deaton, A. (1977) 'Involuntary Saving Through Unanticipated Inflation', *American Economic Review 67*, December, pp. 899-910.

Dell, E. (1973) *Political Responsibility and Industry*, London, George Allen and Unwin.

Dhalla, N.K. and Yuspeh, S. (1976) 'Forget the Product Life Cycle Concept!' *Harvard Business Review 54*, January-February, pp. 102-12.

Dow, S.C. and Earl, P.E. (1981) 'Methodology and Orthodox Monetary Policy', Paper presented at Cambridge Journal of Economics Conference on The New Orthodoxy in Economics, Sidney Sussex College, Cambridge, 22-5 June.

Dow, S.C. and Earl, P.E. (1982) *Money Matters: A Keynesian Approach to Monetary Economics*, Oxford, Martin Robertson (New York, Barnes & Noble).

Downie, J. (1958) *The Competitive Process*, London, Duckworth.

Downs, A. (1966) *Inside Bureaucracy*, Boston, Little, Brown and Company.

Duck, S. (1983) *Friends, For Life: The Psychology of Close Relationships*, Brighton, Harvester.

Duhem, P. (1906) *The Aim and Structure of Physical Theory*, translated by P. Weiner, Princeton, Princeton University Press.

Earl, P.E. (1980) 'A Behavioural View of Economists' Behaviour and the Lack of Success of Behavioural Economics', University of Stirling Discussion Papers in Economics, Finance, and Investment, No. 85.

Earl, P.E. (1983a) 'A Behavioural Theory of Economists' Behaviour', in Eichner, A.S. (ed.) (1983) *Why Economics is Not Yet a Science*, Armonk, NY, M.E. Sharpe.

Earl, P.E. (1983b) 'The Consumer in his/her Social Setting: A Subjectivist View', in Wiseman, J. (ed.) (1983) *Beyond Positive Economics?* London, Macmillan.

Bibliography

Earl, P.E. (1983c) *The Economic Imagination: Towards a Behavioural Theory of Choice*, Brighton, Wheatsheaf (Armonk, NY, M.E. Sharpe Inc.).

Eden, C., Jones, S., and Sims, D. (1979) *Thinking in Organizations*, London, Macmillan.

Edwardes, M. (1983a) *Back from the Brink: An Apocalyptic Experience*, London, Collins.

Edwardes, M. (1983b) Interview in *The Guardian*, 24 March.

Evans, G. (1980) 'A Bottleneck Theory of the Cross-Sectional Variance of Inflation', University of Stirling Discussion Papers in Economics, Finance and Investment, No. 82.

Fishbein, M.A. (1963) 'An Investigation of the Relationships Between Beliefs About an Object and the Attitude Toward that Object', *Human Relations 16*, August, pp. 233–9.

Frankel, M. (1955) 'Obsolescence and Technical Change in a Maturing Economy', *American Economic Review 45*, June, pp. 296–319.

Garfinkel, H. (1967) *Studies in Ethnomethodology*, Englewood Cliffs, N.J., Prentice-Hall.

Godley, W.A.H. (1979) 'Britain's Chronic Recession: Can Anything be Done? in Beckerman, W. (ed.) (1979) *Slow Growth in Britain: Causes and Consequences*, Oxford, Oxford University Press.

Gold, B. (1981) 'Changing Perspectives on Size, Scale and Returns: An Interpretive Survey', *Journal of Economic Literature 19*, March, pp. 5–33.

Gouldner, A.W. (1954) *Patterns of Industrial Bureaucracy*, New York, Free Press.

Grant, A.T.K. (1977) *Economic Uncertainty and Financial Structure*, London, Macmillan.

Hannah, L. (ed.) (1976) *Management Strategy and Business Development*, London, Macmillan.

Hare, P.G. (1980) 'Import Controls and the CEPG Model of the UK Economy', *Scottish Journal of Political Economy 27*, June, pp. 183–96.

Hartley, K. (1969) 'Estimating Military Aircraft Production Outlays: The British Experience', *Economic Journal 79*, December, pp. 861–81.

Hayes, R.H. and Wheelwright, S.C. (1979a) 'Link Manufacturing Process and Product Life Cycles', *Harvard Business Review 57*, January, pp. 133–40.

Hayes, R.H. and Wheelwright, S.C. (1979b) 'The Dynamics of

Bibliography

Process-Product Life Cycles', *Harvard Business Review 57*, March, pp. 127-36.

Hirschman, A.O. (1970) *Exit, Voice and Loyalty*, Cambridge, Mass., Harvard University Press.

Hirschman, W.B. (1964) 'Profit From the Learning Curve', *Harvard Business Review 42*, January, pp. 125-39.

HMSO (1978) *A Review of Monopolies and Merger Policy*, Green Paper, Cmnd. 7198, London, HMSO.

Holland, S. (1975) *The Socialist Challenge*, London, Quartet.

Holmes, P.M. (1978) *Industrial Pricing Behaviour and Devaluation*, London, Macmillan.

Hope, M. (1976) 'On Being Taken Over by Slater Walker', *Journal of Industrial Economics 24*, March, pp. 163-79.

Hughes, A. and Singh, A. (1980) 'Mergers, Concentration and Competition in Advanced Capitalist Economies: An International Perspective', in Mueller, D.C. (ed.) (1980) *The Determinants and Effects of Mergers*, Cambridge, Mass., Oelgeschlager, Gunn & Hain.

Ikeda, K. and Doi, N. (1983) 'The Performance of Merging Firms in Japanese Manufacturing Industry: 1964-75', *Journal of Industrial Economics*, March, pp. 257-66.

Jefferson, M. (1983) 'Economic Uncertainty and Business Decision Making', in Wiseman, J. (ed.) (1983) *Beyond Positive Economics?*, London, Macmillan.

Jones, R. and Marriott, O. (1970) *Anatomy of a Merger: A History of GEC, AEI and English Electric*, London, Jonathan Cape.

Kaldor, N. (1970) 'The Case for Regional Policies', *Scottish Journal of Political Economy 17*, November, pp. 337-48.

Kaldor, N. (1978) 'The Effect of Devaluations on Trade in Manufactures', in Kaldor, N. (1978) *Further Essays on Applied Economics*, London, Duckworth.

Katona, G. (1976) 'Consumer Investment Versus Business Investment', *Challenge*, January/February.

Kay, J.A. (1977) 'Inflation Accounting: A Review Article', *Economic Journal 87*, June, pp. 300-11.

Kay, N.M. (1982) *The Evolving Firm*, London, Macmillan.

Kay, N.M. (1984) *The Emergent Firm: The Role of Bounded Rationality in Economic Organisation*, London, Macmillan (forthcoming).

Kay, W. (1983) 'Guinness Looks to its Head', *Sunday Times Business News*, 30 January, p. 59.

Bibliography

Kelly, G.A. (1955) *The Psychology of Personal Constructs*, New York, Norton.
Kelly, G.A. (1963) *A Theory of Personality*, New York, Norton.
Keynes, J.M. (1979) *The Collected Writings of John Maynard Keynes XXIX The General Theory and After: A Supplement*, London, Macmillan/Royal Economic Society.
Kitching, J. (1967) 'Why do Mergers Miscarry?' *Harvard Business Review 45*, November, pp. 84–102.
Klein, B. (1977) *Dynamic Economics*, Cambridge, Mass., Harvard University Press.
Knight, A. (1974) *Private Enterprise and Public intervention: The Courtaulds Experience*, London, George Allen and Unwin.
Koestler, A. (1975) *The Ghost in the Machine*, London, Pan Books.
Kuehn, D. (1975) *Take-Overs and the Theory of the Firm*, London, Macmillan.
Kuhn, T.S. (1970) *The Structure of Scientific Revolutions* (2nd edn), Chicago, University of Chicago Press.
Lakatos, I. (1970) 'Falsification and the Methodology of Scientific Research Programmes', in Lakatos, I. and Musgrave, A. (eds) (1970) *Criticism and the Growth of Knowledge*, London, Cambridge University Press.
Lamfalussy, A. (1961) *Investment and Growth in Mature Economies: The Case of Belgium*, London, Macmillan.
Lancaster, K.J. (1966) 'A New Approach to Consumer Theory', *Journal of Political Economy 74*, April, pp. 132–57.
Leibenstein, H. (1966) 'Allocative Efficiency vs. X-Efficiency', *American Economic Review 56*, June, pp. 392–415.
Leibenstein, H. (1969) 'Organizational or Frictional Equilibria, X-Efficiency and the Rate of Innovation', *Quarterly Journal of Economics 83*, pp. 600–23.
Leibenstein, H. (1976) *Beyond Economic Man: A New Foundation for Microeconomics*, Cambridge, Mass., Harvard University Press.
Leijonhufvud, A. (1977) 'Costs and Consequences of Inflation', in Harcourt, G.C. (ed.) (1977) *The Microeconomic Foundations of Macroeconomics*, London, Macmillan.
Littler, D. and Pearson, A. (1972) 'Uncertainty and Technological Innovation', *Management Decision 10*, Summer, pp. 111–16.
Loasby, B.J. (1967a) 'Making Regional Policy Work', *Lloyds Bank Review*, January, pp. 34–47.
Loasby, B.J. (1967b) 'Managerial Decision Processes', *Scottish Journal of Political Economy 14*, November, pp. 243–55.

Bibliography

Loasby, B.J. (1967c) 'Management Economics and the Theory of The Firm', *Journal of Industrial Economics 15*, July, pp. 165–76.
Loasby, B.J. (1971) 'Hypothesis and Paradigm in the Theory of The Firm', *Economic Journal 81*, September, pp. 863–85.
Loasby, B.J. (1973) *The Swindon Project*, London, Pitman.
Loasby, B.J. (1976) *Choice, Complexity and Ignorance*, Cambridge, Cambridge University Press.
Loasby, B.J. (1983) 'Knowledge, Learning and Enterprise', in Wiseman, J. (ed.) (1983) *Beyond Positive Economics?* London, Macmillan.
Lowe, A.E. and Shaw, R.W. (1968) 'An Analysis of Managerial Biasing: Evidence from a Company's Budgeting Process', *Journal of Management Studies 5*, October, pp. 304–15.
Malmgren, H.B. (1968) 'Information and Period Analysis in Economic Decisions', in Wolfe, J.N. (ed.) (1968) *Value, Capital and Growth: Papers in Honour of Sir John Hicks*, Edinburgh, Edinburgh University Press.
March, J.G. and Simon, H.A. (1958) *Organizations*, New York, Wiley.
Mariti, P. and Smiley, R.H. (1983) 'Co-operative Agreements and the Organisation of Industry', *Journal of Industrial Economics 31*, June, pp. 437–52.
Marris, R.L. (1964) *The Economic Theory of 'Managerial' Capitalism*, London, Macmillan.
Marshall, A. (1890) *Principles of Economics*, London, Macmillan.
Marshall, A. (1923) *Industry and Trade* (4th edn), London, Macmillan.
Meeks, G. (1977) *Disappointing Marriage: A Study of Gains from Merger*, Cambridge, Cambridge University Press.
Meeks, G. and Whittington, G. (1975) 'Giant Companies in the United Kingdom 1948–69', *Economic Journal 85*, December, pp. 824–43.
Miles, C. (1968) *Lancashire Textiles: A Case Study of Industrial Change*, Cambridge, Cambridge University Press/NIESR.
Miller, S.S. (1963) *The Management Problems of Diversification*, New York, Wiley.
Minsky, H.P. (1975) *John Maynard Keynes*, New York, Columbia University Press (1976, London, Macmillan).
Minsky, H.P. (1982) *Inflation, Recession and Economic Policy*, Armonk, NY, M.E. Sharpe Inc. (Brighton, Wheatsheaf).
Moritz, M. and Seaman, B. (1981) *Going for Broke: The Chrysler Story* New York, Doubleday.

Bibliography

Moss, S. (1981) *An Economic Theory of Business Strategy*, Oxford, Martin Robertson.

Mueller, D.C. (ed.) (1980) *The Determinants and Effects of Mergers*, Cambridge, Mass., Oelgeschlager, Gunn & Hain.

Myrdal, G. (1957) *Economic Theory and Underdeveloped Regions*, London, Duckworth.

Neild, R.R. (1964) 'Replacement Policy', *National Institute Economic Review* No. 30, November, pp. 30–43.

Nelson, R. and Winter, S.G. (1982) *An Evolutionary Theory of Economic Change*, Cambridge, Mass., Harvard University Press.

Newbould, G.D. (1970) *Management and Merger Activity*, Liverpool, Guthstead.

Newman, N. (1982) 'Dunlop's Tight Turn', *Management Today*, November, pp. 51-7.

Nolan, V. (1981) *Open to Change*, Bradford, MCB Publications. (Also available in *Management Decision 19*, No. 2, pp. 1-96.)

Overy, R.J. (1976) *William Morris, Viscount Nuffield*, London, Europa.

Penrose, E.T. (1959) *The Theory of the Growth of the Firm*, Oxford, Basil Blackwell (2nd edn, 1980).

PEP (1965) *Thrusters and Sleepers: A Study of Attitudes in Industrial Management*, London, George Allen and Unwin.

Perrow, C. (1970) *Organizational Analysis: A Sociological View*, London, Tavistock.

Polanyi, M. (1958) *Personal Knowledge*, London, Routledge and Kegan Paul.

Popper, K.R. (1976) *Unended Quest: An Intellectual Autobiography*, London, Fontana/Collins.

Porter, M.E. (1980) *Competitive Strategy: Techniques for Analysing Industries and Competitors*, New York, Free Press.

Posner, M.V. (1978) 'Wages, Prices and the Exchange Rate', in Artis, M.J. and Nobay, A.R. (eds) (1978) *Contemporary Economic Analysis*, London, Croom Helm.

Prais, S.J. (1976) *The Evolution of Giant Firms in Britain*, Cambridge, Cambridge University Press.

Pratten, C.F. (1972) 'The Reasons for the Slow Economic Progress of the British Economy', *Oxford Economic Papers 24*, July, pp. 180–96.

Quine, W. van O. (1951) 'Two Dogmas of Empiricism', *Philosophical Review*, reprinted in Quine, W. van O. (1961) *From a Logical Point of View*, pp. 20–46, New York, Harper and Row.

Bibliography

Radner, R. (1975) A 'Behavioural Model of Cost Reduction', *Bell Journal of Economics 6*, Spring, pp. 196–215.
Reader, W.J. (1981) *Bowater: A History*, Cambridge, Cambridge University Press.
Reid, S.R. (1968) *Mergers, Managers and the Economy*, New York, McGraw-Hill.
Reid, S.R. (1976) *The New Industrial Order*, New York, McGraw-Hill.
Richardson, G.B. (1969) *The Future of the Heavy Electrical Plant Industry*, London, BEEMA.
Richardson, G.B. (1972) 'The Organisation of Industry', *Economic Journal 82*, September, pp. 883–96.
Rothschild, M. (1973) 'Models of Market Organization with Imperfect Information: A Survey', *Journal of Political Economy 81*, November, pp. 1283–1308.
Rowthorn, R. and Ward, T. (1979) 'How to Run a Company and Run Down an Economy: The Effects of Closing Down Steel-Making in Corby', *Cambridge Journal of Economics 3*, December, pp. 327–40.
Ryder, D. (1975) *British Leyland: The Next Decade*, London, HMSO.
Salter, W.E.G. (1966) *Productivity and Technical Change* (2nd edn), Cambridge, Cambridge University Press.
Selznick, P. (1957) *Leadership in Administration*, Evanston, Illinois, Harper and Row.
Shackle, G.L.S. (1949) *Expectation in Economics*, Cambridge, Cambridge University Press.
Shackle, G.L.S. (1961) *Decision, Order and Time in Human Affairs*, Cambridge, Cambridge University Press.
Shackle, G.L.S. (1974) *Keynesian Kaleidics*, Edinburgh, Edinburgh University Press.
Shackle, G.L.S. (1979) *Imagination and the Nature of Choice*, Edinburgh, Edinburgh University Press.
Shackle, G.L.S. (1982) 'Sir John Hicks' "IS-LM: an explanation": a comment', *Journal of Post Keynesian Economics 4*, Spring, pp. 435–8.
Shaw, R.W. (1980) 'Price Controls and Inflation', *Economics 16*, Winter.
Shaw, R.W. and Sutton, C.J. (1976) *Industry and Competition: Industrial Case Studies*, London, Macmillan.
Simon, H.A. (1957a) 'The Compensation of Executives', *Sociometry*, May.
Simon, H.A. (1957b) *Models of Man*, New York, Wiley.

Bibliography

Singh, A. (1971) *Take-overs: Their Relevance to the Stock Market and the Theory of the Firm*, Cambridge, Cambridge University Press.

Singh, A. (1975) 'Take-overs, Economic Natural Selection, and the Theory of the Firm: Evidence from the Postwar United Kingdom Experience', *Economic Journal 85*, September, pp. 497–515.

Singh, A. (1977) 'UK Industry and the World Economy: A Case of De-Industrialisation?' *Cambridge Journal of Economics 1*, June, pp. 113–36.

Singh, A. (1979) 'North Sea Oil and the Reconstruction of UK Industry', in Blackaby, F.T. (ed.) (1979) *De-Industrialisation*, London, Heinemann/NEISR.

Slater, P. (1977) *The Measurement of Intrapersonal Space by Grid Technique*, New York, Wiley.

Spero, J.E. (1980) *The Failure of the Franklin National Bank: Challenge to the International Banking System*, New York, Columbia University Press.

Steer, P.S. and Cable, J.R. (1978) 'Internal Organisation and Profit: An Empirical Analysis of Large Companies', *Journal of Industrial Economics 27*, September, pp. 13–30.

Steinbruner, J.D. (1974) *The Cybernetic Theory of Decision*, Princeton, Princeton University Press.

Steiner, P.O. (1975) *Mergers: Motives, Effects, Policies*, Ann Arbor, University of Michigan Press.

Stewart, A. and Stewart, V. (1981) *Business Applications of Repertory Grid Technique*, New York, McGraw-Hill.

Stout, D.K. (1977) *International Price Competitiveness, Non-Price Factors and Export Performance*, London, NEDO.

Sunday Express (1982) 'The Evolution of a Car', *Sunday Express Magazine*, 26 September, pp. 28–30.

Sutherland, A. (1959) 'The Restrictive Practices Court and Cotton Spinning', *Journal of Industrial Economics 8*, October, pp. 58–79.

Teece, D.J. (1981) 'Internal Organisation and Economic Performance: An Empirical Analysis of the Profitability of Large Firms', *Journal of Industrial Economics 30*, December, pp. 173–200.

Thackeray, J. (1982) 'The American Takeover War', *Management Today*, September, pp. 82–6.

Thompson, S. (1981) 'Internal Organisation and Profit: A Note', *Journal of Industrial Economics 30*, December, pp. 201–12.

Turner, G. (1969) *Business in Britain*, London, Eyre and Spottiswoode.

Bibliography

Turner, G. (1971) *The Leyland Papers*, London, Eyre and Spottiswoode.
Tylecote, A. (1981) *The Causes of the Present Inflation*, London, Macmillan.
UMRCC (1981) *Grid Analysis Package*, University of Manchester Regional Computer Centre.
Utterback, J.M. (1979) 'The Dynamics of Product and Process Innovation in Industry', in Hill, C.T. and Utterback, J.M. (eds) (1979) *Technological Innovation for a Dynamic Economy*, Oxford, Pergamon/MIT Centre for Policy Alternatives.
Wack, P. (1983) 'I find by experience . . .' *Harvard Business School Bulletin*, April.
Wallace, F.D. (1966) 'Some Principles of Acquisition', in Alberts, W.W. and Segall, J.E. (eds) (1966) *The Corporate Merger*, Chicago, University of Chicago Press.
Ward, B. (1972) *What's Wrong with Economics?* London, Macmillan.
Whittington, G. (1971) *Prediction of Profitability and Other Studies in Company Finance*, Cambridge, Cambridge University Press.
Williams, B.R. and Scott, W.P. (1965) *Investment Proposals and Decisions*, London, George Allen and Unwin.
Williams, K., Williams, J. and Thomas, D. (1983) *Why are the British Bad at Manufacturing?* London, Routledge and Kegan Paul.
Williamson, O.E. (1970) *Corporate Control and Business Behaviour*, Englewood Cliffs, N.J., Prentice-Hall.
Williamson, O.E. (1971) 'Managerial Discretion, Organisation Form, and the Multi-division Hypothesis', in Marris, R. and Wood, A.J.B. (eds) (1971), *The Corporate Economy*, London, Macmillan.
Williamson, O.E. (1975) *Markets and Hierarchies: Analysis and Antitrust Implications*, New York, The Free Press.
Wiseman, J. (ed) (1983) *Beyond Positive Economics?* London, Macmillan.
Wolf, C. Jr. (1970) 'The Present Value of the Past', *Journal of Political Economy* 78, pp. 783–92.
Woodward, J. (1965) *Industrial Organization: Theory and Practice*, Oxford, Oxford University Press (2nd edn, 1980).
Wool Textile EDC (1969) *The Strategic Future of the Wool Textile Industry*, London, HMSO.
Young, S. with Lowe, A.V. (1974) *Intervention in the Mixed Economy*, London, Croom Helm.

Index

Abernathy, W.J., 149
Adams, A.R., 186
Advertising, 6, 42, 47
Alberts, W.W., 178
Alchian, A.A., 22, 45
Alford, B.W.E., 168
Allan, R.M., Jr., 188
Andress, F.J., 134–5
Andrews, P.W.S., 137
Ansoff, H.I., xiii, 31, 33, 111
Armour, H.O., 162
Arnott, D., 130
Arrogance, corporate, 64
Aspirations, xiv, 27, 44–54 *passim*, 58, 63–7, 69, 73–4, 78, 128, 147, 167
Attitudes, xiv, 73–5, 99
Axford, S., 43

Balance of Payments, 189–90, 194–7, 201, 209
Ball, R., 120
Baloff, H., 127
Bargaining, 23, 100, 201
Bates, J., 83
Bauer, P.T., 192
Baxter, J.L., 198
Beck, A., 73
Beck, P.W., 138

Beynon, H., 130–1
Bhaskar, K., 82, 181
Blinkering/tunnel vision, xvi, 28, 41–4, 46–7, 68–9, 77, 93–4, 109, 159, 185, 203, 207, 214–15
Boston Consulting Group, 7, 92–3, 124–8, 132, 136–9, 155
Bottlenecks, 31, 109, 149
Boundaries of the firm, xv, 21–39 *passim*, 105–6, 122, 164, 174, 176, 188
Bounded rationality, xii, 13, 44, 49
Bowater Corporation, 47, 56–7, 61–2, 70–1, 158, 177
Briggs Manufacturing Company, 113–14
British Leyland (and its prior constituent companies), 17, 63–5, 68, 74–5, 82–3, 100, 120–1, 129–32, 148–9, 165–8, 171, 175–7, 187, 204, 206–7, 210
Brown, W.H., 17
Budgets,
 consumer, 6, 114, 143–4, 146, 148, 195–6
 departmental, 160, 183
Bunzl, 121
Burns, T., 152

Index

Cable, J.R., 162, 173
Cambridge Economic Policy Group, 190–5, 210
Carlson, S., 83
Carter, C.F., 53
Casson, M.C., 59
Central Policy Review Staff (CPRS), 133–4, 146
Chain Letter effect, 179
Chandler, A.D., 98, 120, 156–9
Chandler, J., 54
Channon, D.F., 167
Checkland, S.G., 98
Church, R., 98, 100
Chrysler Corporation, 45, 101, 105, 118–20, 132, 138–40, 171
Clarke, C., 137
Coase, R.H., 21–6, 31, 34, 37, 212
Cockle, P., 54
Cognitive processes, 55–6, 61, 80, 85, 99–101, 119, 160, 180
Coleman, D.C., 98, 105
Competence/incompetence, 8, 48, 76, 80–1, 99, 141, 149, 152, 206
Competition policy, 174, 204–7
Complexity, xii, xv, 1, 27, 38, 40–1, 77, 80, 128, 173, 184, 192, 208
Conglomerate, 111, 179, 207
Constructs, 42–3, 45, 48, 67, 69, 77, 79, 102, 109, 114, 185
  comprehensive, 117
  core, 56, 61–2, 68, 81, 93, 98, 103, 105–6
  systems/subsystems of, 43, 48, 55–6, 61–2, 116, 149
Contracts, 23–37 *passim*, 61, 71, 95–6, 128, 186, 198–9, 212

Convair 880/990 airliner programme, 78, 81, 95–7, 132–3, 170
Coordination of production, 23–39 *passim*, 122, 174, 212–13
Cosh, A.D., 4
Costs,
  adjustment, 99
  decision making, 30, 44, 50
  information, 35
  labour, 126–7, 214
  of building management teams, 68
  opportunity, 80, 210
  shortage, 35–6
  sunk, 84, 96–7, 109, 209
  transactions, 23–4, 29, 36–8, 174, 198–9
Courtaulds Ltd., 212–14
Coutts, K.J., 70, 84, 98, 105, 206, 210
Cowling, K., 173
Crisis, 16, 45, 48, 62, 70, 77, 82–3, 92, 98, 102–3, 122, 132, 158, 189
Cross-subsidisation, 161, 170
Crowding out, 209, 211
Cumulating effects, 2, 6, 14–16, 18, 45, 89, 126–7, 129, 190–4, 201
Cyert, R.M., xiv, 16, 18, 26, 51, 82

Davis, P., 74
Davis, W., 175, 181
Deaton, A., 198
Decision/choice processes,
  compensatory, 49–50
  cybernetic, 46, 51
  deliberative/reasoned, 46, 50–1, 106, 142

Index

lexicographic/priority-based, 41, 49–51, 65, 142–8
probabilistic, 52–3
programmed, 46, 82, 106–7, 142, 159, 174
recipe/rule of thumb-based, 41, 46–8, 66–7, 78–9, 142, 148, 198
De-industrialisation, xviii, 190, 201, 204, 208, 212
Dell, E., 99
Depression, xv, 59, 72–4, 104, 120
Dhalla, N.K., 141
Dimensions of view, 43–4, 48, 55, 68, 79, 137, 149
Dirrheimer, M.J., 159, 162
Diversification, xvi, 5, 7, 10–11, 15, 34, 36, 77, 112–18, 122, 158, 172, 174, 177, 181
Dogma, 28, 58–62, 73, 85, 95, 169, 214
Doi, N., 173
Dow, S.C., xii, 15, 198
Downie, J., 18, 98, 191
Downs, A., 82
Duck, S., 185
Duhern, P., 60, 65
Dunlop Ltd., 121–2
Du Pont Chemicals, 157–8

Earl, P.E., xii–xiv, 6, 15, 50–1, 55, 97, 99–100, 102, 129, 137, 142, 198
Eastern Airlines, 48
Economies of scale, 17, 36, 79, 92–4, 125
Eden, C., 208
Edwardes, Sir Michael, 64, 68, 75, 82–3, 166–8, 210
Efficiency/inefficiency, 158, 193, 197, 200

managerial, 12
structural, 189–90, 201, 209
X-, 18, 48, 74, 193
Environmental change, xii, 5, 23–4, 31, 41, 67, 69, 79, 103–4, 110, 120, 153, 182, 214
Euphoria, 15, 59, 68–72, 104, 106, 115, 158
Evans, G., 198
Evolution, 1, 15–16, 70, 122, 172
Exchange rate, 47, 189, 191–2, 194–5, 198–9
Expectations, 15, 25, 65–6, 81, 110, 114, 116, 185–6
Experience, xiv, 6, 58–75 *passim*, 79, 89, 99–100, 102, 108–9, 114–16, 122, 139, 141, 149, 154–5, 177, 179, 195
experience curves, xvi, 124–39, 151, 155, 184

Finance, 7–10, 12–17, 25, 30, 56, 70–1, 90, 116, 133, 135, 169, 180, 183
Fire-fighting behaviour, 51, 83, 102, 160, 209
Firm
rationale and nature of, 19–26
Fishbein, M.A., 49
Focus, 31, 48, 53, 92–4, 106–14, 138, 151, 171, 207
Focusing effect, 107, 174, 210
Footwear industry, 92, 94–5
Ford,
Henry, 42, 48, 113, 148–9
Model-T, 42, 48, 148, 151
Motor Company, 45, 64, 95, 118, 132, 149–50
Frankel, M., 78, 90–1

Index

Garfinkel, H., 78
Gar Wood Industries, 112, 204
GEC (and its prior constituent Companies), 68–72, 112–13, 117, 121, 158, 161–2, 175, 187, 206–7
General Motors, 45, 118, 132, 157–8
George, K.D., xiv
Goals,
 of managers, 2–5, 7, 15, 26–7, 45–7, 50, 52, 55, 102, 184
 sequential attention to, 51
Godley, W.A.H., 190
Gold, B., 128
Gouldner, A.W., 129
Grant, A.T.K., 101, 198
Growth of firms, xii, 3–19 *passim*, 37, 49, 67–8, 70–1, 181–3, 188
 financial constraint on, 7–10
 managerial constraint on, 11–16, 18, 116
Guinness, 115–16, 181

Hannah, L., 98
Hare, P.G., 194
Hartley, K., 126
Hayes, R.H., 150, 153–4
Hedging, 34, 79, 111, 174, 177, 207
Hierarchies – see Organisations, structure of
Hirschman, A.O., 192, 197
Hirschman, W.B., 127
HMSO, 124
Holding company, 111, 115, 187
Holland, S., 193
Holmes, P.M., 47, 195
Hope, M., 179
Hughes, A., 173

ICI Ltd., 70, 72, 79–80, 158, 163, 165, 211
Identity crisis, xv, 57, 79–80, 115–16, 211
Ikeda, K., 173
Imagination, 41, 56–7, 159, 185
Imbalances, 107, 109–10, 159, 162, 171–2
Import controls, xiv, 191–7
Incentives, 6, 128–32, 140, 160, 168–70, 184, 202–3, 209, 213
Indecomposability, 162–7, 172
Inducement effect, 107, 174, 210
Industrial Reorganisation Corporation, 175, 204, 206
Inertia, xiv, 80, 102, 157, 193, 206
Inflation, 189–90, 197–200, 203, 210
Information, xii, 26, 40, 44, 60, 66, 82, 112, 153, 155, 159, 164, 168, 180
 impactedness, 18, 27–8, 173
 overload, 162
Innovation process, 19, 48, 98, 192–3
Instability and stability, xv, 1–2, 12–16, 19, 24–5, 51, 59, 70–1
Integration, 31, 79, 90, 111, 166, 183–8
 backward, 111
 forward, 36, 111
 horizontal, 206
 spatial, 23, 35
 vertical, 31, 34–7, 47, 205–6
Internalisation of production, 23, 27–38 *passim*, 165, 183
Investment, xiii, 6–12, 21, 25, 28, 30, 65, 70–2, 123, 127, 167, 190–1, 200–1
 defensive, 77, 84–91, 124, 132, 136, 141, 147, 193, 209

Index

enterprise, 84
  in 'pet projects', 162
  by the State – see National Enterprise Board
'Ivory tower' planners, 167–71

Jefferson, M., 53
Jones, R., 68–72, 112, 121, 158, 161, 187

Kaldor, N., 190–1, 201
Katona, G., 198
Kay, J.A., 198
Kay, N.M., 21–2, 31–4, 37, 106, 111, 121, 156, 164–5, 204–5
Kay, W., 115–16
Kelly, G.A., 41–3, 58, 61–3, 74, 82, 97, 116, 208
Keynes, J.M., 8, 25
Kitching, J., 186
Klein, B., 100
Knight, A., 84
Knowledge (see also, experience), xv, 27, 114, 185
  incomplete and dispersed, 168
  objective, 107–8
  specialist, 2, 16, 27–8, 32–4, 162
  tacit, 108–9
Koestler, A., 19
Kuehn, D., 183
Kuhn, T.S., xvi, 78, 92, 102–4, 157

Lakatos, I., 60–1, 76–7
Laker, Sir Freddie, 42, 198
'Lame duck' enterprises, 208, 210, 212–14
Lamfalussy, A., 77, 84–6
Lancaster, K.J., 49
Learning, xiv, 47, 58–75 *passim*, 110, 116, 124–38 *passim*, 171, 174, 185, 199
  by consumers, 6, 90, 135, 146, 196
  -by-doing, 6, 12, 31, 37, 89, 125
  cognitive, 127
  curves, xvi, 124–38, 196
  manual, 127
Leasing, 27, 38
Leibenstein, H., 18, 99
Leijonhufvud, A., 198
Licensing, problems of, 28, 38
Lifecycle
  process, xvi, 141, 149–55 *passim*
  product, xvi, 2, 5–7, 19, 32, 59–60, 106, 122, 135–6, 138, 141–51 *passim*, 197, 206
Linkages, xiii, 22, 30–34, 39, 42, 107, 110–12, 114–16, 120–2, 125, 156, 163
Littler, D., 169
Loasby, B.J., xiv, 18, 44, 62, 64, 82, 93, 110, 113–14, 202–4, 206
Lowe, A.E., 160
Lowe, A.V., 204

Macroeconomic Policy, 71, 94, 146, 190
Malmgren, H.B., 81
March, J.G., 16, 18, 26, 51, 82, 160
Mariti, P., 38, 175
Market forces, 191
Market growth, 150
Market segment, 117–18, 137
Market share, 136–8, 144
Marriott, O., 68–72, 113, 121, 158, 161, 187

Index

Marris, R.L., xv, 2–19 *passim*, 37, 49, 68, 115, 182
Marshall, A., xi, xiv, 19, 102
Meeks, G., 173, 179, 183
Mergers, xv, xvi, 12, 29, 33, 36, 116, 123, 132, 173–88
  bargain price, 178–81
  conglomerate, 207
  'crystal ball', 207
  'golf course', 181
  policy towards, 190, 204–7
  strategic, 174–8
  waves of, 182
Miles, C., 84
Miller, S.S., 113
Minsky, H.P., 15, 71
Monopoly, xi, 19
  legislation against, 5, 69, 170, 204–5
  monopolistic practices, 68, 161, 170, 174
Moritz, M., 45, 101, 105, 118–20, 132, 139
Morris, William (Lord Nuffield), 59, 113, 148–9
Moss, S.J., 22, 31, 34–8, 106–11
Motivation, 192–3, 210, 213
Motorcycle industry, 92–4, 146
Mueller, D.C., 173
Myopia, 64, 77, 84–6, 203, 209
Myrdal, G., 190

National Enterprise Board, xiv, 190–1, 208–11
Neild, R.R., 85
Nelson, R., 108, 112
Nervous breakdown, 154–5
Newbould, G.D., 181–3
Newman, N., 121
Nolan, V., 81

Non-price factors, 138, 143–8, 195–7, 199

Obsolescence, 5, 17, 34, 38, 77, 109, 141–7, 151, 188
Oligopoly, 144, 195, 200, 214
Olin Mathieson, 115
Opportunism, 23, 27–32, 38, 108, 133, 160, 164–5, 173–4, 184, 206, 213
Optimising behaviour, 40, 44–5, 202
Organisation, 2–3, 23, 51, 62
  mental, 61
  problems of, 12–15, 72, 156–72 *passim*
Organisational structure, xiii–xiv, xvi, 29–30, 73, 77, 80, 141, 151–72 *passim*, 184–5, 205
  decentralised, 165, 167–71
  function-based, 156–9, 165
  mechanistic, 152–3, 156
  mixed-up form, 165–6, 187
  multidivisional (M-form), 157, 159–63, 167–72, 174
  organic, 152–3, 156
  production-/region-based, 156–9, 165
  unitary (U-form), 159–62, 165, 168–9
Overy, R.J., 59, 148–9

Paradigm, xvi, 92–4, 200
Pearson, A., 169
Penrose, E.T., 12, 37, 68, 107–8, 115, 122, 182
PEP, 63–4, 85
Perception, xiv, 55, 59–60, 96, 98, 103, 106, 119, 180
Perrow, C., 47–8, 98
Personalities,
  of corporations, xiv, xvi,

Index

19, 61, 154, 173, 185-8, 204
 of individuals, xii, 61
Polanyi, M., 108-9
Popper, K.R., 59-60
Porter, M.E., 138
Posner, M.V., 195
Prais, S.J., 176
Pratten, C.V., 108, 184
Price controls, 197-201
Prices and pricing policies, 96-7, 135, 137, 142-5, 148, 174, 179, 194-7, 207
Product portfolios, 5-12, 75, 115, 122, 156, 177, 211
Product proliferation, 115-19, 207
Productivity, 18, 27, 30, 45, 63, 125, 129-33, 146, 189, 199-203
Profitability, 2-16 *passim*, 48-9, 85-90, 93, 132, 173, 183, 188, 191, 196, 200, 210

Quine, W. van O., 60, 65

Radner, R., 83, 85
Rationalisation, 77, 84, 106, 115-16, 119-22, 157, 174, 184, 186, 206
Reader, W.J., 47, 57, 62, 70-1, 158
Reference group, 56
Reference points/standards, 18, 41, 45, 53, 63-4, 70, 75, 194
Regional policy, 190, 201-4
Reid, S.R., 173
Repertory grid technique, 208
Research programme, xvi, 61, 76-8, 80, 92-5, 98, 102-3, 105-6, 111, 211
Revolutionary Change,
 of organisational structure, 157-8

of strategy, 77, 84, 103-5, 110, 118-19, 174
Riccardo, J., 46
Richardson, G.B., 38, 174
Rickenbacker, 48
Rolls-Royce, 101, 113
Rothschild, M., 66-7
Rowthorn, R.E., 209-10
Ryder, D., 17, 165-6, 171

Salter, W.E.G., 86
Satisficing behaviour, 44, 49-50, 65, 202-3
Scanlon, B., 137
Scenarios, 53-4, 85, 124, 133-4, 146, 214
Scientific behaviour, 41-3, 45, 59-61, 73, 80, 102-3, 211
Scott, W.P., 65
Seaman, B., 45, 101, 118-20, 132, 139
Self-image, 50, 55-6, 80-1, 100
Selznick, P., 42, 112, 150
Shackle, G.L.S., 13, 41, 52, 100
Shareholders, xi, 2-5, 8-10, 16, 23, 169, 177
Shaw, R.W., 145, 160, 200
Simon, H.A., xii, 4, 44, 82, 160
Singh, A., 5, 173, 190-2, 209
Slack, 16-19, 25-7, 29, 45, 75, 100, 120, 178, 183, 190-3, 201, 212
Slater, P., 43
Sleeper, 63, 72-5, 85
Smiley, R.H., 38, 175
Spare capacity/resources, xv, 21, 31-3, 109-10, 117, 138, 174
Spero, J.E., 176
Stalker, J.M., 152
Steel industry, 23-4, 35, 91, 199
Steer, P.S., 162

235

Index

Steinbruner, J.D., 46, 55
Steiner, P.O., 176
Stewart, A., 208
Stewart, V., 208
Stokes, Donald (Lord), 152, 166, 175–7
Stout, D.K., 195
Strategy, xiii, xv–xvi, 5, 22, 27, 31–2, 35–6, 49, 77–89 *passim*, 119, 134–8, 108–10
 choice of, 98–102, 105–6
 formation of, 105–15 *passim*, 200, 207
 segment retreat, 92–4
Subcontracting, xv, 117, 135, 177
Surprise, xv, 24, 51–2, 214
Sutherland, A., 84
Sutton, C.J., 145
Sykes, A.J.M., 83
Synergy, 31–4, 39, 79, 111, 116, 118, 156, 163, 165, 172, 174–8, 181–2, 207

Takeover raid, 4–5, 10, 49, 179–80, 183, 186
Teamwork, 12–13, 16, 59, 68–9, 184
Technological change, xii, xvi, 5, 22, 31, 91, 138, 151, 162
Teece, D.J., 180
Textile industry, 84, 91, 117–18, 174
Thackeray, J., 180
Thatcherism, 192, 200, 213
Thompson, S., 162
Thruster, 63–5, 71, 73, 75
Time horizons, 46, 85–9, 209
Townsend, L., 45, 120, 132
Townshend, H., 25

Transfer process, 19, 75, 89, 98, 191–3
Turbulence, 31, 34, 40, 57, 132, 182, 205–7
Turner, G., 63–4, 70, 117, 120, 152, 158, 163–5, 175, 177
Two-armed bandit problem, 58–9, 66–7
Tylecote, A., 198, 200

Uncertainty, xii, xv, 1, 19, 27, 33, 38, 40–1, 51–6, 81, 85, 142, 148, 177, 181–2, 186, 198–9, 208, 214–15
Unilever, 120, 163
Utterback, J.M., 151

Wack, P., 109
Wallace, F.D., 180, 183–4, 187
Ward, B., 103
Ward, T., 209–10
Wayne, K., 149
Weinstock, A., 69, 113, 175, 206
Wheelwright, S.C., 150, 153–4
Whittington, G., 4, 173, 179
Williams, B.R., 65
Williams, K., 85, 176, 211
Williamson, O.E., 18, 21–2, 26–31, 35–7, 159, 164
Winter, S.G., 108, 112
Wiseman, J., xii
Wolf, C., Jr., 56
Woodward, J., 152–3
Wool Textile EDC, 117
World view, xiv, 69, 77–8, 100, 106, 129, 151, 161, 185, 208–9

Young S., 204
Yuspeh, S., 141